CW00495280

THE BOW END OF RAIN

BY

BERNIE MULLEN

Published by

**MELROSE
BOOKS**

An Imprint of Melrose Press Limited
St Thomas Place, Ely
Cambridgeshire
CB7 4GG, UK
www.melrosebooks.com

FIRST EDITION

Copyright © Bernie Mullen 2008

The Author asserts her moral right to
be identified as the author of this work

Cover designed by Catherine McIntyre

ISBN 978-1-906050-69-6

All rights reserved. No part of this publication may be reproduced,
stored in a retrieval system, or transmitted, in any form or by any means
electronic, mechanical, photocopying, recording or otherwise,
without the prior permission of the publishers.

This book is sold subject to the condition that it shall not,
by way of trade or otherwise, be lent, re-sold, hired out or
otherwise circulated without the publisher's prior consent
in any form of binding or cover other than that in which
it is published and without a similar condition including this
condition being imposed on the subsequent purchaser.

Printed and bound in Great Britain by:
Biddles, 24 Rollesby Road, Hardwick Industrial Estate,
King's Lynn. Norfolk PE30 4LS

For:

Dorry and my father, Hugh

For my sisters:

Faith, Sally, Monica, Dorothy, Patricia and Catherine

For Mully, my husband who has loved me through the years.

For Me,

And for

Joan

Who has led me into Light.

ABOUT THE AUTH0R

BERNIE (Bernadette) Mullen was born in Serowe, Botswana in 1945. She lived with her parents, Dorothy and Hugh Flattery and her sisters in a small village called Palapye. She experienced her first years of schooling in that village and later lived in Johannesburg.

She was educated by the Sisters of Mercy and later, by the Sisters of Notre Dame.

She became a Sister of Notre Dame in 1962 and left in 1970. She met and married her husband, Peter Mullen (Mully) in 1974.

Bernie and her husband returned to Botswana in 1978 where she taught at Thornhill School and at Kopano Primary School in Selebi-Phikwe. Bernie later became the Principal of Thornhill School. She left Botswana and returned to South Africa in 1992 where she became the Deputy Director of the Catholic Institute of Education and later the Principal of St Martin de Porres Primary school in Soweto.

After some time freelancing as a development facilitator, Bernie got ill with cancer. She has recovered and now works for the Salesians of Don Bosco and the Daughters of Mary Help of Christians. She is the development facilitator in the establishment of a skills training centre for young, disadvantaged people who cannot complete their education in mainstream educational systems.

She lives with her husband in Walkerville, south of Johannesburg.

People ask what this book is about.
I say:

Of the Sun I can speak no word
That people know.
I can only feel its pure beauty
Rising in my soul:
My Sun-lit soul.
It keeps its rising sure and safe in me.
It has become my long longing.
It is existence.
And the love I keep receiving and creating
Is of the Sun, the bright, lit Sun.

ACKNOWLEDGEMENTS

T HIS, my first attempt at writing a full scale book has been a long brewed process. It was through my mother's conviction and persistence that she had a story to tell and through her many requests that I write it that I eventually undertook the task. In our last conversation, the week before she died, Dorry was still providing me with snippets for the telling. My own story grew within hers. I thank her with profound love for this gift.

My loving husband Pete, my sisters Faith, Dorothy, Patricia and Catherine, family and close friends, have always believed that I have a gift for writing and they have all been a great source of encouragement. It is through their unwavering faith in the project that I have had the courage to get the book published. I thank them for years of patience and loving support. Sally and Monica did not live to see the fruit of their 'goading' but I know they are there with hands on hips saying, "get on with it!" Thank you for the lectures and rest assured I have listened with love.

To Anne Joannides and Matt Hooper who were my pre-submission editors and who read the manuscript with an objective eye, I owe a great deal. Their first reactions were spontaneously positive and very heartening. Thank you!

To my sister Trish, who listened with care and skill to descriptions of what I wanted to say in her creative sketches, very special thanks. You have your own talents!

To my sister Dorothy, who kept safe all the writing I thought I had lost over the years, thank you for being there for me...as usual!

Joan, you have listened for so long… thank you.

To my nephew, Dennis Tucker, who made this venture possible, my very grateful thanks.

The staff of Melrose Books, who catapulted me into the reality of having a work published, have been a very helpful and efficient team with which to work. I thank you all. I hope this will not be my only experience of working with you.

♥

Come, we'll go on this journey,
You and I,
To a place that's rarely found.
We will look into the mirror's eye,
And delve our night soul's mind.
We'll have no fear;
We'll hear our mercy-pleading cries.
At our journey's end,
We'll find a full, lit peace-place.
We'll breed the knowledge born
That this is truly you
And this is truly I...

I WALK to the pulpit. On the way I kiss Dorry's coffin. The scent of red roses and deep violet blooms rises and remains in the air like memory. Dorry's presence remains and rises in my mind like the bow end of rain. I unravel the sheets of paper and shuffle. The well-ordered accounts of laughter and of sorrow lie neatly before me ready to be read. Water wells. I watch it spread and stream the sheets. I stare for a while and then I begin the story.

Dorry is my mother. For fun, she calls me her precious 'Number Five'. There are seven of us sisters: Faith, Thelma - but we call Thelma 'Sally' because she used to get into a lot of trouble with her given name and it reminds her of punishment at boarding school. Monica, Dorothy, Bernadette, Patricia and Catherine come next and in that order. I call Catherine 'Kate' and Dorothy 'Dotty'. I don't know why. There are nineteen grandchildren and fourteen great-grandchildren.

We are all hers, all precious. We are woven together like an original tapestry; as individuals but at the same time we are integrated into her life's patterns. There seem to be no limits to Dorry's heart. It enfolds, protects, loves, laughs, grieves and fears for all of us. She is like a flute-reed that is hollowed out especially for our music. Our life's music, be it sad or glad, is also her music. She is a maestro in receiving and in giving song to the world. Her gentle yet rich and mellow voice has soothed us through the years.

Dorry is still beautiful although she is eighty. She shrugs off this compliment and says, "Bern, you should have seen me when I was eighteen." I have seen her photographs and yes, she was very beautiful then. She still has a soft mouth and generous lips. Her eyes are deep set and sea blue. They reflect intense laughter, intense anger or sorrow and sometimes a quiet mystery, depending on her mood. I can't look at her without being drawn into them and feeling well known and well loved. In the photograph, her hair is dark brown and waves naturally into her neck. It is silver-grey and white now. Her eyebrows are perfectly shaped and although they are thick, they grow in a well-kept arch. Her chin is carefully curved and gives sensitivity and strength to her whole face. She says her nose is almost Roman but does not have that extra length. She often tells me that Rose, her surname, is royal and that she believes she is a royal descendant. Her skin is a light olive and is smooth. When I look at her now I can see why she shrugs off the compliments. Her neck is wrinkled and the smile lines around her mouth have become deeper and they only disappear when she laughs. These days she calls them her jowls and says it will be a relief when she dies and is released from their downward journey. They end at her chin. She rubs her neck folds with regret and sighs at the flab. I tell her it is good looking flab and she says that I am blind and do not take after her as far as eyesight is concerned. Dorry is five feet six inches and she doesn't know what that is in metres. She had a slender figure and talks about her size thirty-fours with a mixture of sadness and pride. I do not remember her being that slender and shapely. I used to watch her get dressed in the mornings and she always had a deep valley down her back. Her breasts sagged a little. She had a regular ritual for putting on her bra. It was carefully placed back to front and upside down under her breasts and around her stomach. This was so that she could fasten it in the front and swing it around and then loop the straps over her shoulders. I used to be fascinated by the way she wriggled into the cups and stretched the straps. She would let them go with a bang to make sure they weren't twisted up somewhere on her back. She said that this method saved fiddling about and getting annoyed and frustrated by not being able to find the blooming hooks and eyes and breaking her arms in the process. I still put on my bra that way. As she swivelled the bra around I used to watch her tummy creases. She called them her second and third fronts and her baby banks. She now often looks at them with total disdain and tells me how much she hates them and that she has to get on and diet but it is such a bloody burden when you are her age. I call them pudding pantries and she throws back her head and her laughter raises the roof. Sometimes she tells me how she used to lie on the floor and use a rolling pin to knead her tummy back into shape after giving birth to one or other of us. She says I used to sit on her knees and help knead like a baker's daughter.

I phone Dorry two or three times a week. She lives with Monica and Sally in Benoni. I often wonder what people see in Benoni as a place in which to live. Dorry says it is a peaceful place with a lake and the bus service is good for pensioners. When she comes to answer my call she says, "Is that you, Bern? As soon as the phone rang, I said to Monica, that's Bern." It doesn't matter what I talk to her about on the phone, when our conversation closes she always says, "Bye, dear. God bless you, dear. Love you, dear, Bye, bye, bye…" When I hear the click and I also say, "Bye, bye, bye, Mama," I mimic her voice. It just happens and I don't know why. She's been saying 'bye' like that for at least thirty-five years and I have been mimicking her tone of voice and repeating the 'bye' for thirty-five years.

Dorry calls me Bernadette when she is very angry with me. There is no 'precious' attached and no comfort in her voice when she says my name. I remember once when I visited her in Benoni for a week, I bought the wrong kind of bread. She was very annoyed about that because she had sat with a watering mouth waiting for her warm crust of a baker's white loaf. I arrived with sliced brown. She kept telling me how upsetting it was to have to eat sliced brown when there was a shop full of crispy home made loaves just waiting there for the right buyer. I got angry at her going on and on about it. I told her she was a finicky old nag bag. The 'Bernadette' came out at bullet speed and she told me that I needn't think because I was not under her roof permanently where I could be taught some manners, that that gave me permission to talk to my mother like that! I said something a little more spiced with offence and she marched off to her bedroom and said she would never come out of there again. It took a whole hour for her to calm down and for me to knock and say was the bread fully digested and could we go and see what new loaves were still lurking in the shops.

When the days run into one another and nothing specific prompts a change in her eyes or voice tone, she calls me Bern. Dorry and I have an understanding of each other's ways. Sometimes, when we go out for a meal and a chat, we exchange notes and talk about the whole of creation and then I tell about the mimicking and she says I'm mad. Her sea-eyes laugh with her shaking shoulders and she sort of heaves and hisses before the actual sound wave breaks. Her laugh reminds me of those little yellow weaverbirds that nest in my garden. They also wind up and shake and then reach a crescendo before their timbre crashes and peters out. If I had to describe the birds' song and Dorry's laugh visually, I would light some Catherine wheels on a dark night and watch them spin me into a new, brightly lit world. I can't feel sad there because the colours that are spun are so beautiful and dazzling, I can't think of anything else. Her laughter mops me up. She so easily sets me off too and we can chuckle for ages until people think we are crying and begin to stare at us. She always says, "Stop it, man!" She knows that I can't because she can't so we laugh all over again and things get out of control. When this happens, Dorry throws back her head and a sort of screech takes the place of the heave and hiss. I remember being in agony from laughing once when I spent a night at Dorry's house. We shared her bedroom and the pair of us were just drifting off to sleep when she said, "Do you want some milk, dear?"

I said, "From a bottle or from the boobs? I'm fully weaned, you know!"

She said, "But you are still my precious little Number Five." That was the end of sleep for us. The hissing and heaving and screeching went on for I don't know how long and all we could say in between was, "Shut up, man" but we couldn't.

Sometimes Dorry talks to me about prayer. She says she can't pray in silence like me because her mind will, no matter what, turn to things that have made her laugh. It doesn't matter how long ago the funny incident she remembers happened, she just has to laugh about it all over again. She may be in very serious trouble or in a sober frame of mind just before she begins to settle down to prayer but, lo and behold, it is of no consequence. She wants to know if God will punish her for being a laughing prayer disaster. She says as far as she can see, the Church needs cheering up, what with all the 'don't do's' instead of 'do do's'. I think Dorry will make the whole of heaven laugh when she gets there. I have tried to teach her how to be still and relaxed for a time of meditation but it is like asking a fish not to swim. She can't get further than sitting properly and making sure she is in a position of equilibrium before her tummy and shoulders begin to shake. She doesn't start with the weaver chortle but puts her hand over her nose and mouth to try and prevent an outright exhibition. A sort of fizzing whine escapes between her teeth and a rattle in the back of her throat muffles through before the whole laughing cycle begins all over again. What can I do but join in? I tell her that if she can be joyful in God's presence, then she has nothing to worry about in the hell line. I say that if she does land up in the hot place for irreverence, then she will have me for a neighbour. She says, "Well I just don't know what gets into me, Bern! It's too terrible, man!"

The hysteria at the wrong times has always been a problem. It used to make my father furious. It happened regularly at rosary time. Dorry and the seven of us had to kneel on the cold cement floor around our father's bed. One of the things he always preached was that, "The family that prays together, stays together." He was always quick to tell us that the Pope says so too, so it must be true. My father always began the rosary with the sign of the cross but he never pronounced anything properly. "Name the Father, the Son, and Holy Ghost Amen." I always wanted to reply, as if it were a quiz: 'Name the Father'; the father's name is Hugh John. I never got the time because he was already reciting the next bit about believing in the Holy Catholic

Church and something to do with Mary being the blessed every virgin. I used to think that vir-gin was an Afrikaans word mixed up with a bit of English booze; 'for gin' and that Mary and every one else were for gin because it must have done something good to everyone. I nudged and asked Dorry about it during the litany of the saints that we recited like a regimented chorus after the rosary. She said, "Shish, your father will box your ears." Eventually I got so curious that after the rosary I asked my father. He didn't box my ears; he said that if I waited until the cows came home, he'd tell me. I am still waiting. I also asked him why we say 'Hail Mary'; I was afraid of hail even when the hailstones were very small. It sounded like crackers shooting in the sky before it tumbled down onto our roof and banged so loudly that I had to creep under my bed and put a pillow over my head. I couldn't imagine what would happen if it hailed Mary or especially a number of Marys. There would have been no Mary and no roof left. It would have been like the end of the world and judgement day. I was afraid of judgement day because I had not yet had time enough to become a saint. My father said that my imagination would get me into big trouble. It would soon be arriving on the palm of his hand. He showed me where it would land so I gave up asking and remained ignorant about hailing Mary. I thought that perhaps I was stupid. I asked Dorry if she thought I was stupid. She said that I was a curious and innocent child with a hell of an imagination. I thought I was just myself and that nobody answered my questions. Those cows were always coming home but they never really arrived.

The time we all got into trouble at rosary was when Trish, number six out of the seven of us, was being weaned off her dummy. She was the envy of us all because she didn't have to kneel on the floor and get her knees turned into leather and stained with red stoep polish. I used to think that if I ever got lost up there in heaven, I would always be able to find whoever of us went to God before me; I would just have to look for red leather knees.

Dorry tells the story to us. First she wipes her hands on her apron that smells of cake dough and vanilla essence while she seats herself on the big lounge chair. We are all piled up on the sofa opposite her because when she sits like that and sort of wiggles in for comfort we know the story is going to be good. We even squeak a bit like cellophane paper and nudge one another like surprise packets being opened. Trish is already clapping her hands because she knows she is the hero of the whole affair and it doesn't matter how many times she hears the same story; she can't wait for the fun of it. She also knows that she is the one who saved our knees from red stoep polish that night. We were in the middle of the third sorrowful mystery: 'Jesus is crowned with thorns'. I know that I was in the middle of feeling sorry for Jesus and for my sins, including peeping at Lenny's 'thing' behind the water tank. Dorry has never found that out. Dorry also saved God from another litany recitation saga. Dorry clears her throat and launches off:

"So, we are in the middle of a sorrowful mystery: 'Jesus is crowned with thorns".

Trish is the baby of the family, and she is on the bed. She usually goes off to sleep with the singsong Hail Marys, but this night she is restless and starts niggling. Your father's Hail Mary gets louder and more clearly pronounced so we know that he is annoyed. We start to panic and our throats are also in need of clearing. I put my hand into my pocket and to my surprise and relief I find Trisha's dummy. She has not used it for a week now but I think she will be so pleased to have it that she will just put it in her mouth and fall off to sleep. Lo and behold, all hell breaks loose because she sees the dummy and grabs it. Next thing she's up on the bed jumping up and down and shouting with real triumph, "Mommy found my yo-yo, Mommy found my yo-yo!" We begin to weave and snigger and nudge but to no avail. We break out like bubbles sopping from a bottle of lemonade and Sally sweeps us all along in a crazy fit of careless laughter. "Your father is now looking like hell's right hand helper and is threatening us with God's anger and the devil's joy. We can't do anything about either situation because we are already collapsed in a heap on our haunches and our faces are puffed, red and from our open mouths flow fountains of endless cackle." This is the part of the story Dorry loves best. She wipes up her tears with the vanilla apron and says, "Your father eventually joined the heap of frivolous women and gave himself up to the devil's joy and God's anger as well. He said we could say one and a half rosaries the next night and two litanies; that would make up for our lack of respect for the Sorrowful Mysteries."

There is a huge acacia tree in our back yard. I always felt so sorry for Jesus being crowned with thorns like those huge, sharp ones. I sometimes used to have a holy picture of the scene on the bed in front of me during rosary time. I once cried about the whole happening and thought how sad we made God feel. Dorry gave me a good klap and said to stop crying over holy cards. Rather cry because we are all sinners and ask God to forgive us. I cannot understand why Dorry of all people klapped me for crying over the crown of thorns because she has a holy picture of Our Lady of Sorrows over her bed. On the other wall she has the Holy Shroud. If you walk away from it, the eyes follow you. If you look into the eyes, they close and then open. I think it is because God watches everything we do. Dorry has it there because she says she knows sorrow well and that it is a comfort to her. I think perhaps she klapped me because she is cross with my father for making us get red, leather knees. After the time she klapped me for crying over the Crowning of Thorns, the Sorrowful Mysteries lost their attraction. I smile over the picture with the Joyful Mysteries in it. Anyhow, I was talking about the thorns in our back yard. One day I was playing under the tree and I did not watch where I was walking and a thorn went right into my foot. Maria, our maid, came running out and tried to pull it out but it broke off and remained in my foot for ten days. Dorry put poultices of sunlight soap and sugar on the wound. Every day she and my father came to examine it. They always made promises that if I were very brave while Dorry pressed around it, I would get a nice surprise. On the tenth day after Dorry's doctoring and the day before the doctor from the next town visited our clinic, the thorn shot out of my foot like a rocket and hit Dorry in the face. She didn't have time to heave and hiss; the screech came first, the heave and hiss came second and a sweet tucked into a pair of new sandals for me came next. My father said prevention is better than cure and did I see what happens when I don't wear shoes.

DORRY does not need any more sorrowful mysteries. She has experienced her own and from a very young age. Sometimes she talks to me about them. She sits in the rocking chair with her feet up and begins the story. She always weeps when she starts to say what happened when she was three. When she tells it her tone is softer and I feel that she has shrunk and gone smaller and into a world where she does not care to be. Her eyes well and prepare for water. Her voice quivers conversation. She tells that time as though she is speaking about today and not about eighty years ago. Before she opens her mouth and the first words come out, I am floating above her up into the high mists where her voice is thin and unable to move me. I can accept her story there, in the mists because she has no substance, no heart and no reality. She is the story and not my mother. I wonder what she would do and say if she knew where I get to in her conversations. Perhaps it would silence her and isolate her. Perhaps her words would be lost in loneliness. Perhaps, she would weep inside forever and we, her children, would have no history, no sense of her person, no reference for our lives of which she is the root. Here in the mists there is calm and quiet for reception. There is peace in the telling and the hearing. It is her gift.

"So, Bern, I don't have many memories of my mother. She is a mystery to me and I don't know why through all these years I have never found out more about her, either from my father before he died or from my stepsisters and brothers. May, my only real sister, knew more about her than I but we never talked much about our past. I suppose we were not so sure we wanted to remember all that happened to us. My first memory of mother was the time a small brown sparrow - you know those little grey ones with brown wings and tails - was trapped inside the lounge. I suppose it flew in through the window that was wide open. You know how hot and humid it gets in Durban. It was so frantic flying around and hitting everything in its way. I remember running around getting dizzy trying to catch it, stretching up my hands and neck and calling to it. The poor little mite lost some feathers. They floated and twirled around for so long before landing. It was a pathetic sight you know, Bern, when one can't tell a creature not to be afraid when its instincts tell it differently. Anyhow, my mother chased after it with a duster, throwing it at the bird every time she thought it would sit somewhere for a second. I remember the whooshing sound it made every time she flung it across the room. Of course, she kept missing and the duster also fluttered all over the place. I remember shouting to her, 'Mama, catch the birdie! Catch the birdie!' Eventually it got so exhausted it flew into the glass of the windowpane and just sat on the ledge waiting for its fate. My mother (I believe her name was Maude but I cannot be sure. My sister, May, told me it was Maude but I don't remember) threw the duster over it and let me have a good look at it before she set it free. You ask why I do not know for sure what my mother's name was, Bern. I was never allowed to talk about her to anyone who could have given me some history or just some simple information about her. All I know from gleanings of other people's conversations about her was that she was very beautiful, that she was a good 'horse' woman and rode a lot, and that she had a wonderful singing voice. I believe her mother was an Italian and her father a German. To this day it makes me cry. Excuse me, Bern; I can't carry on for the tears, you know. It's so long ago but it always makes me cry. Anyway, let me wipe up and finish the sparrow episode because it all happened on the same day Maude ran away and left me alone in the kitchen with the umfaan. You know, it is a terrible thing that I don't remember more of my mother. It makes me feel lost and empty. It makes my roots fragile and unsafe. I would rather have known the worst than be left with a mystery for my history. I sometimes wonder what I would be and where I would be if I had all the pieces to the jigsaw puzzle. I can't imagine Maude being such a terrible person all on her own. It takes provocation and some sort of personal experience that cannot be handled to set off something inside. The heart is so hidden and so complicated. Anyway, here I am rambling on when I said I would tell about the umfaan. You know of course that an umfaan is the word for a young man in Zulu. The Zulus are such a proud nation and such a colourful people. We loved to watch their dancing and their rickshaw performances. We used to get into the rickshaw cart and scream our heads off, May and I. The rickshaw driver would move us forward and then suddenly let out a yell and a whistle and send the cart rocketing back and we would be almost touching the ground on our backs. Of course we could not really fall out but we screamed anyway. About the umfaan..." Dorry cries again and she rubs her eyes like a small child with sleep in them.

> *My mind gains height and I am floating in the clouds.*
> *I feel soft mist moving on the far grey sea*
> *It breathes a gentle blindness*
> *And blankets thought to cover me.*
> *Beyond, in distant land,*
> *I hear gull flakes weave and tumble,*
> *Fall and weave and tumble*
> *In time eternal*
> *With the far, grey sea.*

I say, "Tears are good for you, Mama. They wash the sadness clean. Best they are shed and not stored for sickness."

"Yes, I know," she says. "It is strange how one can be affected by something for so long. It is like bruising life at the roots. The plant can't grow to expectations." We clear our throats and Dorry sets her chin and shoulders. Her hand moves over the velvet of the rocking chair as though to steady life and the world around it.

"Maude straightened the room after the sparrow episode and then began to brush off her clothes. The sound of that made me afraid somehow. I know she was smartly dressed and her high heels clicked and scraped as she chased around. I remember she put her hand on my head. She sighed deeply and said, 'Dorry, Mama's going to see a lady get married. And be a good girl now. Mama is coming back.' There was also a man in the room. I think he came in after the sparrow had gone. There was a brown leather suitcase in the corner next to him. I began to scream and Maude could not comfort me. She tried to pick me up but I kicked and screamed to such an extent, she had to let me down to the floor. She said she was going to the shop to get me sugar sticks. You remember those candy-striped sticks you kids used to eat? They were two for a penny in my day. Maude brought me a green and a red one. She peeled off the paper for me but I threw them at the wall and carried on screaming. I must have known in my bones something was very wrong, Bern. I just couldn't be placated. Anyway, she called the umfaan, who used to work for us, and told him to look after me until somebody came to fetch me. She picked up the suitcase and gave it to the man. They walked out of the door together and that is the last time I ever saw my mother. The sparrow was free. She too would soon be free: of my father, of May, of me. For a short time her words drifted back, 'Be a good girl, Dorry, be a good girl. Mama is going now. Mama is coming back soon.' I ran to the door and tried to reach the handle that would take me to her but I could not reach or turn it. Sometimes even today I can get that fearful, trapped feeling you know, Bern. It paralyses a person and prevents one from taking some sort of effective action when one knows one should. It makes one feel small and insignificant, somewhat like that small sparrow in a large, incomprehensible world. When one can't find the nest one's world doesn't make sense. Life seems to hit one in the face for no reason."

I remain high above in the clouds; adrift with Dorry's telling.
I feel soft mist moving on the far grey sea
It puffs out comfort, screens the sorrow
And keeps the peace for me.
Icy shore sands mound and tremble
Slip and mound and tremble
Beneath my cold, wet step
And keep me conscious
Bound forever on,
Forever silent of the white, gold sun
Once shone.

I wait while Dorry shifts and rearranges her feet. They tap-tap at the ground but there is no dance in them. They provide rhythm for her sadness and courage for the telling.

"All was dream, Bern… The umfaan lifted me and laid me on the dark wooden table. He lifted my dress. He murmured and sweated. I was dazed and my being left with my mind that floated above the terror. I felt no pain. I did not hear the sound of my own horror. All was empty and emptied. There is nothing else I can remember about that day. I awakened to the sound of Grandmother's voice. Soothingly and comfortingly it called me back to reality. Back to the other pain and back to my mother's absence. I cried so… 'Granny, Mama's gone! Mama's gone!' Granny's big brown eyes answered my tears. 'Yes baby, yes, Mama has gone. Did the umfaan hurt you? Did the umfaan do bad things to you?' I don't know what I answered. May told me years later that I had been raped. It makes me shudder to think of it now but I don't remember being hurt. I just remember the umfaan lifting my dress and fiddling with me. I laid my head on Granny's shoulder and cried until I fell asleep. The sleep did not bring fairy tale comfort and magic healing. It brought broken and tremulous dreams. I was so lost. I knew that mother was never coming back. She would remain only in the world of my heart's memories, she and her transparent straw hat. To this day I hate floppy brimmed hats. So, Bern, there is a pocket for tears in my soul and I cry inside, always inside, where there is nobody to see nor to hear, nor to stop their free-falling. Such young sorrow is a mystery. That was my first sorrowful mystery: the mystery of my mother, Maude. I used to sit under the mango tree and imagine her riding, fully dressed in her riding gear and always singing soothing songs to her horse. When I got a bit older I often sang, 'Come into the Garden, Maude.' But she never came. She became an imaginary figure with whom I spent time, but she never spent any with me. I once asked Granddad about her and he told me, 'You don't want to know anything about her; she was no good, no good at all.' Somebody else, I can't remember whom, told me that Maude had run away from Dad three times and that he finally divorced her. I never saw nor heard from her or about her again. So, Bern, I can tell you nothing about your grandmother. She is the missing part of me, your own mother."

13

I am missing in the clouds, lost for reply,
lost for all but the mists that hide.
I feel soft mist moving
On the far grey sea
Reaching for my heart
That's travel touched and tempered,
By the far grey sea
Feathered rain winds
Some salt into my eyes
And tear waves break to cry
Of sorrows heaped and hoped
And borne before the tide
Can lift moving mist
From the far grey sea

I say, "Mama, perhaps it is time for a cup of tea. We can get our composure back. This conversation is a hard business." Her feet continue their tap-taps, her fingers fiddle and her eyes trickle-shine: her tears trying to keep their place. She nods and I take her hands and help her to move. We walk slowly into the garden and sit beneath the trees. We hear the chortle of the weavers. I tell her about them and the Catherine wheels. Her cheeks turn pale pink and her shoulders would-be wobble.

"Bern, I swear I don't know where I got you. I must have had an off day or found you in the cabbage patch or something. You're crazy, man! Where's the tea?"

I KNOW Dorry's face, her hands, and her smell of lavender and palm olive soap and her feel. Her favourite dress is the brown one with little moon buttons all the way down to the hem. When I sit on her lap, I play with the buttons and I love their smooth, glass feel. They mirror my happy moments with their clear and simple colour, always just there for themselves, like the moon-man providing laughter and cheese for everybody. I can slide behind their unruffled bulge and lock in my own laughter and peace. I can see the whole world through them and nothing can change or spoil. I can nestle into Dorry and she carries me, invisible and feather-light, wherever she goes. They have a way of comforting me when I feel sad. I know that I can escape into their amber glow whenever I please. I do not play with them often, nor do I usually sit on Dorry's lap when she has the moon button dress on. It is her best dress and she wears it when we go to the hotel for sundowners or to church or to any other special outing. We all go with her to the sundowners because they are from six to eight in the evening on a Friday. We are never too late for a good night's sleep.

These days, I don't play with the buttons because they remind me of the time I lost Dorry. We are left to play at the sundowners. We love to play slip-slip on the shiny, green stoep floor at the hotel. We come home with green socks, green knees, and green hands. My father often tells us to behave and to sit like real ladies and sip our cold drinks but as soon as the sundowners make him happy and we hear laughter, we take liberties. We take off our shoes and slip-slip away in our socks to our hearts' content. My friend, Dianne, once slipped so hard that she broke her arm. She didn't slide properly and so tripped onto her elbow. We wrote "snake-socks" and drew socks that had turned into snakes all over the plaster. All the writing and the snakes were green, of course, so that she would remember not to trust green stoeps and green polish again. Dorry says that to this day it is a good reminder to everyone.

I feel a bit of sticky polish that hasn't been rubbed in properly. It is too late though because I'm already on the ground and my funny bone is not so funny. I laugh-cry and run around looking for the brown dress and the consolation of the moon buttons. I tremble inside like hopeless leaves clinging to an autumn tree, insecure and terrible, afraid of ground death and the absence of green hooded growth around them. I am empty, alone and exposed without my moon-buttoned amber world. I am in a leg and shoe maze that moves like seasickness. The smell of sweat engulfs me. Suddenly I find the brown dress and grab the skirt. When I look up through my eye rain, I see no moon buttons. The face that stares down at me is not Dorry's. My whole world is collapsed into a chaotic swirl with no Dorry to smile me back into calm. The huge hands of my father sweep me up to shoulder height as I reach top C screech. There is no comfort in that because he klaps me one for not listening to the slip-slip warnings. While I am struggling with the funny bone and the klap, Dorry shimmers through the tear view and takes me down from the height of my distress. She slides me over the moon buttons. They don't feel round, and smooth and soothing. They catch my legs and poke at my knees and their glad moments have gone forever. When Dorry wears her brown dress I never sit on her lap. I feel alone and left out as though she has deserted me in spite of her still being here, still going for sundowners and telling me not to slip-slip. It's as though something happy and present has become the sad past. Just like Dorry's mother.

♥

It does not occur to cosmos
That the grass is taller
Or that khaki bossies (bushes) prick and choke.
Their flowers beautifully bloom
In the end of summer's scents.
They bring bright, little colour-hearts
To approaching winter's gloom.
Long may the cosmos grow?

I HUM many tunes when I walk along the road that leads to our village. There is a reason for this humming. The melodies flow easily through my mind and need no conjuring. Perhaps it is because the hot air sneaks through the long grass and causes rhythmic waves across the fields. The birds swirl and dive like Catherine wheels, then disappear into shadow for some small morsel with which to feed their young. Above the wind's sigh and the birds' chatter, I hear the echo of heavy wooden clubs. They thud in hollow tree trunks to stamp the corn. The women move with grace and keep a time. Their bodies bend and straighten. Their clubs lift and thud. They sing of the land, of the sun and of the rain. They tell of the cattle that feed so freely on the long grass. They pause to laugh at the children's play. I am glad I came this way. I blend as they do with the summer's sounds. I feel safe with them.

When I pass the first few huts, I catch a glimpse of brilliant white among the clump of syringa trees. This is Nancy's house. Mr Morey is her father. We call him Mr Snorey because that is what he does when he is in the bioscope. He laughs at everything and then he gets tired and nods off to sleep. Thomas, the man who shows the movie pictures, wakes him up when the snoring gets too loud for us to hear what is going on in the film. He sits up straight and complains that he hasn't had his beauty sleep. I stand beneath the tall windmill that turns the pump for the cattle's water. The water spills into the troughs and I put my head under it. It cools my face and hands.

The front door of the house opens. Nancy beckons to me and I run across the burning sand to where she waits. "Come, the house is cool." I sit in the dark shade of the stoep and rub my eyes because the wind blows fine dust and music through the gauze. When I can see again Nancy is standing with her best tray and best tray cloth. On it is a tall glass of cold milk. Beside the milk is a small plate of Nancy's biscuits. "Have them all, Bern," she says and smiles as she sits to see that I do. The cold glass comforts my hot hands and the smooth milk soothes my dry throat. We talk of this and that, of Saturday's tennis match, of Auntie Shaw's raffle and of the heat. We rise and Nancy picks up an orange. She grows them on her own trees at the back of her house. I receive its brightness. I press it like a treasure against my cheek. I give her the sign of gratitude and leave her smiling at the gate. Along the road, the soil changes colour. My shoes no longer smear with red and brown but with fine white shale dust. I am no longer wrapped in the sand's soft feel. The stones are hard and coarse. The noise they make beneath my feet seems foreign and unwelcome. I change my way and walk along the bush path to keep my peace. I pass clusters of village huts. The women cook and stamp the corn beneath a morula tree's shade. Thin dogs lie in the sun and pant. Naked children weave among the goats that bleat and panic. A group of children sit upon a donkey's back. They kick and slap and goad. It does not move. Dorry says my father is as stubborn as a donkey because when he decides that he will not do something, you can talk or shout or cry and he will not give way. The children whisper among themselves and suddenly beat a tin behind the donkey's back. It stands still. I smile at its triumph. I do not smile at my father's stubborn triumph. He makes Dorry unhappy with his mind that will not change. I greet the children and they greet me. They know that I am the Radibatana's child. They call my father the Radibatana, the father of small animals. When he speaks to the people you cannot tell if he is English or a Motswana. He speaks so fluently and he knows their ways. He sits around a fire with them and talks about God. They listen and some of them become Catholics. He is very proud that he is like the apostles who fetched people off the beaches and from the hills and made them follow Jesus. When Dorry is cross with him she says if he preached as much as he drank whiskey, the whole world would be Catholic.

When I reach the water tank for trains, I stop to rest. The tank stands at the beginning of the station. The train lines stretch into nowhere. I find a place against the huge cement block that supports the tank. My clothes cling because of the heat. My feet throb because of the small coal stones. My mind begins to drift. From behind the slab appears the eldest man of the village. His face is crinkled like old leather. His eyes are deeply set and they have a dark brown glow in them like the light of Wisdom. His hair is very white and he has no teeth. He holds on and bends over his walking stick like an empty sack because he is so thin and frail. His old leather shoes have worn thin and dust has hardened in crevices that his hands cannot polish. His shirt and baggy trousers are faded and frayed. His hands are bony and furrowed like his forehead and face. If he points at something, they shake.

"Dumela Ngwane." (Hello, small child)
"Dumela Tslala ya me." (Hello, my friend)
"The sun is hot, small one! The sun is as fierce as fire."
"Does your corn grow, old one?"
"The rains must come. We must have many rains."
"The corn is higher than I am?"
"The corn grows well."
"The season for growing is still young."
"The rains must come again soon."

I fear when the land gets too hot. The Radibatana broods like one who is distant so that I cannot sit near him. The old man looks at the clear sky. He smiles like one who knows my fear. He laughs and tells me of the time I chased and milked his goats. I put the milk into an old bottle and stored it in Dorry's fridge. She was very angry!

"Ye little gods, what have you been doing?"

"I brought us some milk."

"You also brought us some germs. You'll get diphtheria if you carry on like this. Have you been drinking this milk? Have you given any to your sisters?" I watch my kindness flow out into a desert of no appreciation. Suddenly my world seems flat and sore. There is no comfort in kindness. Dorry gets cross.

"I don't know what you kids get up to in the bush. You stay home and play in the back yard. There is plenty for you to do there. You also stole this milk. Never let me see you doing such a thing again. Your father will take the belt to you."

My adventure with the goats and with the old man has never been forgotten by anyone. My father tells the story to all that come from the city. It is like a village tradition to tell stories of the things we did and what happened when we did them. My father says he had to pay Tsalala for the milk and for the running the goat did. I still chase goats and sometimes catch them but not for their milk. I like to get close to them and to smell their smell. To me it is like being close to the land and close to God.

When Tsalala has rested and has laughed about the goat, he leaves and limp-walks towards the river. I cross the railway lines that divide the village. On this side stand the railway houses. They are made of iron. Next to that is the hotel that reflects the 'Lion Beer' sign. The station buildings and platform are in front of it. When the trains stop for water, the people get out and follow the sign to the pub. They say it is a good watering hole. On the other side of the lines are the club, my father's store, the dipping troughs and Thomas Shaw's shop. He is a tall man with blond, wavy hair and a fair skin because he comes from England. He laughs a lot and rides a bicycle wherever he goes. He has deep blue eyes. Aunty Shaw is his mother. She has white hair because Thomas got lost in the war and she worried so much. Thomas loves the children of the village. He calls me 'Shortie'. He allows me to play under the table in his office. He has a large suitcase of stamps there. I arrange them in patterns on the floor and he tells me stories of the lands from which the stamps come. When I bring my friend Dianne with me, we tell each other the stories. If we do not remember the lands and Thomas' stories, we tell our own. Sometimes I want to tell of the land of Nobody. I go there often. It is the secret place where I cannot be seen or heard. When Dorry and my father fight, I go there. I listen to my father's mad words. His voice shudders through the floor. Its sharp vibrations coil within my brain. His words puff out like a poison adder that strikes me to the quick. They wound my sense and I am left bleeding here within my head. I begin to think of other things and of other times and I stifle out the word poisons like a trained flame snuffer. I am well protected. Nobody knows this Nobody land. Once I fell asleep here and Dorry looked for me for a very long time. She was so pleased when she found me under her bed. She does not know that 'Nobody' land is also under her bed, where I feel safe because the cool, cement floor supports me in its strong, calm silence.

Down the sand road past my father's store is the Freemans' house. Mr Freeman owns two shops and a wholesaler's warehouse. His home is grand. It has a thatched roof and a stoep that goes all the way around it. It has a grandfather clock in the lounge and a very shiny table where a tin of sweets is kept. Dianne Freeman is my friend and she gives me sweets every time I go there. Many people are afraid of her father, the rich man, because he speaks roughly to those who work for him. When I sleep at his house he tells of the day's business. Mrs Freeman rings a bell for dinner and when we sit at table, she rings again and the servants bring the food. The cook's name is Cabbage. If the rich man does not like the food, he calls the cook and says his name is Cabbage because he cooks like a cabbage. I get afraid and ashamed when he calls the man a cabbage. His wife says, "Never mind, Berna, his bark is worse than his bite!" At Christmas time, the rich man gives a party for the children. He dresses up in Santa's clothes and arrives on a horse or on the rail track mender. Auntie Shaw leads us out to the station and we 'jump, jump, sugar lump', until we see his red and white figure coming down the track. We get very excited and a little afraid because he makes us sit around the Christmas tree in his garden and begins to call our names. He asks if we have been good all year. I think of the goat's milk and the suckers I steal from my father's shop and I get scared to answer. I take Dianne to my father's shop and we play in the store room and when my father is busy we open a new box of milk suckers and I put some in my brookies around the waist and then we leave the shop through the back door. Once, Dorry caught us stealing the suckers and she gave me a klap and asked me if I had no mouth and tongue to ask and say please may we have a sucker?

I sometimes get a doll and dolls' clothes at the Christmas tree party. If Dianne and I run out of dolls' clothes Dorry sits at her machine and makes us more. She uses scraps of material from my father's shop. He gets samples from the travellers who come from Johannesburg and sell him goods. She says our dolls are the best dressed in the world. We are very proud of them. When there is a village bazaar to raise money for the soldiers in the war that is in England, Dorry makes piles of dolls' dresses. We get two-and-six to spend and Dianne and I go early and stand with our fingers on all the dolls' dresses so that when the bazaar is opened we are never too late for the fashion buying.

When the afternoons are too hot and we are not allowed to swim in the rich man's pool before four o'clock, we play in the lucerne patch. Dianne is the farmer and I am the hen. We take all the eggs we can find from the hen houses and I make a nest in the lucerne. I put the eggs in it and then I cluck the way the fowls do when they lay their eggs. I lead Dianne all over the patch before she finds them. I do not know why we play this game, but we do. Dorry says, "Ye little gods, man, you kids are mad!" My father says I will grow feathers and he will have to make me live in the hen house. I still play the game but I watch for the feathers. They have not grown yet. Sometimes, my father takes me to the hen house and shows me how to put the fowls to sleep. We sit on a log and when the kippies start pecking at the mealies he scatters around our feet, he whispers to me to keep very still. Then he shows me how to put my hands next to his over the kippies' heads. He suddenly lunges forward and grabs a hen. She squawks and struggles in his hands but he moves them along over her wings and puts her on his knee. He gives her to me and scatters the mealies again until he has caught one for himself. He tells me to sit quietly with the hen until she has settled down. He then takes the hen's head and pushes it down gently. He folds her wing over it. He tells me to copy him. I do. He then moves his one hand in a circle over the hen's tucked away head. After a few minutes he stops and just sits. The hen does not move. It just sits too. He says, "This is the way to put fowls to sleep, even in the day, if you do this to them, they fall asleep." I like to be near my father in the hen house because he is gentle and he shows me the habits of hens. I think I am clever when I show Dianne how to put kippies to rest. I tell her that my father has special magic in his hands so if it doesn't work with Dianne she will not think my father is fooling me. I do not have to worry about being fooled because we often put the hens to sleep and we never get tired of watching how they sit with no heads on our knees.

Our home is small. We have a row of beds on our stoep because there are only two bedrooms. We sleep in a row and Dorry says goodnight to us in a row. My father says goodnight in the lounge. We line up to kiss him and hug him. Sometimes we sit around him next to the fire and he tells us stories. He tells us about a boy and girl who followed a trail of sweets to the house that was made of cake. They got captured by a witch and nearly got baked in an oven. He says we must have our wits about us in the bush. He explains that snakes are to be feared and carefully avoided. We should not run when we see one. We should just stand still and let it pass like a ship in the night. I ask him what a ship in the night means. He says it is when we see somebody and know that they are there but we do not make friends. We just let them come and go. My father always coughs when he says God bless you before he gets into his bed because he smokes so much. I hate the smoking. I feel sick when he spits phlegm into the potty beside his bed. I cover my head with a pillow in case I have to be sick in the potty too. I keep a handkerchief dipped in lavender under my nose so that the smell of the smoke does not make me ill. I want to cry when my father starts patting his pockets for the SRV cigarette box. Sometimes he cleans and refills his lighter and puts new flints into it. I can't watch him without having to keep the tears from welling up. The smoking spoils my whole life. At supper or dinner I eat very fast in case my father begins the cigarette ritual at the table. He coughs and blows the smoke all over the food. Sometimes a bit of phlegm sticks to his bottom lip and I have to run outside and be sick in the long grass. He says I am growing up full of nonsense. I think I am growing up full of dirty smoke. I see myself walking around our home with a cloud around me. It seems to smother my thoughts and makes me want to breathe deeply all the time. There does not seem to be enough air. When it is very hot, the tin roof creaks so loudly that it drowns out all the other sounds. There is no air and so the smoke cloud hangs even closer to my head. I have to go and sit in the syringa's shade and think that I am up in the clear blue sky where the air is fresh and very far from our house. Sometimes I lie under the syringa and the clouds move. I move with them. I sit on top of them so that they do not hang around my head. They take me to a place that is quiet and peaceful. Nobody else goes there. It belongs to me. I am alone in it but I am not lonely.

♥

WE are in my study again. Dorry has a far away look in her eyes. My mind runs.

In passages of flutes,
Varied music rises
Like aromas of rare spices
From the East;
They blend intricacies of
Sweet, spiced flavours
For the senses and the soul.
In passages of flutes,
The mists exude mystique
That gives new breath
To sacred moments of discovery.
New freedom songs can find
Fresh melodies in which to coax
The wearied spirit into play.

"So, let me tell you, Bern:

My father, Thomas, travelled a lot and was often away from home so after Maude's departure May and I were sent to live with Grandma. I remember her coming to fetch us. Her smile was warm and she made us feel loved at once. She was good to us and we grew to be happy in her home. There were also our cousins, Sylvia and Alfred, staying with our grandparents and we all had such wonderful times playing together. Granddad always had time for us and took the trouble to tell us stories. There were several aunts and uncles too -

my father's brothers and sisters. They arranged tea parties for all of us kids and played house-house with us as though they lived in our world as well. We had a real little stove and tiny pots in which we cooked vegetables from Grandma's garden. We enjoyed them even though they were subjected to some horrific recipes we concocted. I remember us being a large family, especially on Sundays. Granny's sisters and brothers, girlfriends and boyfriends all came to Sunday dinner. Granddad always used to sit with us kids. I don't know why he never sat in the dining room with all the other adults. We used to have our meal in the kitchen. He always had time to laugh with us and we loved him so much. I suppose he was there to keep us in order. After the meal and puddings he used to cut us thick slices of home made bread. I never questioned why he did that after our meal but we enjoyed the smell and taste of warm bread. To this day, Bern, I love freshly baked bread. You bring me that home-made loaf from the bakery and I can finish the whole thing in a day. I can gorge on bread and feel nothing about that extra fat roll I am putting on. The temptation is just too much for the mind, Bern! Grandma sent us to St Joseph's Catholic School in Durban and I used to get off the bus outside the cathedral and linger outside there for some time before walking the rest of the way. I always wanted to go inside and see what was going on. One day I did venture in and there was what I now know is Mass being celebrated. I felt drawn to pray and to listen to what the priest was saying and doing even though I could not understand the language or see properly because the priest had his back to the people. I felt that God lived there and so I wanted to come each morning before school. This I did and felt that the tears and the sadness I carried inside was somehow held and heard. Because I went to Mass each morning and because I was taught Catholicism at school I presumed that I was a Catholic. When I told Granny about going to the Catholic church for Mass, she told me that I was not to go again and that I was a Protestant, not a Catholic. This was sad news for me and although I obeyed Grandma, I missed the comfort of knowing that God was near and that I was being comforted and cared about in the secret place inside me.

"I have not said much about my father because, as I said before, he was hardly ever home. I loved him so very much and he was a gentleman. When he did come home, he took us out and spoiled us too. He was a wonderful dad and a very good eldest son to my Grandma. Dad always took her to the market on the Saturdays he was with us. The goods were sent home in a rickshaw so that Dad and Grandma could go to the horse races. This was very much against all the house rules as Granddad was dead against gambling. They never told him where they had been but I am sure he knew in any case.

We had lots of huge trees in the yard and one old silver oak from which was hung a swing. There were two large mulberry trees from which we plucked leaves for silkworms. We had enough worms to start a factory. We were never short of fruit with mango, avocado and guava trees on the plot. May and I used to climb them and sit and eat the fruit until the juices ran down our arms and our dresses were stained yellow. I remember Granddad showing us the one tree in the garden that we could not climb. It was a wild fig tree. I am not sure why he forbade us to get up it but we were always tempted. I suppose once you tell people not to do something, then that something becomes an attractive alternative. Anyway, this day May and I decided we were going to risk the forbidden tree. Makes me think of Adam and Eve, Bern; I am sure they enjoyed the dare and the risk. Aren't we humans in the end, man! May encouraged me and I climbed right to the top. She also got quite far up and then hung onto a branch and swung down and dropped to the ground. You know my determined nature, Bern; I fancied this no end so thought I would try it too. May said, 'You can, Dorry, you can do it!' I needed no more egging on so up I went and followed May's instructions. As I was to swing down, my skirt caught on a branch and there I hung like a sack of potatoes! We screamed and cried so that Granddad heard the palaver and came out to see that we were up to. May tried to hook me off but luckily she couldn't because I would have broken my neck or something. Granddad went to the hedge near the tree and picked a nice cane. He got me unhooked but I got a bottom warming for my troubles. That was the only time I can remember being smacked by my Grandparents.

The incident did nothing to deter us. We were all up there at the first opportunity. It is funny how kids do things that are potentially dangerous and have no thought about the consequences. They don't even entertain the idea that they may really get hurt. They are so naively invincible. It is a wonder that none of you got into serious trouble the way you carried on riding through the bush and picking all sorts of berries. You used to swim in the mud pools, you know, Bern. The goats and donkeys had first gone and heaven knows what got mixed in the mud. My hair stands on end when you tell about these things. Still, I am grateful that we lived in such a small, bush village and yet so much went on there for you kids and for us adults too. Anyway, I was saying, we built a tree house in the mango branches. We had furniture up there and real cups and saucers. We made our brand of tea and played there so often it became like our other little home. Life was good and my mother's going got to be not such a terrible thing, until Granny died."

Dorry sighs and her eyes begin the bright shine. I recede into shadows that, like the mists, are hiding places for my mind - containers of truth not easily heard, not comfortably retained.

My world is dark,
Yet even through this pitch, black night
The sun's memory lies yellow in my mind's eye.
It cannot be blotted out,
For just one rain instant.
And when the day returns,
The white-light sun is born again.
It belches out rude heat.
The little bush-flowers wilt and wither.
Memories of safe, warm
Sun breathes that scented spring
Has died and gone away again...

Dorry is back with the tap-tap and the finger fiddle. I say, "Mama, are you comfortable? Do you want to call it a day for now? Perhaps we can talk tomorrow?"

"Bern, you know what I say? I say, what one can do today, must be done today. One never knows where one might be by tomorrow.

I think that too often we put off things and then never do them because of tomorrow. Your father was a tomorrow man and what did he get for it? Nothing much and an early death. No, man, I must tell you now. Strike while the iron is hot, not so?

It was a terrible day for May and I when Granny passed away. All this lovely life came to an end. There were no more talks and stories. There were no more sweets and hugs for girls who were good. There were no more exciting times waiting for my father to get back from a work trip. There were never any more Granny's eyes to sparkle when she and Dad had won some money on the horses. My dad took me to her bed. There was a sickly sweet smell about her. My father suddenly said that he would be back in a minute and left the room. I stood over the bed and stared. I could not believe how still she was. Neither could I understand the yellow colour of her hands and face. Suddenly, out of nowhere came this loud swishing noise and Granny moved in the bed. She shrank into a small, shrivelled figment of her old self. I flew out of the room and ran down the front steps. The house was built on a sort of stand and I crept under there. I was so frightened. I don't remember how long I was there but my father called and called for me. Eventually I came out from under there and he picked me up and asked me why I was hiding. I told him Granny tried to get up but couldn't and that she went small. He said I was to go and say goodbye to her. He carried me back to the room. He held me over her face and said to kiss her because she was going away. To this day I can't look at the dead without struggling to overcome the sick feeling of cold dead lips on mine. It was such a terror for me, Bern. I suppose my father believed it was the right thing to do. He hugged me afterwards and told me that I could go and play games outside.

I sat under the mango tree and noticed that the breeze still moved among the branches, that the branches and leaves still rustled, the sun still shone, but my beloved Granny was placed in a box with shining handles. I never knew exactly what happened to her but I gathered from the conversation that a snake had bitten her and that she was given too many antidotes. She kept saying that she wanted to go to sleep and that she should be left alone. I was never told that she was dead, just that she was sleeping and would never be awake again.

She was taken away to sleep somewhere else. A horse drawn hearse came for her and she was put into a glass carriage and taken away from me. It seemed that all those I loved were taken from me and that nobody understood how hollow this left my mind and heart. I often sat under the mango tree during that time and thought that those four black horses had taken Granny to my mother and that they had both left me. The silky fringed drapes that hung over the horses waved a little in the wind like a farewell that was only half hearted. She was going away and would never come back and so, Bern, life again was sorrowful and a mystery."

I try to find my way to soft mind-pools.
The cattle bells drum such loud and restless cries.
Stumpy grass graves lie across the land.
In their grass memory,
Lush times died with spring.
Donkeys bray moronic psalms
And tell their hunger to the moon.
The great sun-mother does not listen.
Today the clouds were winded by again.
In my heart there also lie some memory mounds.
They plot across my soul in distant laughter lines
Like little tin soldiers,
Monuments to bravery all neat and white,
All seemingly restful.
They plot a cross so clearly against the sky.
Between are trimmed earth patches
Where bright smiles once grew from nothing
But a glimpse of someone loved.
Those birthplaces were so bountiful,
Those smiles I grew.
But now,
My garden grows in the naked sun.
I hear those beasted bells begin.
Dust rises with my fear:
There'll be no bow at the end of rain.

I say, "Mama, let's go in, it's time for you to watch 'Bold and Beautiful'. I don't know how you keep up with all the messes and the mischief!" Dorry needs no encouragement. She is already out of her chair. I hear the sound of its rocking long after we enter the house.

"What is for dinner, Bern? This talking and crying makes one hungry," she says.

♥

M Y little sister, Patricia, has deep auburn hair and green eyes. My father calls her Trish Wish, Dorry calls her Trisha and I call her Trish and sometimes Trisha. I do not know why she is not confused with all her names but she isn't. She has freckles and a cheeky face. She has chubby legs and when she walks she puts out her arms to balance herself. Dorry ties a bow in her hair like she does in mine. Trish looks good with a green bow on her head because it matches her eyes. Her nose is shaped like Dotty's and is longer than mine. My father says she will be looking down it giving people the evil eye one day. When she laughs, I laugh because she has a chuckle and it is catchy. We play mud pies in our back yard even though she is much smaller than me. She likes to mix up the sand and water and make a good mess. Lena, our maid, is always with us when we play in case there are thorns from the big acacia tree. The wind blows the seed pods around and I love to hear them pop. Sometimes I put some of them in a bag and rattle them. Trish claps her hands and gets excited and wants to rattle them too. When Lena rattles them she sings and makes music. Trish tries to sing with her but she is too young and cannot keep the tune. When she runs, I get worried because her legs can't move fast enough and she looks as though she will topple over any minute. My father says God help us with another rooikop. Dotty's red hair is lighter and Monica's red hair is changing to blonde but her freckles do not change. Dorry says rooikops know how to stick up for themselves, so passop, and she points her finger at my father. Trisha also points her finger at my father and he laughs and says, "Here comes a handful." When Dorry goes to tennis she takes Trisha and me with her. Trisha sits in her pram and Lena and Dorry take turns in pushing it through the sand. The sand makes a crackling noise through the spikes and it sounds like another kind of music. When we get to the tennis courts, we play on the swings and the seesaw with the other children. I love to watch the people play tennis. I love the sound of the popping balls as they are hit across the net. I love to hear Mr Morey say, "Damn good shot!" and Dorry say, "Oh sugar!" when she hits a ball into the net. Mr Morey shouts, "Forty love!" when Dorry serves a good ball and the people on the other side cannot return it. He only whispers, "Love forty!" when she and he have a bad game. Dorry sighs and says, "Ye gods, man!" Sometimes my father comes to tennis but he cannot play well and gets very angry when he loses a game and so Dorry says, "Do something else! Sport is for fun not for fury!"

These days, when Dorry plays tennis, my father plays golf. He is very proud of himself and tells everyone how he shot a hole in one. Trish and I follow my father around the golf course sometimes. Lena pushes her pram and my father gives me a short golf stick and a ball. I try to hit it as he does but I cannot swing the stick high enough. He says I will get it right one day and I must not give up. When my other sisters are home from boarding school they also play golf with my father. Sometimes we take his golf bag and clubs without asking him and we play all day while he is at his shop. Lena does not bring Trish and she does not tell my father. Trish is two years old and will be three in August. It is my worst month because the wind blows and the dust gets into my eyes and everything is covered in sand, even our stoep. It makes it slippery and if we run on it we slip and fall. Dorry sweeps it three times a day. I have to hold Trish's hand when she walks on the August stoep. Our skin gets very chafed in August because it is also very cold in the mornings. Sometimes there is a long icicle on the end of the tap in the back yard. We go and break it off and play with it until it melts. Dorry mixes Germolene, paraffin and wax together and puts it on the stove to melt. She uses it to rub on our skin. She makes a big pot of it and leaves it in the bathroom so that when she has dried us she rubs her mixture on everywhere. Sometimes Trish cries because she does not like the feel of the stuff or the smell; I am not sure. Trish cries even more when Dorry makes us wear little bags of camphor mixed with garlic. She pins them on our vests and says it is because there is diphtheria going around and she does not want us ill. She takes us to the doctor for injections. Trish cries a lot and I try to be brave but I also cry. I love my sister Trish and we are the only two children in the house because the others are at boarding school.

Sometimes Dorry visits Mrs Freeman and she takes us with her. Mrs Freeman admires our bows and clothes. She says Dorry is such a wonderful mother with all these children. She says Dorry is the best dressmaker she has ever met, what with all these dresses and dungarees and even swimming costumes! She picks up Trish and puts her on her knee and makes her laugh. I go and play with Dianne in the playroom where there are many toys and many dolls. We do colouring in and try to be neat and not go over the picture's lines but we can't. We come and show our pictures to Dorry and Mrs Freeman and they say we are very clever and the pictures are beautiful. I know we are very clever. Mrs Freeman gives us cool drinks and cake. Trish makes a big mess and Dorry says, "Ye gods, Doris, look at your carpet!"

Mrs Freeman says, "Never mind, Dot, she is enjoying her cake!" Dianne's little black and white dog Scrap comes and licks up the mess and Mrs Freeman says, "You see, Dot, all gone in a flash!"

When it is very hot and Dorry takes us out, she puts bonnets on our heads and Trish looks funny with hers on because her bow makes it stick up like a clown's hat. I take off my bow when I wear a bonnet. Our bonnets have flaps at the back of our necks so that the sun cannot burn there. Dorry says we will get sunstroke and that would be the end of us. I would not like to be ended by the sun.

♥

Sun strengths fail
Wide eyes shut
And in silhouetted leaves,
Green blood flows unseen
Yet believed by black, mottled blossoms:
They fruit and scent the air.

Then, with no light seen shone,
The moon with night rises.
Vacuumed in its dark, care-mantle,
She grows a loved flamed smile;
Night makes her laugh
With nothing.

WHEN I walk on the moon, soft dust rises like the thin sneeze blanket that enfolds me when Dorry uses her powder puff. She mindfully turns and pulls off the lid in a smooth sliding movement so that none of the precious contents is spilled. It is like opening a treasure. It is like a delicious ritual that introduces life's special moments of magic. She lays the leopard-patterned lid down next to the box so that I can see that they are the same height. The lid shines and the yellow and black patches seem to glitter and grow. They dazzle my eyes until I am sure a real leopard will emerge from the box and the magic will be complete. Next she gingerly lifts the puff out of the box and warily wipes it over the side so that all the powder that has gathered on it falls back into it. I stand very close to her so that I can see right into the box and smell the faint mist that rises when she scrapes the powder off the puff. The patting ritual then begins. She slowly and deliberately lowers the puff back into the box and gently pats it until the delicate smell of lavender begins to fill the whole room and makes me feel heady and sensual. I take deep breaths so that my whole being is filled with its sweetness. It makes me feel clean and suddenly full of mystery. I can sit in the lavender haze forever and never grow tired of it. Somehow, it changes my real world of dust and aridity into soothing softness. I think that life will always be gentle and shielding when I feel the powder on my skin. It is a thin comfort-cover that befriends my whole being. Dorry says that the sensorial smell of lavender is good for the body and the mind. She says it relaxes the whole human spirit. I believe her because as soon as I see the leopard powder box come out of her dressing table drawer, my spirit wants to rest in its mist and laze in its scented smoke.

Although I know in my head that moon dust does not arise I allow the mystery of the moon to cape me in cloud. It guards my vision from all the pits and craters that I feel sure will otherwise turn into desolation that will gobble me up in slow shifts of anxiety. It is when I am very afraid that I walk on the moon. I am walking on the moon now; over on the far side where nothing can be heard, nothing but a pale landscape of subdued light can be seen, nothing can touch or be touched and nothing can change. I need the moon's calm consistency and its care.

I sit beside the moon-lake's edge
With my pallid, moon thoughts
And grey the sun a little.
My moon soul limp swims
Directionless, out of time
And white-light waves tinsel in.
My shallow moon perceptions
Surface,
Flash
And die again.

I watch and wait for care waves to curl, clothe me, to bundle and fold me into a ball and bollemakiesie me out of fright. I feel safe in such play.

Trisha is screaming. Dorry is running to her saying, "Dear God, her finger is nearly off! Hugh, her finger is dangling from a thread. Hugh, do you hear me? She's losing her finger! Do something you bloody bastard!" My father raises his head in slow motion. His huge hands fumble at the chair arms. He sniffs in slow motion and passes his arm across his nose. Dorry is bending over Trisha who is lying flat on the stoep floor, her body surrounded by sticky raspberry cold drink, shattered glass and a spurting little finger. Dorry is shouting at my father for giving such a small child a bottle to run around with. She says he is the thickest father on the earth and she is sick of him and wishes she had never married him. My father grinds himself into response like a rusty clock that has had to begin working after being stopped for a very long time. He grumbles under his breath and makes no sensible reply to her spiked cries.

My mind rises.
In silence, I hold up little moon wounds
For, 'plaster please'
And still, ignore the huge one
That turns my mind so septic,
That farms my fear
Of crossing the room divide,
Arriving at the tiny tubes of flowing red,
Of participating in the fright for a lost finger,
And a sister that has died.

I am in a box. I am listening to the people sing and say that God is with me for all eternity. My mouth is opening and closing in a rhythm of pleading and screaming. They do not hear. I am sinking and their singing is softer. Their weeping is louder. My mouth closes. I can no longer scream. Earth drops on top of the box and cracks in my ears. I am drowned in thunder. I am stifled out of life and remain under earth. I see nothing in the hell of dark around me. I am alone and dead. When the sound of songs and spades heaping earth fades altogether,

I hear the ants begin their creep along the coffin. They scrape and gnaw and I know they will eat me up and I will be a bag of bones, alone and scared forever. I am as icy and steeled into extinction just as surely as the sun has set and just as intensely as I fear Trisha will be because my father moves in slow motion and Dorry is frantically alone in her battle to save. I am nobody and nowhere.

The moon's light is silver like the shine that hangs on Christmas trees reminding me of life, not death. My mind's mayhem is drawn to its healing. I wander along the ashen grey moon path that leads me deeper into the mist. There are no spades or songs or ants here. There are no fathers that move in slow motion and no mothers that are frantic and alone. There is no little sister bleeding with a finger hanging onto life by a thread. Along the way I come upon an apple tree. Its fruit is silver, like the moon's light. I stand and stare and then make a place to sit beneath it. I see my feet fold into silk-sand and feel its balm soothe and unfetter breath that was so locked up in fear. I look up at the apples. They dance in silence and in stillness. They seem to beckon me into adventure. I reach up and pick one. Its silver glows in my hand and tells me of bright days and no dark nights. I cuddle it to my chest and close my eyes. I fall asleep in its silver comfort.

"Hugh, take the child! She is bleeding badly! Here, first stick your fingers in your glass of whiskey. I don't know where the Dettol is. Here, dry your hand on this cloth; it's clean. Sit on the chair and try to keep Trisha's finger on! Just hold it gently together and apply a bit of pressure to try and stop it bleeding. I will have to run and find the plaster." Dorry is breathless and in breathless whispers, she prays, "Dear God, what next, man? Oh, God, look at this mess now. Our Blessed Mother, Queen of heaven, protect my child. Help Hugh to stop the bleeding, holy Mother of God! Hugh, are you listening to me? Sit here dammit!" My father is deliberate but hesitant in his actions. It is as if he knows the saving of Trisha is beyond his ability to co-ordinate what he must do. In slow gestures that seem to steady him, he picks up Trisha and lurches forward to the chair. I am not breathing because I think he will fall over and break her little finger right off. I fly up to the moon again and my head runs around itself and turns into a red balloon so that I can't escape the terror of no finger on my sister or no sister at all. Dorry runs and shouts at me from the door. "Bern, you stay there and help Daddy watch the finger. Hold Trisha's hand and try and keep her quieter!" My legs move. My head remains within itself and I do not know how I get from the stoep bed to the chair where my father is rocking Trisha and she is screaming for Dorry. I lift my lead head while he goes to fetch Dorry and to tell her that we have stopped the bleeding. We haven't. The small red centre has grown and soaked up the white little paths. Trisha is screaming again.

I hear Dorry's running steps that patter along the stoep. She swoops up Trisha and rushes out of the door. It squeaks open like a dying hen that is about to have its head chopped off. She does not stop to catch her breath. Trisha lolls along like baggage under her arm. She shouts at my father that she is going to Mrs Oudendaal for help and plaster. She tells him to get a feeding bottle and fill it with sugar water while she is away. He tells Dorry that together we stopped the bleeding and used his shirt to make a bandage. The door bangs his words shut from her ears and her jogging figure disappears down the sandy path that leads to the station and to Mrs Oudendaal. My father sits on his chair and bows his head. He mumbles about women that do not hear. I go and lie on the bed but first I pull down its quilt and cover my head and my ears so that I cannot hear my father's complaints and I cannot see his drying red shirt and I cannot hear Trisha's cries fading with the figure of Dorry down the road. I do not know how long Dorry and Trisha are away. I lie in the dark silence and listen for their return. I am afraid to listen and afraid to block sound from my ears. I do not want Dorry to shake me out of the covers and to tell me that Trisha has gone to the ants underground. I don't want to see her face blotched with tears. I do not want her to bring Trisha's finger back all blue and dead and separated from her hand forever.

My father sits and snores. His head lolls over the glass in his hand until he wakes himself up to save it from falling to the ground. He slurs at me to fetch the feeding bottle full of sugar water. I unfold my tangle and I am strangely cold even though the hot night wind is blowing gently through the gauze. The cold is from within. I get the bottle from Trisha's cot and take it to my father. He looks at it as though it is a foreigner and pushes it towards me. He shows me how much sugar to put into it and how much water to mix with it. I go like a foreigner with the foreign bottle and do as I am told. I go and sit on the bed and shake the bottle until the sugar has dissolved. I hear Dorry's footsteps crunching the pathway. I freeze from the cold within. Dorry sees the bottle and brings Trish to me. She smells clinical and clean and I know that Trisha's finger won't be lost because Dorry and Mrs Oudendaal have fixed it. There is no soaked bandage. There is a small plaster covering the wound. She says that Mrs Oudendaal poured liquid paraffin over the wound and it stopped bleeding immediately. She will keep the plaster on to keep the wound clean and the finger in place. Trisha is saved from sure death in a box with hungry ants.

It is a long time since Dorry sent me to bed. I am listening to Trisha's breathing and I am watching her hand that is spread on the pillow next to her half-hidden cheek. She is pale and peaceful. Her hair is gleaming and smells of fresh shampoo. Dorry splashed a bit of lavender oil that she keeps in a blue bottle for special occasions, on her pillow to make her sleepy and calm. Although my head has stopped swelling and tottering like a red balloon, it stills aches. Before I close my eyes I let my moon tears fall safely onto my pillow. When Dorry and my father come to see if I am asleep, I keep my eyes closed and my head tucked into the pillow because my tears are my own and they are secret. Perhaps one day I will understand why my tears cannot be seen. Dorry says we all reach the bow end of rain if we never expect anything good in life because then life is always a lovely surprise.

When Trisha visits me these days and we talk about the past, she says she does not remember anything about nearly losing her finger. She only remembers seeing blood and her precious, cool drink run away from her across the red stoep floor. I tell her about the red balloon. She says I am a little crazy but she enjoys being at the centre of the story and she enjoys the feeling of being loved by her sister for so long.

Dorry is a Catholic now. She became a member of the Church when she met my father. She sings all the old Protestant hymns while she bathes us: 'Abide with Me', 'Onward Christian Soldiers', and 'The Lord is My Shepherd'. She also knows new hymns that Fr Murphy teaches us: 'Daily, Daily, Sing to Mary', 'Oh Sacrament Divine' and 'God Bless our Pope'. It is always a mystery to me how the city of Rome has a panting heart. The first line of the hymn says so, "Deep in the panting heart of Rome..." I ask Dorry and she says it's an image of a people who are dedicated to the Church. This is not a help to me. I still do not know why Rome pants and why we ask God to bless the Pope because of it. The dogs pant in the heat and spit drips from their pink tongues. My father says that is the way dogs keep cool and sweat. They get up to drink water after panting for a while and then back they go to do some more. This is the only kind of panting that I have seen and so I will never understand about Rome and the Pope panting. Perhaps Rome and the Pope have many dogs and it is hot there.

When Father Murphy comes, my father brings out the special bicycle that he keeps in the shop store. I shine the spokes and wash the tyres and the frame. There is a steel spanner that I use to tighten up all the bolts. It is a game for me to find which hole in the spanner fits which bolt. I always get it right and I am proud of myself. I fasten the air tube of the pump to the valve of the tyre and the sound of the air being forced into the tube is like the strange sound of San music to me. I sing off key songs in a made up language and pretend I am a San child. I shuffle my feet in time to the music. My father says I'd better be careful or my skin will change colour and I'll be taken to the desert to live with the San people. They sleep with their heads perched up in their hands and their elbows make a stand for it. They do this so that insects and even worse, scorpions can't crawl into their ears and bite them to death. I would not mind being a San child except that I like wearing clothes and I like bathing even though Dorry scrubs me pink. I always pump the tyres extra hard because Father Murphy is a bit fat and I am afraid he will feel the sharp stones shocking the saddle when he rides through the bush to visit all the people. When he arrives, my father meets him at the station. He comes from Francistown. There is no church in our village. Father Murphy is always laughing. You would think that there was no sorrow in the world, just smiling Irish eyes everywhere. The way he speaks is like music to me, not like the pump San music, but like music played on a piano so that the tune is easy to follow. He sings, "Have you ever been across the sea to Ireland?" He tells us stories about that country and he says it's greener than "How green is my valley." I am never sure what that means but I believe that it must be very green. He says there is no dust that funnels up into whirlwinds in Ireland. I think I would feel safer there because when the winds blow here I get into a big cardboard box so that I can't see the poor sand being swept away to places that it doesn't know and doesn't want to go to. I can only hear the sand slap into the box but it can't sting me. Dorry sings 'Oh Danny Boy' with him. I feel like crying because Dorry has a beautiful, tender voice like I imagine that her mother's used to be. It seems to wash over me like silk, better even than the moon buttons do. There is always something sad about the way she holds her head and about the way her eyes shine while she sings the words that tell about how whoever wrote the song visits dead people including Danny Boy. Father Murphy harmonises with her and I long to go to Ireland that is such a sad-glad place.

When we have lunch, Dorry starches the best and only serviettes. She folds them like church towers and puts them into glasses at the side of our small plates. We have a jug of fruit drink or ice water on the table as well. We have two knives on the right side, one for bread and one for dinner. Dorry calls all this etiquette. Monica ruins the whole thing because when we sit down and my father says grace and Father

Murphy blesses our food, she shouts, "Oh! We are having serviettes today, Ma!" Dorry goes red and almost lifts her skirt to cover her head. Father Murphy pretends not to notice and my father coughs as though he has a lung disorder. While we are shuffling about trying not to think what will come next, Father Murphy blesses Dorry. He says, "May you live to be a hundred years and an extra year to repent!" We laugh and the quiet that follows is because Dorry's food is good. Every now and again Dorry's shoulders shake so that we know Monica is not really in trouble.

We have Mass in our home. The people come from the village and we all kneel on the stoep. Dorry puts a table at the one end and we watch Father Murphy take out the candles, the chalice and the books with God's words in them. He arranges them in silence and my father starts up a few Hail Marys in case we begin to talk and not pay attention to our faith. My father stays with Father Murphy at the table because he is the server. His knees are spindly and after he has knelt for some time, they begin to creak when he gets up to light the candles or to take the water to wash the priest's hands. We get taught that the washing of hands is to remind us that Pilate washed his hands of Jesus when he could have helped him not get crucified. It is also a sign that God washes away our sins. I often ask God not to forget to wash away the time I peeped at Lenny's thing behind the water tank. I tell Father Murphy about it when I go to confession. I have to kneel on the rug next to him and I put my hands together and lean on his knees. He never says I am a naughty girl or that God will punish me. He says that God forgives all the things we do but that I must try never to peep again and, most of all, I must never touch anyone else's thing because it's a sin.

At night Dorry tells us stories about all the saints. Maria Goretti was killed because she wouldn't touch a man's thing. St Bernadette, the one I am named after, saw Our Lady in a forest and Our Lady helped her to live better with her asthma. She also started a special stream of water for sick people. If they believe and have faith, wash in or drink some of the water, they can get cured. The stream is still there today in a place called France. I often kneel behind the boiler and ask Our Lady to show herself to me because I am trying to be a saint, too. All I see is the sunlight and my eyes remain scrunched up because it is so hot next to the boiler. I ask her to give me a secret message for the world, like the children of Fatima. She never answers. During rosary I cry because the sorrowful mysteries are so sorrowful and Our Lady and Jesus had to put up with so much suffering when all they did was to be good and holy. My father sends me out of the room and Dorry comes to find out why I am crying. I tell her and she klaps me on my bottom and tells me that I am to become a saint by doing what is right and not by crying over the rosary and holy pictures. I am not sure if I want to be a saint any more. You get klapped and you don't have visions or get special messages. I also get disappointed on Pentecost Sunday because the Holy Spirit is supposed to come blowing in like the wind and sit on our heads like a flame. We are supposed to speak strange languages. None of this happens. Father Murphy tells us how it happened long ago. He says the spirit works in us very quietly and we hardly notice that he is there but it shows in how we do good works.

♥

"LET me tell you, Bern. Aunt Agnes looked after us for some time after granny died. We were kindly treated and enjoyed being in our new home and school. Daddy visited us as often as he could. Life and the games we played continued in a new rhythm and routine that made us feel safe. I remember one of the routine things was for my father to clear our tummies out of worms every few months. I suppose it was because of all the fruit we ate straight from the trees. Anyhow, my cousin, Alfie was my favourite and we got on very well. He did all sorts of things for me. He took special care to make sure I got my homework done right. He used to help me to read. Anyhow, when the worm muti came out, I absolutely shrank, as I hated it so much. On this one occasion Alfie said he would help me to hide if I cleaned out his silkworm box. I don't know why we kids kept so many worms. You would think that they would remind us of the worm muti, but no, we loved to watch them get fatter and bigger and then spin their silk cocoons.

There was a large dining room table in Aunt's house and it had a velvet green cover that reached the ground over it. I remember that I often played under the table and was fascinated by the tassels. I used to get them knotted together for some reason and aunt gave me lectures about that. Anyhow, the muti time came and Alfie hid me under the table. My father knew I was there of course, so my hard worm clean up did not earn me freedom from being dosed. I remember the thrill of hearing dad shout, 'Where is Dorry? It's time to keep the worms from growing! Does anyone know where Dorry might be?' I held my breath. Eventually dad bent down and said, 'Come on out of there!' I had to get dosed anyway. This never stopped Fred from asking me to clean out the silkworm boxes. It was quite a job, you know, as sometimes they were so small one could hardly pick them up. I got clever about that. I just put the new leaves on top of the small worms and left them to crawl out of the old ones. Fred had about six or seven boxes of them. We always fed them on mulberry leaves because they grew in the garden. Anyhow, I got fed up with this whole business of emptying all the boxes especially the ones with the biggest worms in them. I had a bright idea: I would just let them climb onto the mulberry tree and when they had finished feasting I would put them back in the box until next feeding time. I did this and when I came back to get them all back into their boxes, the birds had eaten them all! Ye gods, man! Alfie was very angry and of course I had to do my homework alone. They were like his babies, you know, and he had got attached to them, having watched them grow and all that. I kept my own silk from then on. Alfie was also an orphan. His mother died at his birth. His father was a sailor and only came to see him when his ship was home. Alfie and I got into trouble once with our milk cow. She had a new calf. We decided that we should break some branches off a tree and feed them to the calf. We were shooing, shouting and poking the branch through the gate when it gave way and the cow came after us! You have never seen two kids run like that. I remember getting a head butt in the bottom. I have been terrified of cows ever since. When you were two or three you were afraid of cattle as well. I don't know if I passed my fear on to you but your father always had to pick you up when there were any cattle in sight. You were like that until you were about six.

Anyway, I was telling you: I loved school, Bern. We were still at St Thomas when we stayed with Aunt Agnes. I was good at writing and when I was older, my handwriting was put on the school display board as an example of how one should form letters. I loved my work and I always came top of the class. I used to be called the teacher's pet but I wasn't treated any differently. I was just good at what I was given to do. My teacher, Miss Edgecombe, was always there because she moved up from class to class with us. As we grew so she taught us in every standard. After every exam or test I got sweets or something because I came top. I never got big headed about it, Bern. I never knew what big headed meant. I just loved my work and enjoyed school I remember this one time in particular. It was the end of a year and I came top again. Miss Edgecombe brought a beautiful doll for me. It was dressed like a first aid nurse. I adored it and played hospital until I made everyone sick and tired. I will tell you more about school when I was sent to the orphanage.

Just as we began to think the world would never change again, we heard that Daddy was getting married and that we would have a new mother. We were to go and stay with our stepmother, Mini, so we could live with dad, too. We were very happy to be having a mother that would be permanent and that would stop our being passed on from one parent to another. We were ready to love her and to begin a new family life with her and our father. Our dreams were not in keeping with reality. We were soon sadly disillusioned. Mini had a little girl of two years old and I was chosen to be the nursemaid. May became the housemaid. Daddy, being away for such long intervals, knew nothing of the new arrangements. It was easier for Mini to beat May and I about than to explain her needs or to tell us what it was that we were not doing to her satisfaction. She hit us around every day. There was always something to earn us her wrath. Our new 'granny' was also an invalid. She could not walk, so I had to go and clean and cook for her each day after school. There was a step aunt living in new Granny's house and she too had to be fed. I cooked under instruction from her but never seemed to get anything right. God help me if I got things wrong! God help me again if things were not done immediately and perfectly.

I remember Bern, that once I burned the spinach because I was busy scrubbing the floor and forgot the time. Not knowing how to fix things and make the spinach presentable, I washed it in cold water. Of course it was a mess! Stepmother was called and Aunt Eunice announced that I had tried to poison her. I was kicked and beaten until I bled. I remember the hatred in my heart that hatched stronger at each nauseating blow. I felt so helpless and humiliated and yet so determined not to give way to tears, as this was a messenger of weakness. I would be strong for May and for myself. God would cure me of all that went wrong and

Dad would be proud of me no matter what was done to show me up. May and I often vowed that we would survive and show everyone who we were in the end. When we passed each other in the house, we whispered, 'I'll pray for you, if you'll pray for me.' And we did. Our prayers were answered one day when Dad came home unexpectedly. Stepmother (I'm sorry I call her that all the time, but sometimes I cannot bring myself to name her), she doesn't deserve a real name. She reminds me of the ugly mother in Cinderella. I remind myself of Cinderella - the poor girl who got all the blame for everything that was wrong and who had to take responsibility for the whole world's mess.

"When we stayed with our Aunt Agnes, we were always spick and span. She made clothes for us and made sure that we went to town and to school looking our best. Stepmother never did anything for us and soon I was down to one dress and one uniform. I was also growing and began to bulge out of them. I went to school looking like a neglected child. My teacher, Miss Edgecombe, drew me aside one day and told me that I looked dirty and that I smelled bad. I was so ashamed. I never got over the humiliation. I washed my dress every night after that and went to school in damp clothes on some days, as they did not dry enough overnight. One day I went to school with bloodstains down the front of my dress. Stepmother had given me a punch in the nose because she said I did not make her coffee strong enough. I don't know why she hated us so much. I told Miss Edgecombe that I had had a nosebleed on the bus. She said that I had been looking much better and that I was much cleaner these days. That made me feel happy in spite of my aching face. I wonder now how she did not notice the bruises on me. Perhaps she did but did not feel she could ask questions."

Among the high peaked mountains
I make you my mother
So that the thick disguising mists don't matter:
You sheep lead me, kraal toe!
I am securely penned in your womb of wounded truth.
On the clouded cliffs, I watch you
While you wander through the treacherous ravines.
You give me gifts

To open wide the gates that petrify your pain.
In a small flower's heart
I make you my friend
So that I see through you the sun's light shines.
Here, in my mind, we talk and laugh
And blow some little purple petals
Into the freedom of the wind.

I say, "Mama, listen to the thunder, it is going to rain." Dorry does not answer. She tap-taps and finger plays. She sits in silence for a while. She says, "I was allowed a slice of bread and syrup when I got home from cooking and cleaning for Step-grandmother. I was always so hungry and so stole some butter to go with the bread. Sure enough I got beaten for that too but I still could not resist the butter. I still love bread and butter.

It wasn't too long before Stepmother had a baby boy from Dad and so May and I got even busier. Our Stepbrother, Aubrey, was a beautiful baby with blond hair and blue eyes. I really loved him and my Stepsister as well. As time passed things began to change. May was taken out with Mini; I want to say Mini Rat not even Mini Mouse, in the afternoons and never came home until I had put the two little ones to bed. Stepmother then started going out every night with a Frenchman and with a bus driver who lived next door. His name was Mr Ackerman and he was married to a weedy little lady. She complained and so got beaten up by him. I could often hear her screaming and begging for help. I felt afraid and helpless and understood what she was suffering. I was always too afraid to tell anyone what was going on. May and I never held conversations while stepmother was in the house. We were too afraid of being accused of talking about her or of making a noise. May was taken out of school when she was in Standard Four. She was not allowed to go on to Standard Six or Eight so that she could be a nurse and get a job. She became the housemaid. Stepmother wrote a note to the Principal at St Joseph's to say that May had to leave school because the doctor ordered it. Stepmother also told Dad that Sr Margaret-Mary had asked her to visit the school and recommended that May leave school. I don't know what reason was given but dear softy Dad believed the lies and May never finished her schooling.

I used to pray to Jesus to somehow end it all. He did. One day Stepmother beat me and knocked me to the ground. She used the bamboo cane that left welts on the back of my legs. While I was down on the floor I noticed her hairy leg and before I could control myself and think of the consequences, I bit it. Of course she beat me even harder but it seemed worth the pain, Bern. When Dad came home she reported that there was a wild animal in the house and that its name was Dorry. She showed her wounded leg and waited for my father to beat me for my bad behaviour. Instead he unleashed his anger on her and asked what I was doing on the floor and what the welts were doing on my legs. I told him of the treatment she gave us when he was away. There was a storm that rose like a hurricane in the house. I stared in awe and amazement at my father. I had never heard him shout at anyone so violently. After that May wrote him a letter and told him about the men she was visiting and going out with. She gave it to me to post. Dad came home that weekend. We were so afraid that he had not received it before coming home. Dad left as usual on the Sunday night. Then on the Monday morning May told me that Dad will be waiting outside the convent for me and that I was to tell him that Mini would be going out that night. I saw dad standing a little way up the road when I came out of school. He was under the big clock on the corner of Grey Street. I gave him the message. He told me that he would be in the lane around the corner from our house and I was to tell him as soon as Mini left for her evening escapade. Mini took May with her of course. When Mini set out, I went to the back gate but was afraid to open it and look down the lane as it was already dark and I had baby Aubrey on my hip trying to carry him along with me. Dad gave a little cough and I rushed out. Dad was waiting with another man. They sent me back inside and set off. It was much later when they returned to the house with Mini and May. All four sat at the dining room table. The man with my dad turned out to be a lawyer and he asked many questions. Mini said she had delivered some sewing to the man with whom she was sitting when Dad arrived. He was a Creole and very dark. He turned out to be the caretaker of the cemetery. May and I saw him a couple of years later. We avoided talking to him. Of course stepmother never did any sewing at all. May and his daughter were sent out as soon as Mini arrived at his house and were given money to buy

51

sweets. His name was Mr Le Bond or something like that. There was a hell of a do too because Mini was pregnant with Dad's second child while this affair was going on. There was a controversy about whose child it really was.

My father decided that he would have to take Mini with him to the sites, as she couldn't be trusted at home. He worked for the Provincial Roads Department and so they supplied prefab housing on the sites. He took the two little ones as well but for May and me it would have to be a new home again. Mini kept telling us that we would be very sorry to go into a children's home, but May and I knew very well that nothing could be worse than living with our stepmother with all the beatings and near starvation. We were skinny, puny looking little things, you know, Bern. I remember that May first menstruated on a Saturday morning but she still had to do all the chores around the house. Mini sent her to the butcher and she fainted. The Butcher carried her home and Dad put her on the deck chair to rest and relax. Along came Mini and got hold of a wet dishcloth and smacked her in the face with it. She screamed to May to get off her backside and stop creeping up her father's arse. Dad was watching and saw the whole episode. Bern, he grabbed hold of Mini and gave her a damn good hiding. I had never seen Dad so violent. I was terrified but happy that you know who was getting a bit of her own muti! May told Dad that he should not hit women but he said, 'It's alright, May, I know much more than you think!'"

> *I see some wounds in trees,*
> *The fire has been,*
> *It's scarred the growth paths*
> *But they survive the black,*
> *The leaves bud green.*
> *I look into your eye-scars,*
> *There green, a little dull shone:*
> *Your tears have being.*
> *But then some smiles,*
> *I hear your heart laughs,*
> *Love survives*
> *No matter what the fires have done.*
> *I say, "What happened after that, Mama?"*

♥

Sometimes the sky laughs.
It splits the clouds into free, smile games.
Sometimes the sky cries.
It spills the clouds onto hot, dry land.
Life is born.
Love grows.
Hope remains the feeding fountain.

I AM excited because Dorry and my father have visited Miss Viljoen. She is the village teacher. Dorry says I am just old enough to start going to classes even though my birthday is only in June but perhaps she will take me after Christmas. Dianne is also going to school after Christmas. I have got a new dress and new shoes for school. I have got a new ribbon for my hair. Dorry has put them in the cupboard and I open it and look at my clothes every day. When Dianne comes to our house to play, I show them to her and she says she will have to ask her mother to make her new clothes too.

Our school is at the far end of the village, near Mr Morey's house and near the police station. The red sand road that leads to its gate is lined with syringa trees. Around each tree is a circle of whitewashed stones. The prisoners from the jail behind that police station keep them painted. They also paint the stones that surround the gardens outside the jail and the police station. They have little bushes with purple flowers on them. There are only five prisoners in our village because the people do not steal and do other bad things. They are peaceful people and respectful people. My father says they have to keep the stones whitewashed to remind them that Jesus whitewashed their souls and it is time they thought about that seriously. Dorry says my father talks bloody tripe and why tell kids such bull. I say nothing but I think that the stones look beautiful next to the red sand and the green trees. I think they help to keep the rain water around their roots.

Our school has only one classroom because there are few white children in our village. The many black children go to their own schools where they learn and sing and play in their own language. Aunty Shaw has a school for them near the river. She takes me there and the children stand in rows and dance and clap and sing. They say, "Welcome visitors," in English and I say, "Thank you," in Setswana. Sometimes I play with our cook Polokwane's children. He brings them to our house. They do not wear clothes; it is too hot. They wear a piece of cloth in front of their 'things' and a small square cloth to cover their bums. When they run, their little squares bounce up and down but they do not care. Dorry says it is called culture. She says our culture covers up everything. My father says it saves all the washing and saves arguing about who has how many dresses and it saves money because people do not have to pay for material. Some other black people always wear dresses that touch the ground. They wrap their heads in cloth called doeks. When they go to the toilet they just sit in the road and widdle because nobody can see anything. When they stand up and walk again there is a small puddle that is gobbled up by the sand. My father says there is no knowing what some cultures will do. One just has to accept them as they are. I do not know what my culture is. I do not think we have one. We never have drums and sing and dance and clap they way the black people do. Dorry says God needs variety and that is why we are all different. I do not know what variety is. My father says it is complicated so I keep quiet because I do not know what complicated means.

Our classroom smells of plasticine and Radiant Readers. I love their smell. When I open the pages, their scent makes me feel that I love school even though I cannot read or write. I have a slate and a piece of charcoal. I practise my writing on it. I do not write letters but I draw. I draw Dorry and my father and Trish. I draw huts and donkeys and goats and syringa trees. I sometimes draw cattle even though I am afraid of them. I draw some birds and the sky with clouds. I show my pictures to Miss Viljoen and she says, "Dis nou mooi nê!" She tells me to come and stand next to her with my Radiant Reader. She says I must look at the apple on the first page and say 'aah vir aapel'. When I go home and tell Dorry that I am learning 'aah vir aapel' she says, "What the hell is that language?"

My father says, "What can you do with a bloody Dutchman teaching English to English children; they will turn into mongrels and then what?" Dorry says it is better than no teacher at all. I do not know what it is. I do not like school anymore. My father says Miss Viljoen is in love with Koos Van der Merwe and will be leaving our village. Soon she will be living in Mafikeng. He says perhaps I will learn English now. He says it is a good thing Koos came along and saved his child from language lunacy. Dorry says my father is full of tripe. I do not know who will teach me anything now. I will have to wait and see. My father says there is a new addition to our village. She is living at the hotel with her dog. Dorry says she knows and her name is Mrs Johnston and she is the teacher.

When I walk to school early in the morning I sit under one of the syringa trees and wait for Dianne. Sometimes other children wait too. When it is time to go into our classroom, Mrs Johnston rings a bell and her small dog with the flat face and sticky-out teeth barks. Her dog's name is Pepper because she says it is full of spunk. Mrs Johnston says he is a rare breed. He is Pekingese. We take off our shoes outside the classroom door and we wipe our feet with our handkerchiefs to get all the sand from in between our toes. If we don't, then we get blisters because the sand rubs against our skin and it gets red and sore. Dorry says I should not wear sandals and my father says my skin will toughen up but he will give me some new takkies if I want them. We beat our shoes against the classroom wall or steps and then put them on again before we make a straight line outside the door. Mrs Johnston counts us and calls out our names to see if we are there. She makes us stand next to our desks and arranges us according to our age and size. The children who have been in school the longest sit at the back and Dianne, a girl called Willie and I sit in the front.

Before we begin our lessons we sing 'God Save our Gracious King' because our country is protected by Britain. Aunty Shaw has pictures of our King and our Queen and their three children, who are princesses and a prince. Above Mrs Johnston's desk hangs a picture of the King. She says he looks down on us with concern for our future. I do not know what concern is. I ask Dianne and she says she thinks it is like kindness when we get sweets for being good. I think that if the King ever came to our village I would get sweets for his concern and they would come from England and be famous sweets. I would never eat them. I would put them in a special box and show them to people who come to our house.

Pepper sleeps under Mrs Johnston's desk. He grunts and snores and has bad dreams. When he gets up to have a stretch and scratch, he squeaks and yawns and spit drips onto Mrs Johnston's shoe but she does not notice. She has a bottle of Eucalyptus oil on her desk and she notices when Pepper farts because she clears her throat and her nose turns up with her head that turns to the side and her handkerchief gets out of her pocket very fast. It gets put over her pointed nose and her chair grates loudly as she gets up. She knows Pepper has made the stink but she blames somebody else. She opens her bottle of oil and walks down the rows of desks and sprinkles it all over us. She stops at Alistair's desk and says, "Who has made the classroom smell so dreadful?" Alistair jumps up and pulls his feet cleaning hanky from his pocket and begins to chew the corner. He cries and says that he did not make a stink. Mrs Johnston says that somebody did. Gideon stands up next to Alistair and says Pepper bombed the place. Mrs Johnston turns bright red and claps her hands at us because we laugh at Gideon. Alistair does not laugh. He cries louder and louder until Mrs Johnston puts her oil back on her desk and tells us to make a line in front of the room. She then tells us to go and make two lines outside the toilets, one for girls and one for boys. We all have to go, one by one. We all have to wait back in the line until everyone has been. Sometimes Gideon takes a very long time. Mrs Johnston tells him not to sit around in there all day and he says he has a sore stomach. Alistair is in and out of the toilet very fast so that we do not think he was the bomber. When we come out of the toilets we have to go to Mrs Johnston, who has sunlight soap in a dish. We have to wash our hands and then dry them in the sun. We wave them about and sometimes the boys slap us with wet hands and say sorry it was an accident. When Gideon comes out, we clap and Mrs Johnston makes us march around the school yard. She says it works off some mischief.

When we get into the classroom Mrs Johnston says it is imagination time and reading time. My Radiant Reader does not have letters like aah vir aapel in it. I have a new reader with no writing. It has pictures of balls and dogs fetching them. It has a picture of a boy and a girl and their parents holding hands. There is one of a lot of sand and wavy water. Two children are building a castle of sand. It does not look like the mud pie sand in our back yard. It is white and clean. The children have on swimming costumes. They have small spades and buckets and a wheelbarrow as well. Mrs Johnston tells us about the sea and the seaside that is called a beach. She says if we look out to the water that is called the sea, we will never be able to see the end of it. She says the earth has more sea than sand and land. She stands us in a row and shows us how to be waves that break on the shore. She gets a piece of rope and moves it to show us how the waves move and why they break on the shore. She makes the sound of the sea while she is showing us. Dorry says she will take us all to the sea one day. My father says you never know when the cows will come home and perhaps we will see it one day. I long to see the sea and to hear the waves break like Mrs Johnston shows us.

At break time we play cowboys and crooks. I am always a cowboy and my name is always Roy Rogers. Dorry loves Roy Rogers and his horse, Trigger. We see him at the bioscope on Fridays. I also love him. Trigger saves him when the crooks hide behind the bushes and knock him off his horse and he lies unconscious for a long time. Trigger nudges him and pulls his clothes until he wakes up. Dianne likes Roy Rogers but she loves Gene Autrey. She says he's better because he sings, "Get along little Doggy, get along, get along." He sings it when he is in his truck. There are no doggies, just cattle. Dianne says he is an American cowboy and that is the way they herd cattle. The cattle in our village are not herded with songs from a truck. They are allowed to walk through the bush and the herdsmen are small boys with long whips. They whistle and crack the whips over the cattle to make them go where they want. Sometimes they in-span the oxen and make them pull wagons or sledges. They pile the wagons with wood for fires at their huts. Sometimes the wagons are full of watermelons or sacks of sorghum. The front ox has a bell around his neck and when the cattle are in the bush, the herdsmen know where they are. I am afraid when the cattle run through the village. They have long horns and I think they are chasing me. I climb a tree when I see them in the road near our school. Dianne and Willie also climb trees and we wait until the dust and the cattle have gone before we get down and go home.

Ted is my cousin and he comes to visit us from Ghantsi. He has many cattle and he herds them from Ghantsi to Lobatse. It takes many weeks in the bush and Ted and his brothers ride on horseback. They have to go slowly so that the cattle can graze on the way. They take them to Lobatse and sell them to the abattoirs. They get slaughtered for beef that we eat except on Fridays because we are Catholics. I ask Ted to make me guns and holsters so that I can really look like Roy Rogers. He is very clever and also knows how the leopards got their spots and how the tortoise came first in the race against the rabbit and how Hansel and Gretel fooled the witch who wanted to roast them in her oven. Ted tells me these stories while he carves my guns out of wood with his penknife and makes my holsters out of cardboard and sews them up with string. I also ask Ted to make up a cowboy song so that Gene Autrey is not the only cowboy who sings. He tells me to fetch some paper and he writes words on it. He cuts out the words and says I must go and plant them near the tap in our yard so that they get water and grow. He says words grow songs and I will see the song come up after seven days. I fetch Dianne and Willie and we watch for the song to grow every day. They also plant words that Ted has written. No songs grow and Dorry says Ted is teasing us. We are not sure if he is or not and we look for the songs a long time after he has gone back to Ghantsi. My father says I will have to make up my own cowboy song. He sings, "Home, home on the range, where the herds and the antelope play." He says I could sing about lions in the bush chasing the calves for supper. Roy Rogers would come and save them and herd them away to a proper kraal.

Mrs Johnston is asking Gideon where New York is. He says he doesn't know. She says he should try and find out in his atlas. He says his atlas is at home. She says is his brain also at home? He goes red and looks sulky and hangs his head low. Mrs Johnston tells him he has such a face on him and he had better change it. Gideon says he hasn't got a face and Mrs Johnston says, "What have you got, a flat pan?" Gideon says he will give her a flat pan and tell his father if she makes fun of him again. Alistair takes out his hanky and begins to chew the corner and I ask to go to the toilet.

When it is very hot we sit under the syringa tree in the road outside the school gate. Dianne opens her lunch tin and I take mine out of its brown paper bag. I show Dianne my sandwiches and she says they are lovely and thick. The jam oozes out from around the sandwich sides. Dianne's sandwiches are very neat and have no crusts. She has cheese and ham. She says she will swap me for one of mine. I like her lunch tin and look at the biscuits Mrs Freeman makes. She makes enough for me, too. When my Aunty Maxi comes to visit, Dorry lets her make my sandwiches and I never eat them because Aunty Maxi's fingers are bright yellow from the cigarette smoke. My sandwiches remind me of smoking and coughing. I eat Dianne's and she eats all mine. We also share the toffees and apples in her tin.

Sometimes Mrs Johnston takes us outside to play games. She says we have to keep fit. We hold hands and jump up and down or weave in and out of a circle. We play leapfrog. I hate holding Stephan's hands. They are very rough and dry. I hate his hair oil smell. When it is hot and the sun shines on his head, I feel sick. I try and get away from him and stand next to Gideon or Michael. I tell Dorry about Stephan and she says we must love everybody and I will have to learn how to put up with rough hands. My father says I should wear gloves like the Queen and I will never have to feel rough hands again. Dorry says I must not listen to tripe.

On our way home from school we stop at a certain tree and climb up as far as we can to pick the wild berries that pop out of their skins. They are small and yellow and taste like mangoes. We also pick brown berries from the bushes that grow between the paths. We put them in our lunch tins or paper bags and when we get home we wash them and put them into a glass of milk and drink and chew at the same time. Dorry says we will get worms. She gives us worm medicine sometimes.

We are not going to school today because my father says King George has died and we have to respect him by having a public holiday. Dorry says we should go to school. She sends a note to Mrs Freeman. Mrs Freeman also says we are not having school today. There is sad music on the radio. The flag at the police station is hanging half way down the pole and my father says that is a sign of mourning and respect for a famous person's death. He says the flag will hang like that for ten days.

Aunty Shaw has had a letter from the King's palace. It says that we are having a new Queen. Her name is Elizabeth. Dorry has to make me a Girl Guide uniform because on the day Elizabeth becomes the Queen we have to have a celebration and a ceremony at the police station. We have to march and salute and a new Union Jack will be raised. The Police Band will play 'God Save Our Gracious Queen'. We will be given Royal coffee mugs. My father says he will use his for his shaving things. Dorry says hers will stand on the mantelpiece. I say mine will be put in a box in my cupboard in case Trish finds it. All the mothers in the village will make tea and cakes for after the ceremony.

We are all standing in a straight line at the police station. I look very smart in my Girl Guide uniform. Dianne looks just as smart as me because Dorry made her uniform too. We all have on white socks and black shoes that have been very well polished. Aunty Shaw is reading a letter from the Queen to all her subjects. I do not know if I am a subject like History or Reading. We march behind the Police Band. They play marching music and have rifles against their shoulders. They have khaki uniforms and felt hats that are clipped up at one side and nearly look like Roy Rogers's cowboy hat. Some police are on horseback. My father says they are the mounted police because when you get onto a horse you are mounting it. I mount Dianne's horses and we go and ride on the golf course. We do not ride fast. We walk or trot.

After the marching and the Queen's letter we sing, 'God Save Our Gracious Queen' but Alistair forgets and sings 'King'. Gideon gives him a poke in the back. Alistair begins to look for his hanky but his mother comes and gives him a pat on his shoulder and he joins in the singing again. We stand very still and straight while the new Union Jack goes up the flagpole and the police salute and fire twenty-one shots into the air with bullets that cannot kill because they are not real ones. My father says they are called blanks. When we have stood in the hot sun and respected our new Queen, we go to the tables with cakes and sweets on them and we get our Royal coffee mugs that say 'Her Majesty Queen Elizabeth II'. There is a picture of her and of her crown. We are given our cake and sweets and cool drinks. I am very happy that we are Girl Guides of the Queen.

When we get home, my father switches on the radio and we can hear the horses carrying the new Queen along the hard roads in London. We can hear the Queen swear her promise to be good and to rule over us in a kind way. Dorry says that when I was a baby the Queen passed through our village and held me in her arms. She was a princess then. I am very pleased about that. I tell Mrs Johnston what Dorry has said and she says I am famous and should never wash again.

I am very confused because Mrs Johnston has been teaching us Geography. She tells us about other lands and London. She tells us about many other cities in many other lands. We are also learning where things grow and how they get onto our tables and into our pantries and lounges. She says sardines come from Natal and the Cape in South Africa. They also come from Sardinia over the sea somewhere. She asks me where oranges are grown. I tell her that they grow in Mrs Oudendaal's garden. She laughs and says don't I listen to anything she says? I know oranges grow in Mrs Oundendaal's garden because I have seen them there and she picks me one like Nancy Morey does when it is a hot day and she sees me passing her house. I tell Dorry about the oranges and she laughs too but says I will know more about Geography when I am older. My father says Mrs Johnston knows nothing about oranges; she never visits Mrs Oudendaal.

When we have sports day, we do not have it at our school because the yard is too small so we have it at the tennis club. All our parents come to see us run and do high jump and long jump. Dorry, Mrs Freeman and Aunty Shaw make cakes and tea and give us sweets as well. My father stands at the winning post when I run my races and he shouts for me to win and run faster. He is very proud of me because

I win all my races and I also jump the highest and the longest. He says I am his little nun and his little sprinter and that I take after him. He picks me up and walks home with me on his shoulders because he says I am a champion. I get prizes when I win. I get a small tennis racquet and a tennis ball. I get a new pair of takkies and new white tennis socks. Dorry says I am a clever girl. She is proud of me too.

Mrs Johnston has been in love for some time. She has not told anyone and so we are all surprised when she writes her new name on the board. It is Mrs Loveday. My father says she could not love a day in her life. Dorry says she is leaving the village and going to Johannesburg with Mr Loveday and that one day I will also have to leave our school because it only goes up to Standard One or Two. I do not want to leave our school because I want to stay in our village with Dianne and Dorry. I want to play in my father's shop and have suckers and play hen-hen.

♥

I chose a daisy for my vase;
Small and bright,
It unfolded yellow.
It sent me tears and joy;
Kisses from the sun.
It coaxed my smiling from its smother-shell.
It breathed bare beauty for a while
And then, some petals fell.
My daisy died a simple death.
My wounds were not of simple sorrow bred;
I sang a dirge for its funeral
Though other daisies grow.

"WELL, it wasn't long before May and I were taken to
Cambridge House in North Ridge Road. I believe it is an
old age home these days. We became boarders because Dad paid
nothing for us. It was a hostel for girls. Life there was good, Bern.
We had good food and went out to school every day. I was very sad to
leave St Thomas but got used to the North Ridge government school.
We made new friends and life was lovely really. We had a dance
every Saturday night, just among ourselves. There was also an annual
dance and we invited visitors and boys as partners. It was always a sit
down dinner dance and the music was good. We were also allowed to
have visitors from seven to eight every Tuesday evening. The bigger
girls were allowed to have their boyfriends on Saturday nights but
I didn't have one until I was fourteen. I was rather advanced for my
age, Bern; most girls were older than I. My first boyfriend's name

Dorry, aged 18

Dorry and Hugh

Dorry and Hugh's wedding day

Dorothy, Faith, Thelma, Monica and visitor

Trish age 2, Bernadette , 4, Dorothy, 7-8

Bernie, age 5

Cath age 2, Trish, 4, Bern 6-7

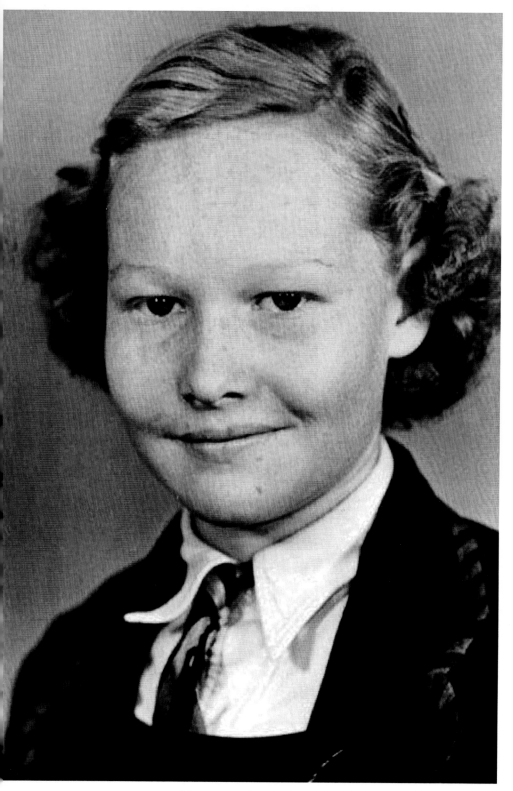

Monica, aged around 9-10

was George and my best friend, Chamita, also fancied him. She had a boyfriend too and I rather liked him so we decided to swap! Next visitors' hour, I sat next to Ernest and Chamita sat next to George. I don't know what the boys thought but things fell into place and stayed that way until I left the hostel. Chamita married George in the end. I was also extremely fond of another boy called Johnny Tilbury. Whenever I heard his motorbike coming along I used to fly to the gate and onto the pavement to chat to him. I went out with him when I was sixteen and had left the hostel to go back home and live with Dad and Mini again.

If only I had realised what opportunities I would miss by going back home, Bern. The matron gave me a choice. She said I was doing very well and could go to college and be trained in a vocation of some sort and she told my father that I had the most beautiful singing voice and that she could arrange for it to be trained. I chose to go home because I thought I was grown up and could do as I pleased and go out with Johnny when I pleased. So silly, we teenagers, hey, Bern? Instead, I became a sales lady at Stuttafords. I had to pay in half my salary to Dad, dress myself and pay bus fares. All was very cheap in those days so I managed quite well. I could buy dress material and May used to make them for me. Once she made the dress too tight and refused to take out the seams so I climbed into her and we had a real brawl on the floor. Luckily, our uncle came to visit and separated us; otherwise I think you would have had a murderess for a mother!"

When Dorry sings, her voice washes over me like a liquid moonrise. It coils around my mind in waves of calm and healing balms that transcend all other sound or cures for crying. It oozes into every heart crevice with its low and clear melody. I can take time to stare some secrets into space and feel secure in their rising with her song. She does not need to be asked for song. It is like her laughter, always at the ready to 'break' what is bland. She sings at any time, when she is baking or sewing or sweeping the thick dust off the stoep. Sometimes my father, Dorry and the seven of us gather around the piano. Sally plays 'Silent Persuasion' and Faith plays 'Silent Confession' and Monica plays her piano accordion. She is very good at it. Her fingers just know what to do and the treble notes and bass buttons make many songs. She is proud of herself and has to sit very straight when she plays because it is bad for your lungs if you slouch. Sometimes Faith and Sally play a duet and my uncle plays the violin. They play at our village concerts. When my father asks us to stand in front of the mantelpiece and sing like his little angels, we sing 'Silent Night', 'Ave Maria' and 'Come to the Station, Jump from the Train'. It is a hit on the radio and my father loves it. He gets very cross when the radio crackles and he can't hear properly. He says short wave and long wave radio is a problem and what is wrong with the manufacturers? He shows me how short waves and long waves bend in the air. I am very ignorant because I can't imagine waves floating around in the air and making tunes and songs. He sings 'Come to the Station' when he has his whiskey on the stoep. I do not understand the song. My father says it is about a soldier in love. I always wonder how a soldier can 'lay down your arms and surrender to mine', when they are attached to his shoulders. My father says I will understand when I am in love. I do not want to be in love. It is always soppy and people kiss and cry all the time. I cannot read music so I stand at the piano next to Sally. She calls out the chords to me and I watch her fingers on the keys. She tells me stories about ebony and ivory. I love to listen to her. She has done many exams in music and says she will one day be a concert pianist. She learns it at school. The nun who teaches her says she is gifted but she also hits her over the knuckles so that Sally hates piano lessons. She gets honours for her exams but the last one she took, she only got a credit because the nun hit her so hard the night before that her hands were swollen and she could not manoeuvre her fingers as adeptly as she should. Now, when I ask her what she will be one day, she gets a far away look in her eyes and says, "Whatever the mood moves me to be." My father plays the piano too. He cannot read music but if he hears a song that he likes he can just play it. He calls his style of playing: 'vamping'. He vamps 'Old Auntie Cathy' for us and makes us laugh. He says that old Auntie Cathy is so dumb; she stirs her coffee with her own big thumb and something to do with her toe as well. He says that the words of the song get rude so he stops before the bad part and makes us very curious to know what else Auntie Cathy does. He says he will tell us when the cows come home.

My father bought Dorry a set of music books and a long tape with red and green stripes on it. She says it is the 'Johnny Ralph's' method of playing and learning piano. You don't have to understand all the theory that Sally and Faith learn. You just follow the instructions and the stripes and a song happens. When Dorry and my father fight and we are afraid, I hide under the bed but Sally plays 'Silent Persuasion' and tries to persuade them not to shout. Monica also shouts. She tells them to stop fighting. I do not know what Faith does. I don't know what Dorothy does either. I think they just sit and wait for the storm to be over and then get on with life again. Sometimes when the house is quiet and I am alone, I play the piano. My fingers just seem to run along and a melody comes into my mind. I think I am like my father and I just play a song when I like it. Sally also teaches me. She practises with me every day when there is a concert in our village. We play two duets and we are very proud of ourselves. My father says he is very proud of us, too. He calls us 'my girls'. I don't know why Dorry does not sing at the concerts. Maybe she is too shy. I don't know what I would do without her beautiful voice. It is a treasure to me.

♥

Inside my heart wells worry
For a world that is yet to happen.
Horizons of hope envelope
And unfold me.
I wait with new music
To play, to sing
To dance in the halls of new knowing.

I walk in the spirit of courage
To do, to work,
To create new being
In the mind of closed ways
Tired of trying.

THERE is a thin, red line creeping up Dorry's arm. Today it is longer than yesterday. Her hand has a bandage around it and she is in her bed because she also keeps coughing. When she coughs, she cries. My father is at Number Two Store working in the butchery. It closes at lunchtime for an hour and he comes home. Dorry says I must go and fetch my father immediately. She says he must tell Mr Freeman that she is very sick and that he must take her to hospital in Serowe. I run to my father and tell him what Dorry has said. He says, "Bloody donders se hell!" He puts on his hat and he goes to tell Mr Freeman what he has to do. Mr Freeman says he must go straight away. There is no doctor in our village today. Mr Freeman says that he will phone Doris, his wife, to see what she can do to help. He goes to the shop phone and turns the handle very fast. He speaks to Mrs Freeman. He tells my father that he must bring Dotty and Trish and me to their house because Doris will look after us while Dorry is in the hospital.

My father is helping Dorry to walk to Pedro the truck. He has put a mattress in the back so that she can lie down and not have to sit all the way to Serowe. The road is sandy and there are many corrugations on it and when we are having fun, we open our mouths and sing on one note and our voices shake like opera singers because of the corrugations. Dorry's voice is soft and she is breathless. She sounds as if there is something stuck in her throat. My father looks very worried and we are worried. He tells us to squash together in the front of Pedro so that Dorry can be comfortable. He puts a warm blanket over her. She asks if my father has packed enough clothes for us and he says yes for now but if we need more he will see Doris and bring them later when we need them. Dorry cries and says he must look after us well and see to it that we have everything we need. My father says she must rest and not worry about the kids.

My father helps us out of Pedro. Mrs Freeman and Cabbage greet us. Cabbage takes our suitcases and takes them to the back stoep. It is a cool place and there are four beds in a row made up with eiderdowns and feather pillows. Our beds only have sheets and blankets and a quilt over them. The stoep has a thatched roof like the rest of Mrs Freeman's house. When I come and stay with Dianne, we sleep on the back stoep. We listen to the wind's soft music through the gauze. We hear the crickets and the frogs. We answer the frogs and they go quiet for a while. Then they answer us and we laugh at how we have fooled them. Mrs Freeman puts sweets under our pillows and we share them and swap them. Mrs Freeman reads us a story while we eat our sweets and then she tucks us in and switches off the lights. There are electric lights because Mr Freeman has a machine. He calls it a generator and he switches it off before he goes to bed.

My father lifts us up one by one to say goodbye to Dorry. She blows us kisses with the hand that is not bandaged. We blow kisses back. My father drives Pedro slowly and we watch him take Dorry away from us. My stomach feels sick and empty and I want to cry. Dotty wipes her eyes with the back of her hand but she does not cry out loud. We begin to walk along the path to Mrs Freeman's house. Trisha begins to cry and Mrs Freeman picks her up. She tries to comfort her but Trisha cries louder and louder. Dotty stretches out her arms for her and Mrs Freeman gives Trisha to her. It does not stop the crying. It turns into screaming. Dianne comes from her playroom and Mrs Freeman sends her back for a doll for Trisha. She comes running with a rag doll with long hair and plaits. It has red lips and blue, glass eyes. Trisha looks at it and begins to scream even louder. Dotty tells Mrs Freeman she will go outside and take Trisha and me for a walk and when we are used to being in her garden she will bring us back. I am feeling afraid and I am feeling sick. My stomach is sore and my legs do not want to walk properly. Dotty puts Trisha down on the lawn and she takes our hands and walks us around to the swing. Trisha has stopped crying because she is on the swing. Dotty pushes her gently. Mrs Freeman comes out of the stoep door and calls us. She says she has cool drinks and cake for us. My stomach is not so sore and my legs do want to walk now.

At lunchtime Mr Freeman comes home. He says hello to us. Trisha hides behind Dotty's dress. Mrs Freeman says Charles does not bite. He just sounds awful but he is as kind as Father Christmas. Mrs Freeman rings a bell so that Cabbage knows we will have lunch now. She shows us where to wash our hands. We use Lifebuoy soap but Mrs Freeman has Palmolive and it smells very nice. I sit next to Dianne. Mr Freeman sits at the top of the table and Mrs Freeman sits at the bottom. Next to Mr Freeman is a bamboo cane. Dianne asks why the cane is there. Mr Freeman clears his throat and says it is for children who have bad table manners and for children who do not eat their vegetables. Trisha begins to pull Dotty's skirt. Mrs Freeman says, "Oh, Charley, stop your nonsense. You are making the little ones afraid!" Dotty turns red. I say, "Mrs Freeman says that you do not bite!" Mr Freeman puts the cane on the floor and says I have a lot of courage.

I have learned to measure flour for scones and I have learned how much sugar and baking powder to mix in and how much milk to pour into the mixture. I have learned how to make dollops of the dough and place them in rows on a greased baking pan. Dotty has learned how to look after Trish when Mrs Freeman is busy and how to do embroidery. Trisha has learned how to play with all the toys in the playroom. Dianne teaches her how to hold the crayons and she holds her hand and shows her how to colour in the pictures. We have got used to being in Mrs Freeman's house and we have got used to Mr Freeman, who likes us to think he is strict and stern but we take no notice. We know that he is as kind as Father Christmas. I know that when we have the Christmas party, Mr Freeman dresses up like Father Christmas and gives us our presents. I heard Hilton say, "Thank you, Dad," when he got his.

My father has come to take us home because Dorry is well again. He says she is waiting for us and is longing to see us. He tells Mrs Freeman that Dorry had blood poisoning because a thorn pricked her finger when she was gardening in Lecheng. He says she also got pleurisy from neglecting her cold. Mrs Freeman tells my father that we have been very good children and that she will visit Dorry soon. She says our hair ribbon bows have improved and she shows my father how she has learned to tie them. He takes our suitcases and Cabbage helps him to put them in the back of Pedro. We hug Mrs Freeman and Dianne. We say thank you for having us. My father picks up Trisha and she begins to cry, louder and louder. When we reach the gate of Mrs Freeman's house she is screaming.

Dorry runs down the path to our gate. She opens Pedro's door and squashes us up together for a hug. Trisha is still screaming. She picks her up and says, "What has been happening?" Trisha tells her that she does not want Dorry; she wants her lovely mother! Dorry says, "Ye gods, what goes on in these kids' minds, I just don't know!"

Every day Dorry sends Lena to Mrs Freeman's house. Lena takes Trisha with her and brings her back in time for her bath at five o'clock. Before she goes, Dorry tells Trisha that she is going to her lovely mother's house and Trisha claps her hands.

♥

Come stand in line now.
Come wait patiently for the gifts,
For the dreaded gifts of
Hearing, seeing and believing.

Come stand in line again.
Come, hands outstretched for
Understanding, mercy and pleading.

Come sit beside my throne.
Bow down for receiving
The precious gifts of
Healing, learning and loving.

Come, do not falter on the way.
Come, lie beneath my feet
And I will teach you dying.

My father sits on the cement block under the cool shade of
the syringa tree. He sits in silence. He broods and mumbles.
I cannot go near for I am afraid of the 'dark' that hangs around him.
I think that the air is made of iron that cannot be entered. There are
some leather straps hanging from his hands and he has a thick needle
and string that he is pulling through the strips and shaping them into
something. He pricks himself and swears, "Donders se hell se bloody
bastard, and all for the donders se hell se dogs!" His face is red and he
sucks his finger and shakes it in the iron air that does not move. Even

the leaves hang in folded forms. They show the dull side of their faces and cannot open and play in the wind. The iron air has captured them in the cruel heat. I stand stiffly in its prison and long for a cooling breeze for comfort. I stare at the wilting grass and the dying weeds. I feel alone and empty and distant. There is nothing across the divide that conveys any ease. Suddenly my father turns and says, "Come and look here and learn a thing or two about how to deal with rabies." The iron air wants to stifle my breath and weight my feet but I walk to where the cement block has cut out a shape in the air. He shuffles along so that I can sit next to him. I see how neatly he has stitched the leather strips and how they look like a small horse's harness. "There is plenty of rabies out there in the village and out there in the bush. If any dog is seen walking about without a muzzle it will have to be shot on the spot. All the traders have to take their guns to the stores in case a rabid animal goes wandering along and bites the people." The people call my father 'Radibatana' - father of small animals. I think it is because he cares for the people and shoots buck for their pot when the crops do not grow and the rains do not come. He gets mealies and corn from another country and sells it to them. He buys their thin cattle and feeds them with hay that comes in the train trucks. He mixes it with molasses so that the cattle do not get sick and die. He is angry about the rabies because if a rabid animal bites anyone they go mad and die. I am afraid of getting rabies because Dorry says it only takes fourteen days to make you go mad. If you don't have injections within the twenty-four hours after you get bitten then you get put in a box like Lenny and nobody can hear you or help you. I am afraid of the silence in the box and under the ground. It is worse than the iron air. The only thing you can hear is the ants eating up the box before they begin eating you.

My father is holding up the tangle of leather and arranging it in a special way. He tells me to fetch our dog Ruddles, who is lying panting in the heat under the morula tree. I can see him in the heat haze and he shimmers in and out of the iron air. I feel that the air is pushing at me and turning my feet into stones. Stones can't move by themselves; they have to be lifted up and carried or put into a wheelbarrow by somebody who knows where they want to go. I am becoming iron like the air. My father tells me again to go and fetch Ruddles. The tone in his voice says I had better stop being iron and stone, and get going soon. If I don't, he will get angry and the air will suffocate everyone in it. There will be a lot of iron people. I know why I do not want to fetch Ruddles. It is because when he does not listen to my father's commands, he gets kicked or beaten with a strap. I cannot listen to his cries. They make me afraid so that I have to walk on the moon again. They make Dorry shout and she calls my father a cruel, unfeeling bastard. He says dogs have to learn who is boss. Dorry tells him that he must never think he is the boss of anything or anyone while she is around because she will box his bloody ears. I can see her doing that to his ears in my mind. My father's ears grow into big funnels like the gramophone in Auntie Shaw's house. She puts on a black plastic record and winds it up. His Master's voice comes out of the funnel; His Master sings a lot of songs like 'My Love is Like a Red, Red Rose' and 'She Walks through the Fair'. I do not know how His Master gets his voice to come out of the funnel so I stay and look very carefully at the gramophone especially when Auntie Shaw invites me to tea and she goes and finds what she has in her cake tin for me. The funnel and my father's ears look like those purple flowers that grow on our fence. They have a wide and wavy mouth and get thinner and thinner. If you pick them and suck their thinnest part, nectar comes out and you wish you were a bee because that is what they do all day. I don't know what my father would say if he knew about his funnel ears. I do not tell him because perhaps he will say that I am full of nonsense and that my imagination will be my downfall.

I can see my downfall. I am falling down, not onto the sandy ground but down a deep well that has no bottom and that never ends. I just fall and echo in there forever. I never touch the sides or the floor but fast float into nowhere. It is not like Lenny's box because the ants can't get there and the ground never covers me. It is a strange place and a strange feeling to fall forever and get nowhere. I am getting nearer to Ruddles. He lifts his head and licks his lips. He rolls onto his back because he thinks I am coming to play. I call him quietly and slap my leg so that he knows he must come with me. He gets up slowly and yawns. He puts his bum in the air and stretches his front legs. He makes me laugh in the iron air so that I know I will not be choked by it. I take him by the collar and he comes quietly with me. My father says, "Ruddles, sit!" He sits and my father lets him smell the leather thongs. He slowly puts the leather cage around Ruddles' mouth and fastens the strap around his neck. The dog struggles to get the muzzle off but my father tells him that it is better than being shot.

Our cat, Dommie, has no muzzle. She is named after a nun called Sr Dominique at my sisters' boarding school. Dommie is sooty black like Dominique's habit. She has a white face, like the bib Dominique wears. I do not know if the cat is called Dominique because my sisters like the nun or if they think the nun is catty. Sally says all nuns are cats of a special Irish breed. I do not know what special Irish breed is but I believe her because she tells me how they call her names like 'stupid' and they are forever saying, "Mark my words, Miss Thelma, you will amount to nothing." When they say the name 'Thelma', they can't pronounce the 'h' so they call Sally 'Telma'. I wish Sally would tell my father or Dorry about the way the nuns treat her because it is cruel and our priest always tells us that the nuns in the convent are there to love everyone as God loves them. I am afraid of God's love. I think if I tell Sally about falling into the well, she would come with me because nobody can amount to anything in there. Monica says that the God-loving nuns lock her and Sally up in a dark corridor under the statue of Our Lady every night for a week or two if they think she or Sally has been insolent. They say she is insolent when Sally does not answer their questions like, "Did you steal a tickey?" Sally doesn't answer because she is afraid that if she says no, they will tell her that she is a liar amounting to nothing. If she tells them that the prefect in charge of the tuck shop stole the money, they will also say that she is a malicious liar amounting to nothing and they will write and tell my father. When they lock up Monica it is because she just tells them what comes into her head like: "I am not a thief and neither is my sister!" Monica can never keep quiet. She fights with words whenever trouble comes her way. She says she doesn't have red hair for nothing. She says, why people should bully her even when they are older and stronger, she just doesn't know. Monica does not keep her mouth closed at home either. My father says he will donner the living daylights out of her but she just carries on until he gets up and fetches the belt.

I love to play with Dommie. She chases me around if I drag a piece of string along with me. She plays ball with Dorry's tennis socks if she leaves them on her bed while she is bathing. She wrestles with my father's shoelaces while he sits on the stoep. He says she is a sharp cat and a good hunter. I have watched Dommie catch mice. The poor little creatures have no idea that they are being watched and followed. She is silent and creeps along the way the lions and leopards do. Before the mice have any chance to run or dive down their holes, Dommie has them in her mouth. Even though she is very hungry, she does not eat them in a hurry. She lets their tails wag frantically and when they have struggled for a while, she drops them back on the ground. They sit there and shiver for a few seconds thinking that they have had a change of luck. As soon as they make a dash for safety, Dommie pounces again and tosses them up into the air like a bit of rag. They make a little thud when they fall and it makes me feel sick and sad that nature is so cruel. My father says God looks after all the creatures but I wonder why creatures get eaten and tortured. It is a mystery to me. My father says he also loves all people and all creatures. He shoots the buck and ducks. I think he only loves the creatures when he isn't hungry or when the shooting season is over. My father says we all have to eat and that is the way God made us. I do not understand God or the way he made us. I am afraid when my father forgets about loving everything and everyone, like the time our cook, Polokwane, prepared a Sunday dinner for us while we went to church. Polokwane means 'a place of safety' but I think our house is not very safe for him when things go wrong in the kitchen. Dorry sometimes tells us about the 'Mad Sunday' even though it is a long time ago now and I was there with Trisha.

"You know, Bern, your father goes that pale white colour around the lips when he is angry. I do remember a few occasions when that happened. There was the time when you were about six or seven and we came home from church to enjoy our usual Sunday dinner. I think it was just you and Trish with us at home. The others were at boarding school. Polokwane could really cook very nicely and your father always loved his rys, vleis and aartappels so much. I used to make ice cream when the fridge was working well. We had that with tinned peaches for dessert. Anyway, this particular Sunday, Father Murphy was having lunch with the Morey family. I always thank God for that small mercy, you know. I don't know what would have happened if he was with us that day. Your father would have died with rage and embarrassment. He was always so touchy about what others would think if this or that happened. When he is not so angry, he turns red. When he is going to be violent, he turns pale, especially around the lips.

Anyway, as I was telling you, as soon as we get into the house he takes off his hat and calls Polokwane. We go to wash our hands and come straight to the table. We always set it before going to church because sometimes we stay and chat to the rest of the people and then there isn't time before one o'clock. Your father loves to be settled at the table by one. Anyway, here comes Polokwane with a big smile on his face and the meat tray all neatly packed with the potatoes around it. He tells your father that he has cooked impala. As soon as he puts it in front of your father, all hell lets off the devil's language. Ye gods, man! Your father is up in a flash and shouting in Polokwane's language. He informs him that he has the brains of an empty, brown paper bag and that his sense of smell is as rotten as the bloody meat. He stomps around the room with the meat tray, sniffing it and calling it polecat carnage. He says that even the hyenas would run a mile from the stench and does he look like a hyena? He shouts and screams, 'You bloody son of a bliksem se donder se hell se kind!' By this time the odour of sanctity is all over the room because of the to-ing and fro-ing and waving around of the dish. You know how you hate smelly things, Bern, so you are running around behind me with your hand over your nose and heaving like a heavy weight. Trish is under the table because she hates all the shouting and I am behind your father pulling at his shirt to try and catch his attention and stop him from doing any violence. I am just too late though because the whole tray; meat, potatoes and all are turned upside down onto our cook, poor Polokwane's head and he is running and slipping on the gravy all over the floor. By this time your father is hauling him up to give him a thrashing! Poor boy, he doesn't know what has gone wrong. As far as he is concerned the meat is fine and the smell is not important. Between your father and Polokwane slipping and sliding and me pulling and tugging and you heaving and Trish crying from under the table, we had a circus act for Africa. Polokwane broke away but not before your father got in a few smacks. He ran down the road and did not return until the following Tuesday. Your father sulked and swore all afternoon and you kids went and lay down quietly. We did have the peaches and ice cream after the fuss was over and we discovered that we were very hungry. Only your father deprived himself of food. He used to cut off his nose to spite his face quite often, you know, Bern. When Polokwane returned to his culinary skills I made a special cake for him as a kind of sorry from your father. Your father could never say sorry for anything in those days. After that Mad Sunday, Polokwane always asked me to smell the meat before he dared to bring it to the table."

I am walking towards the railway lines with my friend Willie. Her name is really Philomena but it is too long to pronounce all the time so she is happy with her short name, Willie. I do not pronounce it like people pronounce the boy's name, Willie, but like the first letter is a 'V' so it sounds like Villie. I used to call her Phillie, but she said she is not a horse or a mare. Willie is Afrikaans and we have been playing together for a very long time. She has nut-brown skin, green eyes and a turned up nose. If you do not know her you would think that she is looking down it at you. She has a quiet voice and she laughs easily. Her hair is also nut-brown and a bit curly. She wears it with a ribbon that keeps it tied back. Dorry sometimes goes to the store to chat to her mother. Her mother's name is Edna. Dorry can't speak Afrikaans so she struggles to make herself understood but Edna encourages her and they also laugh a lot. Edna reminds me of Jack and the Beanstalk because she is tall and slender but her whole body leans over and her veins on her arms stick out. Edna is always kind to me when I go to play with Willie. I am afraid of her husband Mr Van Eck. He is a huge man and he has a very deep voice. I only say hello to him and then Willie and I go to the stoep or to her bedroom to play. He also shakes a lot. My father says it's the amount of brandy he drinks and one should not say hello before his first doppie. My father does not shake in the morning but I do not say hello until I can smell his first doppie too. He gets angry quickly without it. Sometimes Willie's brother Gideon has to go and fetch his father home from the pub. He once took a wheelbarrow with him because the barman phoned to say that Mr E was beyond walking. Edna gets very shy about her husband's drinking. When Dorry goes to say hello to her at her house, she does not look straight into Dorry's eyes. She looks everywhere else and at the floor as though she is examining a bit of dust or an insect that should not be there. Dorry pretends not to notice and just carries on about the heat and the lack of rain. She tells Edna that she likes the material her dress is made of and who was clever enough to sew it up so well? Edna blushes and says she sewed it herself. Then she lets Dorry look at her embroidery and they discuss transfers and patterns from the Mafikeng sewing shop. Edna never comes to our house. I think she is too shy to do anything besides going to work in the Number Two Store and then going home. She has chickens in her back yard and she feeds them. She calls to them, "Kip, kip, kip, kippies!" They come running from all over her yard, like ours do. Sometimes I wonder if there is also a 'kippie' language. I sit in the hen-hok and make the sounds that they do and then one or two of them come right up to my feet and one special little hen jumps up and sits on my shoulder.

Willie and I are crossing the lines. We take big steps and never let our feet touch the lines because we are afraid of slipping and falling and perhaps getting trapped between two lines at the signal points. We are going to the pub. We know that our fathers are there because the village bell has just rung and it is ten past five. We know that if we stand at the back door of the bar, my father will see us. He will say, "What do you kids want now? Can't I have five minutes peace?" I tell him that we need a cold drink. We like Pepsi cola. It fizzes up very quickly and when we feel naughty we shake the bottles and aim them at each other. We go home with stains on our clothes and tell our mothers that it is everyone else's fault and that we never did anything. As soon as Willie and I are finished with our Pepsis, we go home because it is time to have a bath and get ready for supper.

I am crossing the lines again. I hear Dommie meowing in a strange, mournful way. At first I cannot see her but I follow the sound. There is a train in the station. I look to see if the water chimney is in the engine's tank so I know it will not pull out or shunt suddenly. Dorry often tells me not to cross the lines when there is a train in unless I go right around and do it in front of the engine where the driver can see me. She tells me this because one day my father came home and got sick in the garden before he opened the front door. He said one of the railway workers got squashed in between two coaches when the train was shunting. He had to hold his hand while they called his family. They could not release him from the two coaches because they feared he would break in half. He just had time to say goodbye to his wife. There is no doctor in our village so the vet came to see if he could help. It was no good; the man died stuck and pinned between the coaches and when they released him, my father says his whole stomach fell out onto the track. My father says it is madness to think that anyone can crawl under trains or stand between the coaches and predict when they will suddenly move. The drivers just give a quick hoot and move straight away.

I think I will have to get under the train because Dommie won't listen and won't move. Her meowing is getting worse and I do not know what to do. If I leave and go and call Dorry the train will run her over and squash her to death. I am afraid because not so long ago our dog Mauser arrived home on three legs. He ran across the lines at the wrong time and the train cut off his leg. I sometimes dream of him hopping along and yelping at the front door. My father couldn't help Mauser and the vet was at a cattle station in the bush. My father carried him and put him into the truck. My father took his gun with him. Dorry called me into the house and wiped my eyes with her apron. We sat and took the wiping in turns because we knew what was going to happen to Mauser. He was a playful, loyal dog. My father came home when the moon was busy rising. He sat on the stoep with his dop of whiskey and called life a donder se hell se ding. Dorry sat and cried next to him. My father wiped his eyes with the back of his hand every now and again. I went into the bedroom and crawled under the bed. It is safe for me under beds.

Although I know what happened to the railway man and Mauser, I am crawling under the train because we have had enough donder se hell se dinge and Dommie cannot be the next. I am trembling but I know that I have to be brave. As I reach for Dommie the lines creak loudly because they are contracting after the day's heat. The stones that are packed between the lines are still hot. They prickle and poke at knees and hands. I am feeling sick and I am short of breath. My cold drink wants to fizz up and spill over the stones. I fight to keep it down. I call Dommie. My voice comes out like a croak and a whisper. I think of Dorry and my father and I feel sicker and very afraid. Suddenly, Dommie rushes at me and scratches my hands. She arches her back and hisses at me. Her eyes are wild and she looks at me as though I am a stranger and not the friend who has a lap for her to sleep on. The train whistle makes my heart jump into my mouth and I crawl out from under the wheels. I bump my head on the hard steel of the undercarriage but I do not really notice until I am running home with bleeding hands and a throbbing head. Dommie is running after me with her strange eyes and mournful meowing. Her meowing is like a thin cord of pain in my head and is an echo in my ears. She follows me inside and I go to the bedroom to change my clothes before Dorry finds me in such a mess. Dommie twines around my legs like a snake in the grass. She makes my hair stand on end. It is as if she has turned against me and I have become a mouse with whom she is playing her death games. I am full of goose pimples but I hurry to get out of the dirty under-the train-clothes. I rush to the bathroom and wash. My scratches are red and raw. They are deep but not deep enough to be called cuts. Dorry comes into the room and Dommie begins her meowing and twining around her too. She calls me, "Bern, what is going on with this cat? She is acting so strangely!" I tell Dorry about the train but not that I crawled under it to fetch Dommie. I show her my hands and she says she is calling the vet. Rassie the vet does not take long to come because he lives just across the lines on the other side of our village. He looks at Dommie, who has gone very quiet and who is sitting on the chair as if there was never any meowing or twining or scratching. He tells my mother not to worry too much but to keep an eye on the cat and the kids.

It is eight o'clock and the village bell is ringing to say that the stores must close for breakfast. In the summer the stores open at half past six because the sun is so fierce and the people have to walk a long way to buy their goods. Dommie, our cat, is lying under the syringa. She has started meowing again and her tail is shifting like a whip that is getting ready to crack through the air, the way the long whips of the cattle herders do. A man on a bicycle is riding past our house. He has a bell on his handlebars and he rings it because Dommie has jumped up and started to run after him. I call her but she does not hear or will not listen. I call until she is a small dot that eventually disappears over the hill that leads to the river. When my father and Dorry come home for breakfast I tell them about Dommie. My father says he will go and look for her. He has a frown on his face and he asks to see my scratches. They are swollen and he tells Dorry that she should take me to Rassie. I am very afraid to go to the vet's dispensary. It smells of animals and dip. He sees the sick animals in a small room with one small window. I want to vomit when I go in there. Rassie laughs when I start heaving. He says, "What's a little bit of a dog dip smell on a summer's day?" Rassie is a big laugher; you can hear his gurgling drain sound from far away. If he is in the pub, the whole pub laughs with him. My father says he is the life and soul of any party. He stands with his hand on his hip and tilts his curly head to one side when he thinks about something. When he is frustrated he says, "Jissie, man dis nou vrot!" His green eyes go glassy when he sees Katrina coming along the road. Dorry says he is love struck and should get on and tell Katrina so that we can go to a wedding. When he stands in the evening light while the sun is setting, it shines through his hairy arms and makes him look like our ancestors. My father says we all come from the same ancestors because we were all once apes. He says some of us humans still look like apes. He doesn't say who.

Dorry is talking quietly to Rassie and he starts shaking his head and is saying, "Jissie, man, let me have a closer look." I am heaving and I feel pale and sick. Rassie is kind and takes me by the hand and leads me outside. He shows me where to sit in the shade of a morula tree. It has a green wooden bench under it. He says that he must give me four injections immediately because Dommie must have rabies if she is running around in circles and biting people. He says that after the four injections he will have to give me one a day for fourteen days. He takes me by the hand again and leads me to the steel table in his vet's room. He tells Dorry to lift me and lie me flat and to pull up my dress because the injections have to be in my stomach. Dorry talks quietly to me. I am so afraid that I am lame again like I feel in the iron air. Rassie has a steel dish full of needles. They are covered with methylated spirits. It stings my eyes and makes my nose run. I want to cry but my tears seem frozen inside. Dorry holds my hand. She has tears in her eyes and she looks away from Rassie and the needles. He puts on some thin gloves and his skin sticks to the inside. I can see the thin hairs of his hands through the plastic. I feel ever sicker. I watch him take the syringe out of the dish. He takes a small bottle of white liquid and punctures the top with the needle in the syringe. I think my head has landed on the moon and I am walking up there, slowly, slowly, one foot after the other. I am bouncing like a light balloon in the still silence. There are no needles signs, no wild waves to squeeze the store of vomit that wants to exit like a bullet into the dip bucket that lures all to the edge of its brim. The moon sky is pale with tender light and I am thinking of heaven and how it will be like living on the quiet moon because Dorry says God doesn't like noise when we visit him in church. I wonder how it is that the angels can sing so much without God getting tired of hymns and feeling cross with their noise. I think of Mauser and the man squashed by the train and I wonder where they stay in heaven. I call Mauser in my moon mind and he comes running on four legs as though the train had never been. He wags his tail and jumps for a balloon. He catches at the string and brings it to me, bright blue and unbroken.

I feel the needle sting. The thick liquid squirts into my stomach and Rassie says, "Daar's sy! Moenie huil nie dis niks!" Dorry says I am a good, brave girl and I am being saved from rabies. She says, "Ye gods, man, what a thing to happen, what next, I wonder!" Just as Rassie has finished with the injections and 'moenie huil ne', my father's truck parks outside. I know it is his because I know the sound of the engine. It roars and then rattles out of energy when it stops. He does not knock at the clinic door but rushes in with Dommie. She hangs over his hands, her neck wet with freshly spilt blood. My father's shirt is covered in it. His hands are covered in dark, caked, red. His mouth is tightly closed. He frowns and deep worry gullies dent along his forehead. He puts Dommie down on the floor and she lies like a sack statue. Her mouth is slightly open and her tiny teeth show. Rassie says, "Jissie, Oom Pat! What happened?" My father tells us that Dommie followed that man on his bicycle and when he got home she rushed at him and bit him. Dommie then went running around and bit three other people who were walking back to work. My father only caught her after she had got into the wholesale shed and bitten Katrina as well. He shot her as she crouched in a corner. My father also has scratches on his hands because he tried to catch Dommie. Rassie tells him that he is next with the injections and that he must tell the others who were bitten to come to the clinic as soon as possible because Dommie had rabies. My father says, 'Bloody donder se hell!" Rassie laughs but I can see that he is worried, especially about Katrina.

My father says, "Get a move on with the pricking, man, so I can go and find the people!" My father tells me that I am brave and that he will also have to be brave and we will come to Rassie every night for our pricks. Dorry says, "Ye gods, man, my poor little mite!" I feel like crying because I am a poor little mite. I ask her about being a mite. She says it is another name for a tick. I do not want to be a tick. Dorry explains that she does not want any ticks or mites in her house so I am a poor little might. She says might is someone who is strong and brave. I do not mind being a might anymore. Dorry calls my father a big might although he screws up his eyes and says bloody donder when Rassie gives him the needle. My father says he can understand my pain because it is happening to him just as it happened to me.

My father and I have become friends in a special rabies way these days. When the sales travellers come to his store and show him their stock he tells them the whole rabies story from beginning to end. He calls it the Midsummer Madness.

In my head there is a madness that I cannot tell. It swims around and around and never goes anywhere outside of my head. Sometimes I walk with my head tilted to one side so that perhaps the madness will pour out of my ears but it doesn't. It stays and washes over everything else that enters my brain. It gets into my head from the eyes of cats and dogs. I am afraid of them. I am afraid to call Ruddles and to play with him. When he lies and sleeps under the syringa tree, I walk quietly and slide past him. I park my bicycle as close to the gauze door as possible so that I can move away quickly. If I see a dog coming towards me in the road I run or ride to the nearest tree and climb it because of the madness that may be in its head. The madness stays in my head when I sleep. I dream of thin dogs with red wildness running along their backs and white-hot flames spurting from their mouths. The flames never die or go out. They lick at my legs while I am running. I am running and I can hear my breathing. I am screaming but nobody hears me. I stay in the same place even though my feet are going as fast as they can. Sometimes Dorry comes into my room and wakes me up. She puts her soft hand on my head and says that I have been dreaming and fighting with the sheets. She sits by my side and gives me cool water to drink. Sometimes she sings, in her low soothing voice. Her song is always the same. I call it her bad dream song. It is about somewhere over the rainbow. It makes me feel safe and in a place in the sky that will keep the mad dogs and cats away. I ask Dorry if the injection will really stop the madness. She says, "What next, man! If my precious Number Five was going mad she would have bitten me long ago!" She says Rassie has saved my life, my father's life and all the other people who got bitten. She says, "Never worry again!" The madness stills comes into my head when I am alone on my bicycle riding along the bush paths but it doesn't stay there for long because I believe Dorry and I watch my father. He has not gone mad. He still sits under the syringa's shade and plays with Ruddles. He does not put on the muzzle any more and all the dogs in the village can bark and play again.

♥

Come and see the mud pools
Warm, soft, wet, brown,
Like cow's eyes
Staring into blue.

Come and walk in mud pools,
Tread deep down smooth,
Like worm-silk
Sparkling into blue.

Come and hear the mud pools,
Sing, laugh, splash, speak,
Like owl's wise
Rising into blue.

"BERN, you know what I say, I say: never expect anything good to happen to you. This is because if you don't expect anything good to happen to you then all that does happen is a lovely surprise and all that happens can be treasured like a gift. Take, for example, your sixth or seventh birthday. You so wanted a bicycle of your own. We had one for the seven of you to use. You were riding it since you were a tiny tot. I am not sure how old, but when you got on you had to stand on the top stoep step and climb on the pedal and sort of launch off into a terrible wobble. I always held my breath and waited for the crash but somehow you got into the right rhythm and off you went. I used to kill myself laughing because each time the one pedal went down half your head with its bow on the top disappeared behind the handlebars. Just your forehead and the bow on the top of your head remained in view. You always aimed at the platform outside the shops so that you could break and land in a good position. If you missed and didn't brake in time, you chose the moment to jump off and let the bike go and roll onto its side. You hated that because the dust got into the chain and messed it up. Anyway I was saying about your seventh birthday. Your father told you many times to forget the thought of having a bike of your own because we couldn't afford one. Anyway, the day before your birthday we got a note from Jannie at the railways to come and collect an article from the goods shed. We couldn't believe it but there it was: a green and white size twenty-four bike with a new bell on it. Your Aunt Helen sent it because her Brenda was too tall for it and she thought it a pity that it was just lying around the farm. I am not sure who was more excited, your father or I. We couldn't wait to get you to bed so that we could fetch it from the shop and put it next to your bed. You little beast, you just would not get off to sleep. You must have known in your bones that something was coming your way. In the end, your father went to the shop on his own and I came and sang, 'I was Waltzing with My Darling' and 'Come to the Station, Jump from the Train' to you until you drifted off. Your father was like a schoolboy fiddling with the chain, dusting it off and eventually things got too much for him and he rang the bell. I never saw him shoot out of the lounge so fast before, bike loaded up and all. You came into the lounge sleepy eyed and said you heard a bike bell. Your father shouted that it was not a bike bell but a new bell for the cattle. You know how he used to put one around the bull's neck so that the herdsmen could tell how far away they had walked on the grazing expedition for the day. Anyhow it was, 'Is there some milk please, Mamma? I can't sleep.' You loved milk so. I suppose you needed the vitamins in our dry country. That was a close shave. When you woke up the next morning there was your new bike. I can't tell you how you hopped around and clapped and performed and hugged us to near death. Your father got tears in his eyes; he was sentimental you know. I got you ready for school and saw you off at the gate. Next thing you were back, mud from head to foot. You thought you would try your hand at getting through that long mud pool that formed in the dirt road near the school. In you went. You cried so. I had to give you a bath and a good rub down. I had to take you to school with your new dirty bike and explain to Mrs Johnston - she always smelled of eucalyptus - why you were so late. She came to see the bike and you hid your head in my skirt because it was so dirty.

"Funny little thing you were, Bern. Things had to be perfect and you had to get everything right or there was hell to pay. You are still like that, you know, trying to be perfect. I think you became a nun because you thought that that was the only way to be holy and perfect and a saint. Never mind all the millions of us ordinary people out here who are just doing our best to get to God in everyday circumstances. Anyhow, so many good things happened when I prayed to Our Lady for you all and somehow especially they happened for you. Maybe you were spoilt upstairs I don't know. Your father used to stand at your cot when you were just learning to stand and say, 'Lovey, this child is for God because just look at those deep blue eyes that seem to see through everything.' I think he taught you that you had to be a saint and a nun.

"Another time, when you were three or four, must have been three because you were the baby then, just turning four in the June. We were having a raffle for the soldiers who went to the war. The prize was this beautifully dressed doll. I wanted so much for you to have her. I made a novena to our blessed lady. I said to her, 'Our Lady, please send me the name of the doll, I have to have it for Bern's birthday.' You know we had to guess the name of the doll instead of just buying a ticket that was a lucky number for the draw. I was given the list to sell tickets. Auntie Shaw was in charge and she asked me to see that everyone bought a ticket. You know how hard she worked for the London Missionary Society. One night I woke up with the train whistle. You know it used to echo as it came down the line to the water tank. It was a hollow, haunting kind of whistle. I suppose it was so quiet that one could hear everything clearly. The cattle bells used to sound hollow, too. Anyhow, I turned over and as I was settling down I looked at the doorway and there stood Our Blessed Lady, Bern. She was holding a huge bunch of little white daisies. They were like little

bright stars. They hid her face. I could see her hands perfectly. They were transparent. They looked like porcelain. I could see right through them, right through her flesh and veins. It was so absolutely beautiful. I said out aloud, 'Oh, so the doll's name is Daisy!' She disappeared as suddenly as she had come. I thought in my mind, oh well, this is the answer to my prayer. I can have the doll. I am going to get it for Bern's birthday. I bought a ticket and wrote down, 'Daisy'. There was no doubt in my mind that I was going to win that doll. Next day I went to Auntie Shaw as I had sold all the tickets. I told her the doll's name was Daisy; I was so sure of it. She shook her head and said, 'No, it begins with an 'S'.' I could hardly believe that Our Lady had come with the flowers and I had misread her message. I couldn't think of a single name that began with S. I was sort of shocked, I suppose. Eventually Auntie Shaw spelt out, 'Su.'

I said, 'Oh! Sue!' She shook her head again and then told me the name was Susan. I bought another ticket and wrote down Susan. That was plain cheating, Bern. I began to think that perhaps Our Lady had such clear and pure hands because she was trying to tell me to have pure faith and not to cheat my way into winning that doll. Anyway, the day of the raffle came and four other people also had Susan for the name. I thought I would still win, as we had to have a mini draw to see who would get the doll. A couple, Mary and John, I think they were, had a child called Susan and they won the doll. I couldn't believe that after appearing to me in the doorway, Our Blessed Lady let me lose the doll. I remember trying to fathom out the whole affair and being angry about cheating and losing. The next day, you were playing in the yard and Jimmy Riley arrived in his old Chevy truck and hooted at the gate. He called, 'Where is that little sweetheart?' He always called all kids little sweethearts. I am not sure where he came from. He just sort of grew to be part of the village and the people. He went hunting with your father and lived down by the river. He wore that grey cowboy type hat that became his trademark, so to speak. One could always see the top of it before one saw Jimmy. Anyhow, I called you and he gave you a small suitcase like the size you get when you have gone through the first couple of years at school and have bigger books to put into it. He said, 'This is for you, little sweetheart!' Your face was such a picture when you opened the case and there, inside, was this doll and some dolls' clothes. You kept it for years, Bern. When you were a bit older, it was tears forever because you couldn't get the sewing right and perfect. Dianne used to sit with you for hours stitching up the doll's clothes I cut out for the pair of you. Dianne always inspected your sewing and made you pull it all out when she thought the stitches were too big. You used to fight so to get it all right. You named that doll Susan of course! I have never forgotten that vision in the doorway and years later the one I had in St Theresa's church in Jo'burg where you were at school. I was in deep distress at the time, Bern, and I looked up at the stained glass window and asked Our Lady to pray for me. She swallowed like someone who knows great sorrow and tears fell from her eyes. I thought I was seeing things but I wasn't. I really saw that and whenever great sorrow came - and you know, Bern, how much of that came our way - I remembered that Our Lady had shown me her own tears and they comforted mine. That's why even sorrow can be a gift as precious as your doll and the bike. Sorrow and joy can be a gift of tears. So, Bern, I always say: never expect good things to happen and then they do. Life is just like that. Full of good things not expected. I always tried to appreciate one day at a time. That way I never got bored or if there was sorrow and hardship, it was always bearable and always good came from it."

My bicycle's wheels make music through the sand. I have to pedal hard to hear it because the sand is so thick. The music is like a soft hissing and whistling. The sound of the sand beating on the mudguards makes a noise like a triangle. I hum when I am moving slowly. I sing any words that come into my head when I am moving fast. Sometimes the song that comes into my head is about the earth and how it mothers all plants and all creatures. Mother Earth has room for everything that has been made. When I want to change the music, I get a piece of cardboard and a wooden peg. I fold the cardboard around the wheel frame so that a bit of it sticks out into the way of the spokes. I use the peg to clip it in place and when I begin to pedal again the spokes catch the bit of cardboard and I have a drumming sound amongst the hisses and whistling. I pretend that I am on a motorbike. If I do this at home, Dorry says, "What next, man!" My father tells her that pegs are not meant to make motorbikes and that kids are not meant to ride them but I do not take off the pegs; I just wave and pedal on. He stands and watches with his hand on his hips and his head shaking as if to say: these kids don't listen. By the time I get around the corner, I do not know what he is doing or saying or thinking.

I often ride along the rail track. There is a narrow, stony path beside the lines so that the stationmaster can walk along there and signal the drivers with his green or red flags. He also changes the route of the train by pulling a handle on the side of the track. I can never understand how pulling the lever makes the train go onto a different track. Dorry says it's engineering. My father says it is train business and I will understand when I am older. I am older every day but I still do not understand getting trains from one line to another. If I see the train smoke coming along, even before I hear the engine, I get off the path beside the track because there is no room for the train and me. I am afraid that it will suck me under the trucks or sweep me off my bike or cut off my elbows because they stick out. I am afraid of the great engines when they are standing under the water tanks in the station. The drivers wave when they see me. If I come past the driver's door they pull the hooter and I jump out of my skin. They throw back their heads and laugh. My father makes me walk close to the train engine with him and when they blow the whistle, he calls them 'Donner se helle se kinders' and points his finger at them. They call my father 'Oom Pat'. His name is Hugh but they say he is a mad Irishman and all Irish mad people are called Pat. Sometimes my father stops and talks to the drivers and he lifts me up into the engine room so that I can see how the coal is shovelled and the steam is made and the pistons get ready to push out the steam. The driver allows me to pull the whistle handle and I love hearing the sound echo into the bush. I get proud of myself. The driver shows me how he controls the huge steel wheels and how he lets the pressure of steam build up and how to release it in great white guns of cloud that burst from steam pipes at the sides of the engine. He says it is the way the train burps when its stomach is full.

I think my father tries to burp like that when he has finished his dinner and has to wait for Dorry because she eats so slowly. She tells him to leave and let us eat in peace. He likes to leave the table early and he goes and sits in the syringa's shade and waits for the moon to rise. I never walk too near the steam engines because when the train burps, the power of the steam can blow me away and burn me because the water that is released is boiling. The trains never leave the station quietly. The steam hisses and blasts out its burps and then wheels begin to turn slowly. After the train has moved a few yards, the wheels start spinning around on one spot. It is as though the train has lost its breath and is choking and sneezing to get enough back to move along smoothly. It changes its rhythm three or four times before it becomes a steady song, blowing smoke words out of its throat and getting smaller and smaller as it travels away. I love the sound of the trains and I love the smell of the smoke. I love the green leather and the polished wood in the coaches and I love the feel of it. When we travel with Dorry to Johannesburg, we fight over who sleeps in the top bunk. We have to pick a piece of paper from Dorry's hand. She writes on one piece of paper, 'top bunk' another, 'middle bunk' and the last one, 'bottom bunk'. That way, there can be no fighting over who sleeps where. The way the train movement rocks the coaches soothes my mind and I can sit and stare at the trees and grass. My mind does not have to settle on any thought but can trace the land's shape and the sky's colours where all that is, is a harmony of the spirit. It makes my soul sing.

When I ride my bike-motor-bike along the quiet bush paths, the plovers begin another chorus to warn of my intrusion and to distract me if I am getting near to their nests. Altogether there is a special song and music carrying across the veld and I do not feel alone. Sometimes when I have ridden far into the bush, I find a morula tree and sit in its shade. I hear the other songs being sung. The trees also make their own music; the cattle and goats join in the chorus. The Lourie birds sit in the tall trees and criticise with their "go-way" chant, and Kwe cries sound like I-told-you-spiteful. I think of how Dorry and my father got my bicycle for my birthday and how sorrow is a gift of tears but I do not understand it. I only understand the full beauty of the land and the creatures that sing in it. Happiness comes like the easiness of breath that fills my being with quiet. The quiet floats me into the bark of trees. It carries me along the sounds of growing leaves and I think I can hear them speak leaf-language. It is a very gentle language that moves like kindness through their fragile veins and into their transparent leaf tips where light and love can tremble in the wind. I feel at one with the tremble and language of the leaves. I feel at home with trees and the smell of manure.

Dorry says that manure is the soil's doctor and the small dung beetles push huge pills of it to help the plants and grass to grow. When the rain breaks up the small pills the manure can seep through the tiny spaces between the grains of sand and make new life like a miracle. I have watched the dung beetles roll up the manure until the ball is so big it buries them. They push it along with their back legs like my father pushes against Pedro our truck when it gets stuck. The beetles

battle over stones and tufts of grass to get the miracle pills to where the soil most needs it. I don't know how they decide where the soil is sick and in need but they just do. My friend Dianne says that new life comes from a miracle of love in our mothers' stomachs because that is how we are born. My father says he found us in a cabbage patch and that the stork bird brought us. It is a miracle that it knew where to put us because there are a lot of cabbage patches in this world. Mrs Freeman and Mrs Oudendaal have one. My father's cabbage patch is in Lecheng so I think we were dropped there. I do not know how long we had to lie among the cabbages before he brought us home. I told Dorry that I think we come out of our mothers' navels because I watched where lambs come from. They come from a bag that the mother pushes out of her bum but the lamb can't get out of the bag until the mother breaks it and eats holes into it. She has to chew a long piece of cord that looks like a cross between jelly and rope. It comes from her navel. When she has chewed it all through the lamb begins to bleat and she nudges it until it gets up onto its feet. It falls over a lot but she licks it clean and it keeps trying to get up and then it can stand like a miracle. My father says he will give me a navel salute. I am still not sure where I come from. I think God made all of us. The catechism says so. I think God uses fathers and mothers to make us because Lenny told me when I peeped at his thing behind the water tank that day that things get put into ladies to make babies. These days I think that people make babies and storks deliver them. God makes people love each other so that babies can get into their mothers' stomachs. Dorry says I have enough knowledge about babies for now.

♥

WHEN the circus comes to our village, Mrs Johnston lets us out of school as soon as we hear the circus train whistle. We run all the way to the station to watch the train whistle and steam its way onto the side tracks next to the railway warehouse. The engine shunts forwards and backwards until the trucks are parked exactly opposite the place where the animals can walk off and into the cattle kraal where their cages are kept while the circus tent is placed. There are lions and elephants and tigers. There are ponies and dogs as well. The elephants do not go in cages. They are led around the trucks and help to push them into place. They use their heads. We watch all afternoon. The huge tent lies rolled on the ground and then some workers begin to run with ropes with loops on their ends. They have large pegs made of steel and put the loops through them and hammer them into the ground until the tent looks like a flat circle with a heavy pole sticking up through the middle. The pole has steep rope all around its top and the elephants come and pull the ends that are covered in canvas. The tent begins to rise like an opening umbrella and all the people stand and clap. The workers bend and run under the parts of the tent that have not been pegged to the ground and they help to push up the pole. The tent is bright red and blue and it has 'Boswell's Circus' written on it.

Before we know it Tickey the Clown comes running out of the tent and he does summersaults and takes bright balls out of his pockets and juggles them so fast we can hardly see them touching his hands. He brings out a stool and sits on it and tells us jokes. He calls the workers 'walking chocolates' because they are brown. The walking chocolates tell him he is a white chocolate and he pretends to eat his hand and lets it creep up his baggy red sleeve so that we believe him. Tickey the Clown has a funny face painted on and under his eyes there are big teardrops. Dorry says it is because clowns make people laugh but sometimes they cry inside where nobody knows their sadness. Sometimes I think I am like Tickey because I also feel sad inside and hide my tears in case my father sees them and gets cross.

We follow Tickey down the village road to my father's shop. He jumps on the stacked mealie bags and summersaults off of them. He is very short. My father says he is a dwarf. Dwarves are grown ups that do not get taller than the height of our kitchen chairs. When Tickey gets into the shop my father says, "Donner se hell, who is this?"

Tickey says, "It's me, and what can you give me for a sixpence?" My father looks in his till and gives him a sixpence and we laugh. Tickey asks my father for all his old fountain pens and damaged goods like watches that do not work. The people in the circus fix them while they are on the train travelling from town to town. Tickey leads us to the window of a caravan and shows us that they sell circus tickets there. Dorry comes to the window and buys us a ticket. We go home and bath and get into our best clothes and come to the circus when the sun has set. We can hear the lions roar and the elephants trumpet. We can hear the engine that makes the lights come on in the tent and all around it. We sit in the front row of circus seats so that we can see everything easily. There are other clowns in the circus and one who is a bit taller than Tickey says his name is Sixpence. Tickey gives him my father's sixpence and says, "That is all you are worth, Sixpence!" All the clowns do tricks like making things disappear and then showing us that they are under somebody's hat or pocket.

I get afraid when the lions and tigers come into the ring. The trainer has a long whip and he talks to the animals and they roar but do as he tells them. He makes a lion open its mouth and he puts his head inside it. The people clap and some of them hide their eyes behind their hands in case the lion takes a bite of head. The trainer also lies on the floor and makes an elephant lift its leg above him. I am glad when the animals have finished in the ring. I do not like to see them in cages because they miss the bush and cannot run around and be free and happy. My father says they are happy enough with the circus. Dorry says they are not and they should be in the wild. She says they can never have babies in cages. She says they are worse off than the donkeys in our village. The donkeys are made to pull heavy carts that were the backs of motorcars. They are thin and sick but still they have to pull until they drop dead. I have seen a donkey drop dead and my tears are still in my head because of that.

Some circus people climb up very high and swing upside down on a thin swing. Dorry says they are trapezes. They work up speed and then fly through the air and catch one another. There is a net underneath them in case they miss and fall. A man is climbing a very high pole. We watch him in silence because the clowns show us that we should be quiet. I can see sweat on the man's forehead. When he gets right to the top he shows us in signs that he will do a back flip off the pole and land on a spring mattress underneath the pole. The people clap and whistle. Dorry says he is a madman. My father says he is brave and, wag 'n bietjie, we will see him do what he says. We hold our breath and the man balances himself carefully. He shouts and does his back flip and misses the mattress. The people gasp and there is silence in the tent. Dorry says, "Ye gods, man, how terrible!"

My father says, "Bloody donner se hell!" The clowns run in with a stretcher. They slide it under him and carry him out quickly. The circus band plays loud music and then the ponies come trotting in and ladies do tricks on them but nobody is hurt. Later, before the circus show ends, they bring the man that fell, back. They help him to walk and he claps his hands so that we can see he is okay and we clap too.

In the morning when we wake up there is no circus tent and no train. There are no signs that the circus has been except for the elephant pooh pats that lie in the road. Tickey and Sixpence have gone for another year.

♥

I have lost some poetry;
It was in my head.
I had it treasured and exposed.
I spoke it in my dread.
Hardly uttered, it has hung, unheard.
Life's feeling-fires have burned
Its easy essence early
In its spring.
I have lost some poetry;
It has withered in my thoughts.
It has died.
Will it ever live again?

"You know, Bern, when you kids were small there were seven years of drought. God, it was terrible, man. We used to go on our five-mile drive early in the morning so that we could get back before the sun got too hot. Daddy used to take his gun and see if he could get us a guinea fowl for supper. He used to cheat, you know. He used to leave them with seed every day so that when we came they would be there waiting to be fed. Sometimes he would shoot three of four and give them to the other families. I used to pluck them for Doris. I couldn't bear to think of her posh kitchen getting feathered up and smelling of hot water over 'derms'. She always had that way of being so English. You would think that we were foreigners by the way she acted like the Queen. There are English and English. We are the ordinary English. My surname was Rose, you know, but I say: accept all people and all that happens. It's the way God made

107

things to be. I always wondered how Doris lived in Palapye. It's such a tiny place: just five shops and the station and the water tank for trains. They say her husband Charles owned many farms and many outpost stores. They were the first to buy a car in Palapye. Its number plate was BP 1, like a mayor or something. I remember how upset she was that Barbara was the first to import bunny wool and knit a short-sleeved cardigan. She brought it to the tennis club one Saturday afternoon. She made a point of apologising for the fluff that stuck out like wires because the air was so dry. Doris said not to sit near her, as she couldn't take being shocked. She got more and more annoyed because everyone else came and had a closer look at the wool and congratulated Barbara on the pattern. I don't even know how we played tennis in those drought times. We started at two and played until seven, when we couldn't see anymore. We used to meet Daddy at the hotel and have a sundowner before going home. I could only ever drink half a beer-shandy. You kids used to take turns to have a sip and finish it off. It's a wonder you didn't get involved with alcohol. You must have had a lot of shandy sips in your childhood.

I remember us going to Lecheng, your father's outpost store, and seeing animals lying all over the bush either dying or dead and rotting. The stench was unbearable. Daddy got out of the truck and shot those that were lying there unable to move and gasping for water. It was such a pitiful sight. There was not a blade of grass anywhere to be seen. The sand was so red and so thick that your shoes were of little use if you dared to stand for a few seconds. You had to keep moving, or else your soles got burned. Daddy used to give you kids those thick brown takkies to wear. I used to cut out the toes when they got too small for you. Your feet looked like tortoises walking down the stoep. You always had red toes from the polish. We kept your good buckle over shoes for the bioscope and for coming to the tennis club. You were such a fusspot, Bern, you used to take a hanky and polish them off whenever you arrived anywhere. Daddy and I used to laugh so! God, I used to bath you to death. I used to put three of you in the bath at a time and scrub you from head to foot. If I thought Doris was likely to come for morning tea, you used to get scrubbed and forbidden to go outside until she had gone. One day, she came unexpectedly and, God, were you dirty. You and Dianne were busy

with mud pies. I was so ashamed I could have died! 'Oh Dorry!' she said, 'what a wonderful sight! It's the first time I have ever seen your children dirty. What a celebration! I wondered if they were ever allowed to play!' From then on I didn't bath you every five minutes.

Anyway, I was telling you about the drought. It was a pitiful time for the animals and the people. I remember the ox that got stuck in the mud in the riverbed. There was one small mud pool left for all the herds to drink from. They used to run and you could hear their pathetic lowing from miles away. They could smell the water and it drove them mad. Daddy had to go down there and shoot the poor thing. When he got back to the shop everyone was there, the children included. He had a meeting with them and tried to help with some sort of plan to get water to them. He made a timetable for different herds to visit his well but of course it wasn't enough. The very same day, some cattle ran to the dipping troughs by the railway line and drank the dip! That was a terrible sight. Poor things were burning up inside from the dip and the people were weeping. Your father got drunk that night, too. He kicked Ruddles at lunchtime because he had enough trouble for one day. Your father gets angry and violent when he is upset. It is easier for him to be angry than it is for him to cry. I had to haul him off the dog and speak to him about being so cruel and frightening all the kids."

Cruelty crusts the mind:
It hardens up the heart
And seeds its trouble
In terrors of deeds un-thought,
But so suddenly done.

Cruelty sits in stoic brooding
Knocking at the door of inconsistency
That shuts out promises
Of gentle, safe release.
It uglies up the temperament
That would speak of tenderness,
Of love,
Of hope,
Of peace:
Of rage, just thought but left undone.

"I had to sweep the stoep four times a day at that time. The winds blew all the red sand onto the polished floor. You know we only had gauze around the stoep to keep out the insects. I would sweep and two minutes later a fresh lot of sand would cover the floor. I was afraid you would slip and hurt yourselves. The floor was always so shiny. You know we didn't see a blade of grass in Palapye for seven years. It was just terrible. I prayed to Our Lady and to St Anthony for rain but it was so slow in coming. I prayed to St Jude; you know Jude is the saint for hopeless cases. As true as Bob, after my nine-day novena, there came the rain. We couldn't help crying and carrying on. It was such a celebration and relief. You would have thought that all the grass seeds were as dead as doornails but, lo and behold, a few days after the rain the grass was back. A fine green carpet covered the red desert seashore. It was like a whole new world was born and such terrible sadness lifted. We started going for our five-mile drive in the evenings after the shop closed so that we could see the bokkies with their mothers. Your father shot a female Kudu for making biltong and for some good roast meat but she had a calf. He didn't see it until it was too late. I remember you crying all the way home and refusing to eat your supper. You kids used to go walking after the rain and slush through all the pools on the Serowe road. You had empty cigarette boxes and collected all those little red tick spiders. They crawled all over your hands and you loved to rub their small backs because they felt like velvet. I don't know where the spiders went; after a day or two they would all disappear until the next time it rained.

Near the end of the long drought we used to hear the Wildebeest and Kudu come into the village. Our car, 'Chorry-Chorry-Bang-Bang', was always parked under the big thorn tree outside the gate. The poor animals used to come and moan around the radiator because they could smell the water in there. The lions used to prowl about too. I remember one year when a small child went outside her hut home to go to the toilet and a lion attacked and killed her. This land has seen some hard times but somehow it and the people survive and carry on with everyday things."

Here in the dry Kalahari
On going roads that are
Always coming to water;
Water, always coming,
Never arriving
At these mirage images of true.
Are they also mirage images of me?
Or are they images of you?
Orange earth indentations:
Dams of hope.
Hope dams these empty dreams
Beneath the blue.
The blue beneath looks long…
Looks deep,
Is deep,
Is far too long,
Is far too deep for me.

On the moon, the corn grows to full height, like umbrellas of security. Moon waters feed thirsty roots that spread and dig into life like pigs at parties. They swell with gifting food. The corn is sweet. Moon people sit at fires that let them tell their life stories. Laughter swells rivers along their laughter lines. They suck thick butter from slow-cooked cobs and laugh again before they chew. They rise and dance and sing moon melodies to the music in the corn. Moon dust rises in their praise of moon rains and sun and grass for grazing.

"Your father got so discouraged and surly in the drought. He used to go straight to the pub after five and get home any time after nine. We used to fight because he said the supper was ruined. If I left it in the oven, it dried out and he would not eat it. If I left it on the table until he came home, he complained that it was cold and stale. One day I had had enough of the complaints so I let him sit down at the table. He always sat with his elbows on the table and his hands held up his chin. He would start the slurring and mumbling with his head bent so that I could never really hear his moans. Anyway, he started on the litany of discouragement and I got the jug of milk from the fridge and threw it all over his bald patch. He couldn't believe his eyes. He sat bolt upright and stared at me with his mouth wide open. I started telling him what a drunkard he was and you kids started crying and calling from your beds. It was a cats' chorus. But your father learned a good lesson for a good few weeks. He came early enough for supper and never complained about dry food again for a good while.

For all that, you had a good father. He provided well for you even though we did not have much money. You always got an Easter egg, birthday and Christmas presents; drought or no drought."

♥

The sand dunes shift.
There is no resistance to changing form.
Their substance dances willingly
In the wind;
Their journey unconfirmed.
There is no mapping of their needs expressed.
They are eternal optimists.
They fling their fine, sand-rain
Into the sighs and breaths that move them;
That draw them into being across the plains.
Praise for the difference in the dunes.

MY father sits under the cool shade of the syringa. His hands in prayer clasp, his head prayer-bent. I see the thin hair patch oiled and pressed, like a Sunday best suit. Blue smoke is trailing from his thick, yellow fingers. The evening wind plays games. Swirling smoke patterns weave, waver and wander and then, gone, with an 'Abracadabra'. The smell of one who has had too much whiskey floats and lingers. His sandy socks lie loose about his ankles; coiled cobras, ready to spit fierce fire into eyes. I screw up mine, and watch; not being fooled, not being foiled. I stand silent until I tell his mood sense. The cobras rise in his hands and turn into socks again. He coughs, heaves and hunches. He spits upon the ground. He moves to bury the deed and wipes the ground's face clean. He leaves a little phlegm grave. I watch its funeral until the small mound stops moving. He stoops and smothers the tiny red glow and smiles serenely. I say, "The stars show, even though the sun is not dead and they are so far away."

"Yes," he says, "They are eternal optimists."

"What are optimists?" He sighs at my ignorance. He moves his feet. The cobras coil again. I gain a little distance, waiting for them to strike. He shuffles out his thoughts.

"Optimists are people who see well when their world is dark. They think goodness when there is only trouble and darkness all around. Your mother is an optimist. She never gives up hope, no matter what. Her faith is so strong she can put the devil to sleep any time. She sees goodness, not evil."

I ask, "Why are the stars optimists?"

"Come," he says, "Sit here." Because he smells of whiskey, I pick the place with care like one who is unsure, like the half stars that bewitch the mind. They can be seen and then they can't; they shine and then they don't. "The stars are optimists because they shine light into darkness even though the light is not their own. They are happy just to reflect the light and to pass it on. They don't have to own any of it but they are rich and beautiful with it and because of it. The dark is like evil and the light is like goodness. It is just like God and the devil." He clears his throat like a satisfied orator. I am perturbed. I move a little closer. "Is the night evil and the day good?" He sighs at my ignorance. I do not move. The cobras lie like sleeping sentries. "No," he says, "When people are evil we say that their souls are dark, like night, because goodness in them cannot see the way. The stars are like the goodness that peeps through in people."

I say, "They are very small and the night is very big." I look at his socks. The sentries sleep.

"They seem very small because they shine from so far away. In truth, they are very big, bigger than our whole earth. Sometimes goodness can seem so far away but we can still see it and feel it."

"Which star am I?" The pressed patch moves. He heaves and hunches and makes other little graves. I feel his brief absence like a webless spider. To mend the rift, I give him my handkerchief. He blows and sniffs. The cobras slither down again. "See that cluster over there, near the moon slit?"

I point and nod. "There are six, no seven, no six?"

"Yes, there are six that can be clearly seen. See the seventh?" His voice is urgent. "The one so small and distant; the one that blinks at the night and sends it away?"

I peer and search. The half star blinks and bewitches until I cannot tell it from the darkness. "See it? See the seventh?" His voice is urgent. I look at his socks. I bend and touch the cobra's back. I cover my hands in the good, dark earth. "I see," I say, but my heart is heavy because I am only a half star. He senses my heaviness and tells me that God uses little half stars to make people aware of the light. They are special stars that beacon and blink so that people remember the light when they are lost. They keep their eyes on the star so that they can find God's way again. He says that I am his half star and that I will get him to heaven with my blinking and my beacon. I know that I will have to be a special star that never stops blinking and showing the way because I think that my father is often lost.

♥

WHEN the rains do not come, there is no laughter in the land. The sky becomes a cruel, unyielding master. It lashes out with a bright whip of sun. In spite of its brightness there is a dark mood that creeps into the mind. I cannot sit at the river's edge to cool my feet. I cannot hear the dragonfly's drone. There are no leaves floating on the river's breast or the sounds of drinking beasts. The great, brown life-vein shrinks and cringes in its path of death. Its burned out images press into the soil and leave deep face scars in its wake. Ghosts of old life cling pitifully to the dry clay bank. They are brittle to the touch and have no gentle gifts to give. If I stand in a dry patch of riverbed, I feel the scorching heat filter through my shoes. The sun saps up moisture from my body and leaves me weak and thirsty. I stare towards the sparkle of a small surviving pool and a new pity rises in my soul. The fish snatch at air and writhe for a small space in which to live. Around the pool hangs the dank smell of decay and the glint of dead fish invades my eyes.

From far away I hear the thirsty cattle. They scent the water. They run wildly through the hot bush and their dust billows up and soils the sky's blue haze. The herd clusters at the bank and their lowing sends a desperate cry for mercy. The ox stands hesitantly at the river's edge. I catch the warning in his hollow sound. His great horns jerk up and down and then he plunges his body into the clay. He struggles violently but is trapped in the black mud. His nostrils widen and he rolls his nervous eyes until only the whites show. His lowing takes on a frenzied note of fear. The herdsman's whip lashes out over the heads of the herd on the bank and they turn away and leave their

thirst unquenched. They leave their leader to his fate. The herdsman's wail carries far across the hills. He runs to and fro like a hen that has lost her chicks. His skin shines wetly and the more he runs, the more violently the ox struggles. After a time, the beast is silent. He squats in his grave and tries hard to hold his head up above the mud.

A sudden shadow passes overhead and for a moment a gentler light relieves me. The relief does not last long. An ugly shroud of vultures hangs low over the tired beast. Their raucous shrieks mingle with the cries of the herdsman, who throws pebbles that do not carry far, that sink deep into the mud. The herdsman lowers himself into the hot, dry ground and mourns the loss of his ox. He sways to the rhythm of his dirge and his tears flow freely like a rush of falling rain. A young boy comes and sits at the river's edge. He begins to wail with the herdsman. Together their sound haunts the sky. After a time, the herdsman asks the boy to find my father, The Radibatana.

In the distance, I hear the grumble of an approaching truck. The herdsman wails on a louder note. He knows it is the father of small animals, the Radibatana. He knows that he cannot beat the mud and the vultures. The truck stops. The engine's whine is stilled. The dry grass snaps beneath a firm step. He lifts his sweat stained hat and greets the weeping boy.

"Dumela mosimane." (Good morning, young boy)

"Dumela Radibatana." (Good morning, Father of small animals)

"A o sa tsogile sentle?" (Are you quite well?)

"Nnyaa, ga kea tsoga sentle." (No, I am not well.)

"Dikang ke eng?" (What is the news?). They stand a moment and look at the beast.

"O tlaa fithwa gompieno…" (He will be buried today) .They share a mutual prayer and mutual grief.

The Radibatana raises the gun and points death at the silent ox. The gun blasts its message of devastation among the lands. The sorrow drums begin to beat. A red pool surges up and merges with the mud. Before the smell of gunpowder has left the air, the shrieking cloud descends and rips at red, warm flesh. I leave the funeral with a fearful heart.

I walk towards the store of the Radibatana. The people have gathered outside and the children squash in the pepper tree's shade.

I can see the heat rising from the mass of bodies. I can hear their urgent talk. I can feel their fever. I can sense their fear. The Radibatana comes from the entrance of his store. He stands with his hands on his hips. He mutters at the heat. He flicks his greasy hat back a little and his eyes narrow because of the glare. The furrows on his forehead glisten and the hairs on his hands matt together and cling to his skin. The people weave and agitate and press their pleas upon him. Their headman begins to move among them. The women begin to wail out their distress. Gradually a silence settles. The children stare at the grief of their elders. A small one plays games around his navel. He cannot tell why his belly is so huge and his hunger so constant.

The headman stands with the Radibatana. The remains of a flannel hat hang from his hand. His lips part for a small smile and he shows some yellow stumps that were once teeth. He speaks slowly. The people listen and give signs of approval. He tells of the sun that is very angry at the land. It is a cruel sun. He speaks of the empty breasts of cattle and the empty breasts of women. He shows again the pot bellied children and asks if the Radibatana could save the ox in the dying river. He does not wait for the answer, for they have all heard of the funeral in the mud. The Radibatana sighs like one who has heavy burdens, like the thorn trees that creek and moan in the dry winds. He cannot bring the rain. He cannot feed the children. He cannot lift the oppression of the drought. When the old man has paused long enough, he changes the hat from one hand to the other. The Radibatana must speak now.

"The Radibatana's gun spoke in the river this morning."

"Yes, the beast rests now."

'It is said that the rains have fallen to the south of the village."

"Yes, Old One, but the cattle will not reach the place without water."

"How shall we herd them? How shall we feed them? What will become of the children, without corn?"

The Radibatana bends his head for the Old One's voice is low with sorrow and fear. I can see the fine layer of dust upon his hat. The wrinkles of his neck unfold and black lines of wet earth nestle there. The black lines merge as he feverishly gropes for his SRV. These are his Special Rhodesian Virginia tobacco cigarettes with no filters to stop the dirty yellow stains on his fingers. He lights one and coughs. His face grows red and the veins on his neck stand out like worms that want to escape. The people watch with patience and concern. A ripple of quiet conversation rises and falls with the coughing waves until silence falls again.

The Radibatana speaks loudly, like one who knows his standing among the people. He speaks with words that soften the blows of the drought. He lifts their spirits and tells them that they may take water from his well. He makes a plan for them so that not too many cattle drink from the troughs at once. He prays with them that the rains will soon sing and the land will be saved. The women begin a new song. It holds a story of the one who speaks with wisdom; who shares his water to spare the people, the beasts and the land. Their song moves with them down the village road. The song fades as the heat grows. The sun's heat drives men to desperation. The hunger of children becomes the obsession of women. The thirst of the cattle becomes madness in all. They will not sell the cattle. It is a sign of wealth. It is a sacred sign. They believe that the rain will come and that the cattle will survive.

The village bell rings at one o'clock. It is the time for the shops to close. It is the time for rest. The people lumber home for a meagre meal. The main street falls silent and the fine dust hangs over the trees like a mist of menace.

I make my way home. I see the tall figure of the Radibatana, my father, stoop a little as he walks down the hot road to the house and syringa tree. I enter the back door and it screeches closed. Dorry is already preparing our meal. She asks how the day has been. My father tells her of the ox's death, of the people who weep for cattle that do not have water, of the children with pot bellies. He does not lift his head to speak but rubs his forehead like one that wishes to take the thoughts away. Dorry says that God is with the people and the cattle. God will send the rain. God will make the flowers, the grass and the corn to grow. God will fill the pools and the rivers with water. She speaks like one with longing in her heart and prayer in her mind. He rubs his head like one in a fever. I watch the fever. I fear it. I fear this time of day when the heat is most vicious and the burden becomes too big. The dog begins to pant. He shouts for it to stop. It pays no heed to his complaints and saliva drips like rain from its tongue. The father of small animals rises and kicks the dog until only its pain can be heard. It echoes through the house, through my mind. Dorry runs from the kitchen and begins to scream at him. She rages at his cruelty and his madness. I run. I run hard and hear the thudding of my heart in my ears. The fear grows like fire in my belly. I fear for Dorry and for the dog. I hate the heat and the sorrow that it brings. I think that Dorry knows a different God. I do not know a God that leaves the sky dry and the tears of people full. When I have run a way, I turn again for home. My father sits and broods in the shade of the syringa. I enter the house again. The dog and Dorry are silent. I sit on the stoep and listen to the silence.

At half past two the village bell sounds again. I walk along aimlessly to the dipping troughs. I notice the thick dust that hovers over them and over the kraals that keep the cattle. I sense the urgency of the crowd around them. I begin to fear again. It throbs, like the heat that will not hold rain. I come upon the scene. I stand shocked but my eyes will not close and my feet will not run. The cattle lie writhing on the ground. Their eyes bulge and roll like marbles in a sack. A pale yellow foam slides slowly down from their swollen tongues and their moving mouths. Their bodies twitch and their hooves kick like strange creatures that do not know themselves.

The fathers shake their heads. The mothers hide the sight from small children. They whisper about the thirst that drove the cattle to drink the dip. They point in disbelief to beasts that drank the strong smelling dip that leached them to their death.

The sun beats down with new sorrow. The people hold a new burden. The Radibatana holds it with them. He stands against the iron railings of the kraal and broods. I fear his brooding. I fear for us, for Dorry and the dog. I move away from the people and make my way down to the water tank for trains. There is a little comfort in its shade. I listen to the sound of dripping water and I wish for the sound of falling rain. The memory of it brings a smarting to my eyes. I try to think of other days and other times.

At six o' clock the shutters of the shops go down. My father counts the takings of the day. He shakes his head like one who is discontented. He puts the meagre pile of notes into the drawer. He mumbles of tomorrow and of the rain that will not fall. He lifts his hat from the shelf and sighs. He does not talk to me. He locks his shop and walks away to where the 'Lion Beer' sign flashes out its message to those who are burdened. I go home to Dorry, who cooks and sits and waits. She sits on the stoep and sings a quiet song. Her voice is gentle and deep. It washes over me like balm. I feel a little freer. The terror of the day becomes a little less real and I push away my fear. I become as one with bleating lambs and fresh water streams. I drift slowly to lands where the cattle are strong and fat, where the water pans never dry out, where the rivers are eternal and where the sun goes to sleep.

♥

Do not think this land is dead
Because the black, bold rocks
Betray its face:
There are hidden depths that pierce the dull façade.
The lichens are alive in reds and greens and grey.
They gully and they flow like little rains that grow.
The desert of my heart
Has also bled its flow.

"PULA e yana thata!" The rain is pouring down! This is the cry of people who have done battle with the sun, who know how the soil aches, who pray that the river will never again lose its life's blood and leave the land and the beasts to death. I can hear the rain drum and the rain song. The rain bird's hollow sound has been echoing for days. There are feet swelling and sweat flowing; little volcanoes of emotion that have longed to lift hearts from bondage. Dull brain passion grows a fever. The cattle rush madly with their nostrils wide and waiting. The birds weave and sweep. Dry earth is funnelled up by the fickle wind that taunts, flays, and forms frenzy in the sky. Through tattered leaves I watch the clouds cruise. They billow black. I search for bits of blue as though to satisfy a need for safety. I hear the black grumble and the trees reply; they curl, curtsey and beg to cry. The dark clouds move and I am left in sudden shade. The wind's voice dies. Silence grows. It is not a stillness I can trust. It has a heavy heart. I wait. Violent weavers of destruction crowd out the sun's power that has manipulated for so long. When the land has held its breath for too long and my shade becomes too deep for day, the clouds blink. Light flashes into my mind. Thunder drums into my ears and then the soft sound of dust that feels the comfort of cold rain brings other tears. These are not only mine. Dorry's eyes tell of tired-of-dry-days she thought would never wash away. Joy shocks smiles into my father's face. Furrows filter back life into the brown soil's body and wraps new, green life around the graves of grass.

When the rain has sung its song and the satisfied earth is clean, I can return to the river's edge and witness its re-birth. I can listen for the sound of the dragonfly. The ox's death becomes a distant sorrow. The herdsman sings a new song. He tells of corn that grows to great height. He sings of beer brewing and the time of stamping corn. He shows me how bellies will grow fat again.

My father stands at the edge of his fields. His face has the look of one who is content. He bends and plays finger games with the wet soil. I am pleased I came with him. His harsh words that shuddered through the floor and the kicking of the dog seem to have moved to the moon's far side. He shows me the weavers' new nests. We listen to the lambs and the cicadas. The fogs of fear lift. We are happy with the sky, with the growing, with the land.

We can stand and stare into mud pools that are mirrors for the sun. We have found the bow end and the secret wisdom of the rain.

D ORRY is hurrying around our house. Her movements are frightening because they are not her normal hurrying movements like when she's getting a recipe ready for making us cakes. She's getting out cotton wool and candles. She's gathering bottles of Dettol and some kind of oil. She tells us to stay home because Mrs Bird's little boy has died. She is going to lay him out. She is not sure what diseases are hanging around and so we have to have bags of camphor and garlic pinned to our vests. It stinks and I always want to vomit. I take it off when it's time to eat because I can't stand the smell of food, especially cabbage, with the smell of camphor. The curtains of Mrs Bird's house are drawn. They have been that way for three days. My father's truck, Pedro, is parked outside and there are a lot of people from the village there. They are singing songs in Setswana about people going to their ancestors and about the mercy of the Morena in heaven. I want to cry because I will never see nor play with Lenny again. I am sorry all over again that I peeped at his thing. I ask Dorry where heaven is and what we do there. She points to the sky and tells me it's up there somewhere and we spend our time there being very happy and looking at God. She says it's the communion of the saints. I don't know how I will get there because I have given up trying to be a saint. No more klaps for me, I just get on with every day like everyone else in the village. I am not sure if I want to look at God forever. I have seen holy pictures of him and I can't look at those all the time. Dorry says I will understand death better when I am older.

My father and Lenny's father carry the little white coffin to the truck and place it in the open back. The people put flowers all around it. They already look droopy in the heat. Dorry has her arm around Mrs Bird and leads her to the back of the open truck to where Mr Bird is waiting. Everyone lines up behind the truck and they start to follow it slowly to the graveyard. I can watch everything because the graveyard is across the road from our back yard. There are a lot of graves heaped up with stones that tell you who is who and when they went to heaven to look at God. My sisters and I sometimes go there to have a picnic under the big trees. We tell spook stories and frighten ourselves so that the sandwiches come back home with us in a hurry. They are still singing and praying in between. They take Lenny's small white box and let it down into the hole with ropes. They weep aloud so that I feel the tears running down my cheeks too. The red sand flies up while they cover up Lenny and put the dying flowers on the top and leave him there alone like me in the back yard. I will never forget Lenny and how lonely is dying.

"After Lenny's funeral you kids used to play grave-grave. You had the whole yard filled with small heaps with those bright bellflowers on the tops. I never heard so many funeral speeches and 'Abides with Me'. I began to worry about you, Bern; I took you to the doctor and told him about all the insects, birds and even ants being buried. It went on for weeks. You even had Dianne doing it in her back yard. Doris Freeman said she could not stop her either. You made sure everything was a Catholic too. You baptised the whole of creation before the funerals. Ruddles got you out of the funeral play because he dug up all the crickets and birds and ate them. You worried that they would not be in heaven when you got there and that Lenny would not remember you. It reminded me of when my granny died. I felt sorry for you, Bern, because you were too young to understand what was happening."

I don't know why I go to the graveyard but I do. I go there alone. I feel separated from my home and from the village. I feel lonely and sometimes so quiet in my soul that I think I will never be able to leave the silence of the graveyard and return home to Dorry and the friendship of my sisters. The trees in the graveyard have a deeper shade, a deeper understanding of the need for shelter from the sun that is so often fierce and exposing. The soil is fine and red and soft and when I go beyond the gate there are no other footprints. I seem to tramp into the soil more slowly and more deliberately and as I move among the graves, I look back and see my footprints and the small land slides that they have made. It makes me feel as though my life is also sliding and changing and that nothing ever stays the same. It is strange that I feel safe in the presence of such long and unknown sleep. Dorry tells me that life and love is eternal and that eternal means forever and ever. She says the prayer, 'Eternal rest give unto them oh Lord'. I can never imagine how forever is. I find the days between my birthdays long and nearly forever.

I often sit here at the end of the graveyard that is farthest from the gate. The trees huddle more closely together and I can lean against their barks and listen to their whispered messages in the wind. They whisper the same messages and the same stories. Perhaps that is because I sit and stare at Naomi's gravestone. It is very white except at the bottom where the rain splashes red soil up onto it. The marble glistens when the leaves part and the sun is allowed to play on it. It is like being happy and sad at the same time. I sometimes think that darkness and light always hold hands. Dorry says they cannot be separated. Even in the day there are deep shadows and darkness and at night when the sun sleeps the darkness shows us the moon and the stars. She says life is like that; dark and light with a forever hand hold. It is a sad, glad thought in me; I will never be all sad or all glad. I think I will always be mottled in a mixture with a longing I do not understand. Dorry says the longing is a longing of the human spirit for God. We are made for God. My father says life is a journey to God, and passop vir die honde on the way. It is being full and empty at the same time. I do not understand life. It does not matter where I am or what I am doing, I am always full and empty, glad and sad, afraid and safe, exposed and clothed in my mind's secrets. I keep them to myself because I do not think other people will understand them.

Naomi was four years old when she died. She was dead before I was born but I feel that I know her. My sisters tell me about her and I ask Dorry to tell me her story.

"You know, Bern, it was such a terrible thing that happened the night Naomi died. She was such a precious little thing and always came to play with the kids. She was Monica's special friend. She had big brown eyes and dark hair cut in a fringe. It was straight and long and fell in a shiny sheet into her neck. When she laughed she swung her head and her shiny hair caught the light as it swayed with her.

She and Monica were the same age. Naomi got shot, you know. It was not right the way she died. Alan and Ivy Bradshaw used to pick up their friend, Ted Harris, and go out at night to hunt. They used to blind the animals with the car lights and take pot shots at them. They often brought a buck home. The way they hunted was against the law. This little girl Naomi often spent the weekends with us. If her parents went out at night, she came to stay. I used to allow her to sleep over because what was one more child anyway? You were such a brood of chicks in any case. On this particular night I was in the kitchen making scrambled eggs for supper. We used to have our main meal at midday. Alan and Ivy came to fetch Naomi. It was just getting dark. I could hear the kids begging that she be allowed to stay over the night again. I heard this entire conversation going on but did not go out to greet them. I was busy with the eggs. You know how they stick in the pan and burn so quickly. I never thought to put anything down and rush outside to say everything is all right and Naomi is welcome to stay. It was a Sunday night. I just left it all as it was and they went off with her. It was already dark. We heard a shot but we were not told anything until the next day. The Police Commissioner came and told us that Naomi was shot dead. Alan had his loaded gun in the front of the car between the seats. Ivy was in the back with Naomi. Naomi's little dog was chasing the car. She leaned over to call him. Ted Harris, who was in the other front seat, wondered if the safety-catch was on and so he put his hand down to feel and pulled the trigger by mistake. The gun went off. It hit the side of the door; you know the steel piece along the side. The bullet hit that and shattered. Five of the pellets went into Naomi's heart and lungs. She was killed instantly, of course. We had a little funeral and everything. It was terribly sad. When Alan and Ivy left the village, Ivy brought a little gold cross in a box. She said it was for Monica when she got a bit older. Monica loved it. Some other kids were here playing with your sisters. I put the box on top of the piano. When all the kids were gone, I opened the box to see it again and it was gone. Monica still remembers that. She was so upset that somebody stole her cross."

When the sky turns red and I am sitting beside Naomi's grave, I think that she can see me. I ask her in my mind how it is to be dead and alive in heaven forever. A long road of cloud starts in my head. There are people floating in it. They have wings like the guardian angels, who Dorry says look after us. I have a special guardian angel who follows me to the graveyard and who walks next to me everywhere I go. I sometimes think its wings are all around me so that I can never come to any harm. All the people on the cloud road smile. They have bright rings of light around their heads. Perhaps they are in eternal rest because they do not do anything. I see Naomi with all the other angel-people. She is also smiling and floating. She isn't sad and lonely. I don't know if I am. One day I will be a cloud person but I do not like to think about it.

♥

KATE has blonde hair. It is not the colour of straw but looks very white and it is matted behind her head because she sweats when she sleeps. She has ice-blue eyes that sparkle when she smiles. Her teeth are even and she is chubby and healthy. Her skin is smooth like Dorry's and she is a quiet and calm child. She is also quietly stubborn because when you tell her not to do something dangerous like pull the dog's tail she looks at you with her ice-blue eyes and her ready smile and she pulls the dog's tail and says, "See, it doesn't bite me!" If you try and tell her that other dogs are not like our dog, Ruddles, and that they will bite her, she laughs and her little shoulders shake and she says, "So what!"

Kate is sitting on the floor sucking an ice cube. Mary, our maid, gave it to her. Kate loves ice and is always sucking a lump of it. Dorry gets the cold shivers when I tell her about Kate and the ice because she says people can choke and lose their breath trying to eat ice that way. All it takes is a bump or a slip and then there is trouble of the worst kind. Her words do not stop Kate from the ice episodes. She cries and begs Mary for it when Dorry is not there. I get into my moon mind when Kate puts the lump into her mouth and walks around with it sticking out. Sometimes she doesn't let it melt - she chews it and makes crunching noises; first slow, deliberate ones; and when we complain about her manners, she chews faster and makes a bigger noise to show us that she does not care about our criticism.

I am reading a comic about Superman. I love him because he is so strong and never hurts anyone. He saves everyone from all sorts of trouble. He just puts on his cape and up he goes in a flash. I love it when he picks up buildings or cars that are crushing people. He saves everyone so fast that they do not have time to say who are you and thank you. I ask Dorry why Jesus was not like Superman. Why did he not fly and save everyone from everything that hurts them and why did he die on a cross for all bad people? She says it is a mystery and that Superman is just a play, a play person from somebody's imagination so I must not worry about it and just be thankful to Jesus for all he has done for us. She laughs and shakes her head and says, "You kids! I just don't know where your minds get to!" Mine gets to the moon when Kate eats ice. I get there but my tummy still trembles until she has finished it. Superman is on his way to save an aeroplane full of people. There is smoke coming from the engines. I am holding my breath because I am not sure if he will get there before it crashes.

Kate begins to hold her breath too, because the ice is stuck in her throat. She is gurgling and turning blue. She is crawling around on her hands and knees. I am frozen on the moon. My mouth opens and closes and no sound comes out. I am lame in the legs and cannot run nor reach her, nor slap her on the back the way my father did when Dorothy got whooping cough. Kate has crawled under the divan. I suddenly find my legs and my voice and I scream that Kate is choking and dying. I do not stay to see her death. I turn and run down the road. There is a wind-thunder in my ears and my breath fits-and-starts with the thud of my shoes. There is no Superman to fly around and save me from being devoured by fear and guilt. I have let Kate crawl around the floor looking for air and I have run away. I reach the end of the road and see the river water rushing by like time. I climb a tree that hangs down over the stream and my heart hangs down with it. The long branches play and paddle among the white water tips. My mind becomes a branch and I play with the tips too. There is no peace in it. There is only fear trying to blot itself out. There is a tremulous hope that someone has found Kate and saved her from her airless world. I hold my breath and ask to die of no air too. I cannot go back home and face Dorry. I cannot tell her that I have let my little sister die of an ice disaster. I can see her turn pale and her hands go up over her face and her legs grope for the nearest chair. I can hear her wailing and crying and I can see her telling my father and my sisters that we do not have Kate with us anymore. I can see my father's rage tower over me. I can see him bend and lift me and then I can see nothing. The wind whines on and my fear paralyses thought. It turns into sound: the swishing of cars passing our hearse. The swishing turns to whispers while the red soil is being tossed and the bangs on the box fade with Kate, into silence. It is beginning to get dark and Dorry will be home. I slide down the tree and begin my leaden walk. There is no moon to set my feet free or to soothe my mind into light. There is only dark dread and raw fear. I open the door and sitting on the divan with a piece of ice, is Kate. She shapes her mouth around it and sucks noisily so that a thin whistle curls through the air. There is no shortage of that and death is a bad dream away. She digs her fingers into the little space left, takes out the ice and offers it to me. "Cold," she says. I run into my room and sit behind the curtain. I cry. When Dorry comes home, she asks me what I have been doing and why my eyes are so red and puffy. I say, "I have ice-eyes, Kate has ice cubes and death is a bad dream away." She looks at me with frowning furrows above her eyes. "You're a funny one, Bern," she says. Kate climbs onto her lap. "Are you eating ice again? One day you will choke!" I shiver and my moon mind is ready for a run.

"Bern, I forgot to tell you about whooping cough! You all got whooping cough, but Dorothy got it so very badly! She used to just sort of gurgle and then she'd go clean out, very frightening, very frightening, you know! Daddy and I could never have our meals unless we put the cook next to her so he could shout to us if she went into one of her whoops. We couldn't even hear her cough. She just used to go clean out. Daddy used to run and pick her up and rub her back. One time he ran right outside with her and she'd go gasping with that terrible hollow sound, you know, like people do when they are trying to catch their breath. That is what whooping cough does. I remember once when the priest, I forget his name now, was staying with us on his visit from Francistown. Daddy asked him if he would like to go to the hotel for a drink and he said yes. It was so hot; he said he would love that. We were on the stoep and Dorothy was getting over the whooping cough but I was frightened when Daddy suggested the trip to the hotel. I couldn't stand the whooping and the losing of the breath, you know. I panicked so and was terrified of not being able to get her to breathe again. Now they were going to leave me alone. The road ran right in front of our house; you remember, Bern, with the big thorn tree in the middle of it and the thick sand. Anyway, they had just crossed the road and, lo and behold, Dorothy went into the worst whoop episode of all. I screamed for Daddy. He came running with the priest in full flight after him. The priest got out his rosary so quickly and began pacing up and down the stoep praying like hell was on our doorstep. Dorothy was in such a state, a goner. Daddy rushed out of the door with her and sort of swung her

Trisha, 5 & Bernie, 7

Patricia, age 6, Bernadette, age 9

Right to left Hugh, Bernie, Dorry, Trisha - Durban beach after Hugh's heart attack

Thelma, age 9,. Dorothy, 5, Faith, 10, Monica, 7

Dorothy, aged 10

Home at Palapye

Lady Catherine, age 9 or 10

Patricia, aged 14

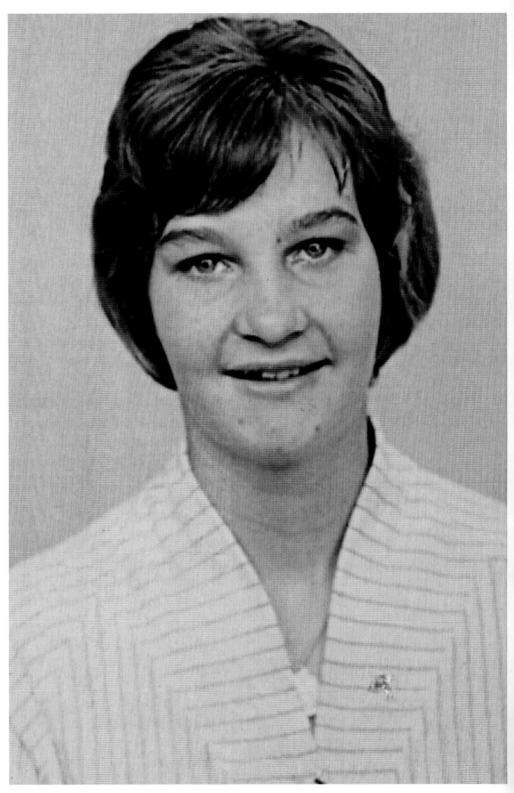

Bernie, aged 16-17

A 'FIRST' FOR B.P.

Sr. Bernadette Flattery (above) is believed to be the first White Bechuanaland-born woman to have become a nun.

She is pictured with her parents at Palapye (in the Protectorate) whom she visited after returning from a Notre Dame novitiate in England.

Born at Serowe, Sr. Bernadette was educated by Notre Dame nuns at Venterspost, though she lived at Palapye.

After the Mass which was offered for her and her family, Mr. Peter Molosi welcomed her on behalf of the community, presented her with a small gift, and asked her to pray that more young women from Bechuanaland would follow in her footsteps.

Sr. Bernadette has been sent to work in Embakwe.

Sister Bernadette clipping

around. I don't know how he got her breath back but she came okay.
Daddy waited a while so that he was sure she wouldn't cough again
and he and the priest went off to the hotel. I prayed the whole time
they were away because, you know, I was not so sure she wouldn't
have another whoop fit. Anyway she was well on the mend from that
last terrible time.

When you were little, Bern, you must have been about three
or four, you got very ill too. You were in such a state. I had to get
the doctor to you. He said you had tick fever. He said that no tick
would ever get you sick again. I suppose you had it so badly that you
developed permanent antibodies. He gave you medicines. You were
very feverish, red and hot to the touch. You looked in a hang of a way
and I was afraid you would die. I was sick with worry. You were in
bed a few days before I was happy that you would recover. The doctor
said you were a strong little bit. People didn't think you were strong,
you know. You had those black rings around your blue eyes and that
pale face. It turned as brown as a berry in the summer but when you
were not able to get out into the swimming pool, it got pale and the
rings seemed blacker. I was always having you examined. I fed you
a couple of spoons of malt a day too. You used to hold your nose and
heave while it slipped down your throat."

Malt time is moon time.
I have to travel there so fast
To beat the frenzy in my mouth and mind.
It lumps and heaps while the spoon escapes.
There is no mercy from mothers who persist that this is good.
Moon malt turns to liquid cream crammed with other flavours.
Moon-flower melon, moon iced cakes, moon marshmallows.
I hurry to the edge of calm.
I cut off breath and swallow moon made butterscotch.
I am freed of frenzy.
My feet are firmly on the ground.

"I took you to my best friend Helen's farm in the Magaliesburg
for a holiday and the rings disappeared while you were there. As soon
as you got back to the village, lo and behold, the rings got back too.

I didn't worry about them too much because you were such a run-about and so energetic. You ran everywhere or rode your bike everywhere. You won every race in the village sports. Daddy was so proud of you girls when you did something and won. Anyway I was telling you. After the tick fever episode, life went back to normal. I was down to the tennis courts and back three times a week. I used to take Lena the nursemaid with me. She watched you all while I was playing. You were safe with her. I never worried about anything but that tennis ball getting into the wrong place for me and me getting it into the wrong place for the other side. I loved slamming those backhands up the tramlines and putting them away. I used to play golf too. I was good at it. All of us ladies played golf together; Doris, Ivy Bradshaw and I. Ivy had a child called Naomi. She was Monica's friend.

I want to tell you now about how you were born, Bern. There was a priest who used to come to our village once every three months. You know we only built a church when you were already a nun overseas. I think his name was Father Fry. He had red hair and a flowing beard. In those days the priests who visited the village stayed in the hotel and not with us. I said to him, 'Father, you know, I don't really want to have any more children; I have got four already and that is enough.' Father Fry got me this book. It was all about the rhythm method of birth control. Of course, I had never heard of such a thing, Bern. I was so ignorant. He told Daddy and me to read it. He explained it all to me. All about the menstrual cycle, how and when you were fertile and so on, you know. I only had five days a month when I was sure I was not fertile. Daddy was good about that and he didn't mind that I could only give him his needs for that short time in a month. We lived like that, kept on like that and I thought I would never have any more children. Then, lo and behold, all of a sudden I was pregnant again! That was with you, Bern. My cycle had changed and you know we knew nothing about cycle changes or how to tell when they would happen. So, there was nothing I could do about it all. Your period just happens at the wrong time and then you ovulate at the wrong time.

So, I was trying to arrange to go to Jo'burg for the birth of Bernadette! I had to see a doctor immediately to see if all was okay. I went to Doctor Friedman; he was in Serowe but came to us every week in those days. I told him I was going to get to Jo'burg but could he see to me in the meantime? The birth date got nearer and nearer and I still had not been able to get a booking into the Queen Vic. They said that the South African government would not take patients from Bechuanaland and I would have to pay private hospital rates. That was so expensive, plus the train fare and paying for my keep afterward until I could get back. Doctor Friedman asked me why I had to go to Jo'burg, when he was here and when there was a perfectly good hospital. He said he would look after me and see me through it all and that I would be put in a special ward so that I was private. So the pregnancy with you was all okay. I played tennis for the first three months but my legs got very painful after that. You know I have varicose veins. It broke me up, not playing tennis. I had to just sit and watch all the others. I still had my tea day. You know, we baked and had to arrange the tea etc. It was lovely and everyone loved my sponge cakes and Swiss rolls. You kids used to stand at the kitchen table and watch me make them. Remember how I used to get them to slide out of the baking tray and onto a damp cloth? I used to spread the jam while they were still warm and then roll them up perfectly. You used to argue about whose turn it was to lick the dish. I always left a little of the mixture in the bottom for you. You loved it so much. You still love anything vanilla flavoured, hey, Bern?

I broke water during the night with your birth and Daddy had to go and ask D'Arcy to come with him to Serowe, as our car was not so reliable. Aunty Flo was up for a week or two to look after the others while I was in hospital. We got there okay and Doctor examined me and announced that he was going to bed. It was a Monday night. I said I would go to bed too and sleep. I had no pain. I slept through the night and had just a dribble. Next morning, doctor came to see me again and I had not had any pain. I had only one contraction. He said that we would have to do something about bearing down when the next contraction came along because he had to go to our village for the clinic that day. So next contraction I bore down. There was hardly any pain and out you came. So your birth was not a tragedy, so to speak. It was not even a normal birth. I was never in pain that was severe. So the matron came in and took you and bathed you and everything. Doctor saw to me and then went off to the clinic. That's how I remember you were born on a Tuesday because of the clinic day getting in the way of no pain and contractions. I stayed in the nursing home for three or four days with you. And then I came home. Doctor brought me home in his car, as he had to go to Palapye for something.

I was very fit in those days and I saw to you and bathed you. The maid was never allowed to do that and then Aunty Flo had to go back to work. When we got back from the hospital, Flo had the four all spruced up with lovely big bows in their hair. I cried my eyes out because they all looked so beautiful and smart like they didn't miss me at all! I only stayed off tennis for about two months and then I went back to it. I took you in the pram. Dorothy was nearly four when you were born so she was walking. I took the maid with me so she could watch over you all while I played tennis. Mr Morey always shouted, 'Here comes Mrs Flat with all her chickens!' I used to pack your bottle because your feeding time was during my tennis time. I used to make sure it was not too hot and try it out then give it to the maid who fed you while I was running around getting the backhands down the tramlines. She used to wave her hand over you while you were feeding to keep all the flies away. The flies were dreadful; they used to cling and stick to a person, especially before the rains. They seemed so lethargic and heavy in their movements. Their buzz seemed lower pitched somehow.

After tennis we used to go to the hotel and if I was very thirsty, I had a cold beer shandy. I could only drink half of the shandy; then I was too full. Daddy used to drink the rest of it. The kids used to have minerals and Monica always had orange juice. Monica couldn't drink anything bubbly: she didn't like it. I don't know why but she didn't. After that we all went home. The maid would push the pram along and all the others walked along. I used to get home and get the kids washed and fed. At night they always had porridge or vet-koeks. We used to have dinner in the middle of the day, with meat and vegetables. Dr Friedman always said, 'Mrs Flattery, if you have a good dinner during the day, then all the children need in the evenings is a glass of milk and a couple of slices of bread and jam.' But I used to make oats or thin mealie-meal. You would go to bed and then Daddy and

I would have our supper. Daddy always had to have meat. Fried meat all the time and after that it was normal living. I used to bath you all by twelve in the day. Dad used to come home from the shop at one. I put the whole lot of you in the bath and dried you all like a factory line. I dressed you all in your knickers and vests and you weren't allowed to go outside in case you got a spot of dirt on them. You used to eat in your knickers and vests in case you spilt something during your dinner. When dinner was over I used to put you all in your pretty dresses. I sewed morning, noon and night. I sewed dolls' dresses and made all your clothes. I made your knickers, vests, dresses, petticoats, and the lot. When you were all spruced up in your pretty little dresses I used to trek off to the tennis courts. Daddy never came with us because he played golf and it began at three. Tennis always began at two. We had all that lovely tennis, Bern."

You've been my mother,
You've watched me grow,
And while the years have passed
You've built your plaster cast.

But I have seen the wound beneath
Your blasé laugh
And when my surgeon's knife
Cuts through,
You bleed a little
Like opened roses do.
I've been your mother too.

"While I am talking about births, I must say I cannot remember too much about Trisha's birth. I know I went to Doctor Gemmel that time. I didn't like Dr Gemmel too much, that I know. I went to Serowe again. It was easier to go there. I think Aunty Joey came down when Trisha came. There wasn't any trouble with Trish either. She was a normal little redhead. It was just a normal birth. Daddy couldn't come to Serowe to visit me in hospital as he had you and the others to look after. What I do remember is that once after I had gone back to playing tennis after Trisha's birth, we went to the hotel as normal for the sundowners and Daddy insisted that the maid go home. We stayed a little later than usual so he let the maid go. He was pushing the pram and I never realised that he was drunk until the pram nearly tipped over. He was plain unsteady on his feet. You bigger children were holding onto the pram. I didn't think a thing until I realised that Daddy had had too much to drink and was wobbling along. I took the pram away from him. I was expecting some sort of argument but he let it go as meekly as a lamb, with no ill feelings."

♥

I carry you in my soul-womb
Where your foetal fire grows
And wanders lost,
In well concealed thought portraits.
Mirage images of who you are,
Hardly visible in mirrored love
Shine through.
So still,
So starkly phrased
In pale, poured lights of fading
Blue...

"You know, Bern, I have not always been a good woman. Do you think God will punish me? There are things I have done that only God and your father know about. Of course, I went to confession and got absolution from the priest. It took me such a long time to get the courage to go but in the end I did. I felt so much better and it was as though a huge weight was lifted from my heart and I didn't have to carry a brick around in my chest any more. You see I was such a good and ignorant Catholic, I didn't know any other way to stop having babies. I fell pregnant six weeks after your eldest sister Faith was born. I knew nothing about breast-feeding, or sex for that matter. Nobody ever instructed me. One did not talk about such things in my young days. It was all hush-hush and find out the hard way. Trisha must have been only about two and we were getting a new priest. The priests came out from Ireland and Urban Murphy was one of them. So, lo and behold, next thing I sit on the rhythm for a while and I in any case became pregnant again. I said to Daddy, 'I am not having this baby. I am definitely not having another baby. No way am I doing it!'

I wrote to Mafikeng chemist, T A Little. I used to deal with them. They sent me my cosmetics and stuff. I sent for a glycerine syringe. Bern, you wouldn't know what a glycerine syringe was but in those days they used it for abortions. You poured glycerine into it and inserted it into the vagina and injected the glycerine into the womb and it causes a miscarriage. So I decided to do it. I spoke to Daddy about it and he wasn't keen for me to do it but I told him I was doing it anyway; whether he liked it or not I was doing it! I inserted the glycerine into my womb mouth and nothing happened and so I gave it another tube of glycerine. Then I started to have pains. I must have been about six weeks pregnant already. I had such terrible pain, Bern, I suffered nearly the whole night and I had to wake Daddy eventually. The next day I had to call Daddy and ask him to get me some hot water that has boiled and bring Lysol and the syringe with it. I was bleeding but that was all. Then lumps of blood were coming out. I douched myself with the Lysol. I suppose I could have burned my insides with it. We used it for douching in the old days.

Eventually, we had those slop pails. You remember them Bern, those buckets? We used them for the loo. Remember those loos we always had built at the back of the yard? They had a wooden shelf across them with the hole in the middle for the loo seat. Those pails used to be put under the shelf in the right place so that they could be emptied every day. We used to wash them out with dip and scrub the shelf and floors with it, too. I was always so afraid of snakes in there at night. We used to take torches down with us and look everywhere before we sat down. Anyway, Daddy brought a slop pail. I began to feel so very, very sick, Bern, so very weak. I had this terrific pain. I sat on the pail and eventually everything came out. It was only as big as a pear. You know, not an avocado pear, but an ordinary pear. It stank something terrible. This was probably the afterbirth and not the baby because I never saw it. The baby must have been much smaller. Daddy got so afraid and I said to him, 'Take it now, down into the yard and bury it.' I knew all the time that I was committing this dreadful sin, you know, Bern, and being so frightened of the Lord for it. At the same time, it didn't stop me from doing it. I suppose I was desperate about having so many children. I stayed in bed for a couple of days and kept douching myself with the Lysol. I got quite well and strong again. I probably saved my life with the douching. I could have got poisoned judging by the smell of it. It smelled so rotten.

I thanked God that the next priest that was to come to us would be a new one so I would not have to confess to Fr Fry, who was our usual priest. I was so relieved that I wouldn't have to tell him about the dreadful thing I had done. It worried me dreadfully, you know. Then came this new priest. My goodness me, I almost wished I had the old priest back. At least he knew that I was not all wicked. It was too bad, you know. I went to confession and had to tell him about committing abortion on myself. He never said anything, you know. He just sat there and whistled long, slow and quietly, like into the air, you know. I thought: good God, I really have committed murder! And anyway, he spoke to me and so on. In any event the very next month I was pregnant again with Cathy so it didn't help me at all. I said to myself that Jesus is showing me that I just can't do what I like, that I will do what he says anyway. Sometimes I have a problem with Jesus, Bern. You would think that I had had enough children and that the bloody rhythm method would work properly, if it were God's natural and appointed way of doing things. I always thought that a good wife should never deny her husband of sex, and your father was never satisfied. Anyhow, now you know the worst thing I have ever done."

The stained glass windows
Give rainbows from the light.
You seem not to see their play.
You sit motionless
In quiet mourning.

Tears try.

I say, "Let them flow."
Then in your open hands
Their small pools grow
Like precious crystals,
Mined in the heart of grief.
Would that I could, like you,
Let my own soul's anguish
Go.

Dorry is very sick. She cries because the pain is terrible. I am under my bed because I can hardly hear her here. I look at the bedsprings and count them. I count them many times. Trisha is in her cot. She is sleeping. I wish I were in a cot and asleep. My father walks up and down the stoep. I hear his shoes squeak then stop, and then squeak. I hear him say, "Sacred heart of Jesus have mercy on us." I hear him say, "Bloody hell se donner se hell, bliksem and to hell with it all." I hear Dorry scream. I rush to the moon. There are no swearwords here. There are no screams and no shoe squeaks. The light is like the early time when the sun is about to rise. The Moon Mountains glint and I walk along the high peaks. I put out my arms so that I do not fall off. There is moon music in my mind. It hums softly and tells of peace. Water runs down from the mountains and sparkles in the moonlight. It does not burble and make a noise like the river in our village. At the bottom of the mountain is a lake that looks like glass. The running water spills into it but there are no ripples that disturb its face.

I think I will stay on the moon forever and become a moonchild. The glass lake cracks and breaks with the sound of Dorry shouting and calling. My father rushes to her side and she tells him to help her and take this away. Take it away and bury it in the yard. I do not know what my father is going to bury. I do not care. I only count the bedsprings and I watch the lines of the mattress that peep out from the blankets that enfold them. I follow the lines with my mind and I sink into the small pits that interrupt them. I hear the back door close. I close my mind. My father comes back later. He stops in the kitchen and he washes his hands. He goes to Dorry and tells her it is done. They pray and say the act of contrition. There is no sound after that and silence hangs down like a heavy curtain.

My father calls me and I creep out from under the bed. He tells me to sit on his knee. He tells me that Dorry is sick but that she will get better. He says he will put me to bed. He takes my hand and walks me to Dorry's bedside. She is pale and her eyes look like the hollows in the mattress lines. They have shadows around them and the blue has turned to grey. Her hands are clammy and her forehead has small beads of sweat on it. She says I must be a good girl and do what my father says. She holds my hands and I feel lost and afraid. There is no warmth and comfort in the holding. There is no bow end of rain.

♥

MY little sister has been born. She is only a week old and she has no name. My father says she will be called Hope. Dorry says over her dead body will he name her

Hope. She says my father is full of bullshit and he hasn't a hope in hell. She says Sally nearly got named Hope, and Monica nearly got named Charity. There is no way she is having Hope and Charity in her house. Faith is all she is having. Father Murphy is arriving on the train this evening and he will come and baptise her. He will not name her Hope. My father says that we will see. He is the father and the boss of the house. Dorry says in your dreams.

Father Murphy will not baptise my sister. He is saying, "Hugh, you are not naming this child Hope. I am sitting here waiting to baptise her but I will never do that until you change your mind about the name!" My father is drinking whiskey on the stoep. Father Murphy is waiting on the stoep. Dorry is smiling and my little sister is sleeping. It is late. My Aunt Molly has been staying with us and helped take Dorry to hospital because it was raining and the roads were so wet and slippery. Dorry was in hospital in Serowe. There is no hospital in our village. I was also born in Serowe, where the Chiefs live. She is on Dorry's side. She says my sister should be called Catherine Mary. I do not know what she should be called. Father Murphy says he will wait until Ireland is no longer green before he baptises her Hope! My father has gone silent. He is sitting with his head in his hands. He is mumbling something about Catholic priests thinking they can do what they like. Dorry is starting to laugh. Aunt Molly has her finger to her lips to stop Dorry because it will make my father very angry. He knows he will have to give in and call the baby Catherine Mary. Dorry says why don't they all give in and call her Mary Catherine?

There is long silence. Father Murphy sits on a chair with his stole and his prayer book, ready to baptise. He puts little pots of oils and cotton wool and salt and a candle on the small table next to his chair. He says, "Come now, Hugh. God is waiting for this little soul." My father says she will be as pure as the lilies in the snow when she is baptised Hope. Father Murphy says he cannot be responsible for Hope lilies in the snow. Dorry sits and looks at him and my father's head has bent lower. Aunt Molly goes to make some tea. Dorry says, "Come now, Hugh, it is eleven at night and the little ones are dropping on their feet and you are keeping your daughter in original sin for want of a name." Father Murphy begins to sing 'I'll Take You Home Again Kathleen'. My father gets up slowly. He holds onto the chair because the whiskey is helping him to wobble. He says, "Bring the child." Dorry darts up and Aunt Molly forgets the tea. Father Murphy says that my father has seen daylight. We stand around my little sister and Father Murphy begins the prayers for baptism. Everyone is smiling except my father. He sighs. My father is very drunk but he is as meek as a lamb. My little sister no longer has to sleep with original sin on her soul. My little sister is as pure as lilies in the snow. Her name is Mary Catherine. My father has no hope! They do not call her Mary; they call her Catherine. I call her Kate.

I help Dorry bath Kate and I watch her when she has her feed. She smells of baby oil and baby powder. She crumples up her face and puts her fist in her face before she cries. Sometimes Dorry lets her cry for a few minutes before she picks her up. She says it makes her lungs strong. I think I must have cried a lot because my lungs are very strong. I take deep breaths and my chest swells up. I show Dorry my strong lungs and she says they are star lungs. Trish also watches Kate. Sometimes we sing to her. Sometimes our singing makes her smile but sometimes she cries. I think it is because we cannot keep a tune for long. We sing 'Twinkle, Twinkle, Little Star' and 'Lullaby my Baby, Close your Pretty Eyes'. When my father sings it we all want to cry, not sleep, because he makes it sound like a sad song, not a soothing one. Dorry tells him to sing outside to the fairies in the sky because her kids cannot take his lullaby voice. She says when he can sing to us without the whiskey accompaniment, she will let him sing us to sleep. My father says Dorry is full of nonsense and a touch of shit but he laughs and takes his singing to the stoep.

♥

"So now, I have told you about the worst thing I ever did and that was the abortion after Trish was born. I just couldn't face another baby, man. We went back to the rhythm method and it worked for a couple of years and then the cycle changed again and there I was pregnant. Anyhow, after I had been to confession and spoken to the priest, lo and behold, here came Cathy! What could I do about it? I had promised never to have an abortion again. I said to myself: Jesus is just showing me that I can't just do what I like about having babies so I just went ahead with the pregnancy. It was not even six weeks after the abortion that Cathy came along! Cathy was a very bad birth because she was lying in bridge position and I always felt when I walked that I wanted to fall over onto my face. Aunty Molly came to us. She came and she said she would stay until the baby was born and she was with us for about a month. Catherine in the meantime would just not come into the world. She decided to take her time, I tell you, no matter what! I was overdue and everything and Aunty Molly said one day, 'Dot, I have had enough of you! Come along, we're going for a walk!' Off she toddled me up the Francistown road. It was such a long walk; I thought I was going to die because I wanted to fall onto my face the whole time.

Anyway, that night the membranes ruptured and I had Dr Slump then. He was a good doctor. I remember it was raining when I went to have Cathy. It poured for days and days. Dr Slump came for the clinic day and after he examined me he said to Daddy that he was going to have to take me into hospital. He couldn't see me having this baby at home and the rain was flooding; the bridges were already covered with water streaming over them. I thought to myself: that will be the day I go over to the Doctor's house and live there for perhaps two or three weeks, you know. I said, 'No way, there is no way I am going to come and live in your house to wait for the baby.' About two weeks after that, Molly took me on that walk and that night the membranes ruptured. It was still pouring with rain. Molly had to come with me to the hospital because of the rain. Koosie Alberts came and got me into his van. Molly and I sat in the back and the roads were just water all the way. I think the anxiety took all the pains away. I said to our Blessed Lord, 'You just get me through this birth.' It took us nearly two hours to get to the hospital. We got there after midnight and I stayed in the labour ward. It was only an hour after I got to the hospital that the pains began. Man, I had a hard time. I laboured through the rest of the night until two in the afternoon of the next day.

Cathy was born at two o'clock. Aunty Molly made Daddy stand outside my labour room door. In those days the husbands were not allowed to come in. She told him to go and stand there where he can hear the cries and the pain. She gave it to him! She said, 'Go and stand there and listen to your wife's crying. She has had too many children! Go on, stand there and hear her!' Shame, Bern, I felt sorry for Daddy. You know I never ever thought it was Daddy's fault that I had a big family. I didn't mind to have it. Then Cathy was born and the nurse said, 'Goodness gracious, Doctor, look at her, all peaches and cream. We don't even need to bath her; she's beautiful.' Of course it was a girl again. Daddy was sure this one would be a boy. More than likely, the one I aborted was a boy. Nobody will ever know that, of course. Anyway I was lying in bed since the birth right until the next morning and I said to myself: I am going to get up and go to the toilet. So Cathy was hooked on the bottom of my bed in her cradle and I got off there and went to the toilet. My God, I never got such a shock in my life. There were sanitary towels lying all over the floor. They all had a blue rim around where the blood ended. I knew then it was the African women who had left them there. You know they get a blue edge around when they bleed. When I came back from there I began to wonder if flies from the toilet were lurking around and I was so afraid that they would sit on Catherine that I sat on the edge of the bed and I kept making sure that a fly didn't sit on her. When my lunch came I had a look at it and it wasn't covered and I just could not bring myself to eat it. It had been next to the sluice room as well. So I told the sister that I couldn't eat anything.

When Daddy came to visit I told him about it all and he couldn't do anything and I told him to bring a net next visit. I said to the sister that I wanted a net for Cathy's cradle. So next time he came the net came too and that was such a relief to me. I decided that I was doing myself more harm staying in the hospital than I would be if I went home. When the doctor came in I said, 'Doctor, can't I go home? I am very well and I will look after myself.'

'Well,' he said, 'I don't think there would be a problem. We will take you home in the ambulance!' So the next day was his clinic day and I sat in the ambulance with Catherine. It was only forty-eight hours after the birth. I was so happy to be home, my dear; at least I didn't have to worry about flies and dirt. Aunty Molly stayed a while with me.

There was trouble with Cathy when the priest came down from Francistown. It was Father Murphy in those days. She was due to be baptised and after supper Daddy told Father that he would like to have her baptised with the name Hope! Well there was such an argument. Father refused to call her by that name and Daddy refused to change it. Molly and I joined in the fight. Molly said she should be called Mary Catherine and I said no, Catherine Mary! Molly's daughter was Mary Catherine. She was born just before you, Bern. Anyway, there was such a row. Father said Daddy could get another priest to baptise Cathy but over his dead body would she be called Hope. I suppose he wanted a Charity as well, as we had Faith already. Eventually Father baptised her Mary Catherine at about eleven that night. It took all that time for the argument to settle and people to give in. Poor Cathy had to wait so long to get into God's family!

The priests started coming to our village once a month and stayed with us. Cathy was only a few months old when she started ear troubles. I never got any sleep. I used to sit up propped up against the back of my bed, holding Catherine. I used to also walk the floor with her to give Daddy some sleep. I put warm oil down her ear and the doctor said to give her a half an aspirin as well. Nothing seemed to help. He gave me drops for her ear but nothing helped. Once I was walking her up and down at two in the morning and Fr Murphy came and said I should go and get some sleep and that he would nurse the Queen, as he called her. He nursed her until the morning. Eventually, after sixteen days of this ear routine, I couldn't take it any more. I went down to Doris. Catherine's ear used to burst and orange liquid would come out. I said to Doris, 'Look at this stuff coming out of Catherine's ear.'

Doris said, 'Oh Dot, take her up to Johannesburg. Take her to a specialist; don't play around here with that ear.' That is when Doris took Dorothy, you and Patricia in for the time I was away. That's when Trisha called Doris 'Mommy' and got to love her like a mother. Doris really spoilt you and I was sixteen days away with the specialist treatment. He gave her some antibiotic that looked like strawberries and he gave me a yellow powder as well. After that I had no more trouble with those ears. About a month after I got back, there was one more ear burst episode and then no more trouble.

Daddy went on holiday by himself after that. I said I didn't want to go away. I stayed and looked after the shop and Daddy asked Ted, your cousin, to come and stay so that he could drive Pedro the truck to Lecheng to deliver the mealie-meal and so on. Daddy used to collect Africans and take them with him and bring others back. I didn't know that he used to charge them for the trips. Ted collected R16.00 from them on the first trip. The passengers always had their money ready so Ted and I shared the proceeds. Daddy never told me anything about it so I never told him anything either. Daddy used to spend that money on booze, of course, and that is why I never heard about it. I never forgot how good Fr Urban Murphy was about nursing Cathy. He even used to feed her for me and sing Irish songs to her and make her smile. He used to have to go back on the goods train. I packed him a basket for his lunch because the train stopped at every siding and shunted trucks on and off. Of course twelve o'clock was the Queen's feeding time. Fr used to break her winds and everything while I did the lunch basket. When she was bigger, Bern, you used to have to watch her suck on her feeding bottle in case she choked. You used to have to sit and watch her suck on a milk sucker, too. I used to give you one to keep her company but it was eaten in a flash. Once an ant crawled into Cathy's ear. I got into such a panic I sent a note down to the golf course to Daddy to come home. Of course, I had put oil down her ear so the ant would have been killed anyway. Daddy didn't even bother to come home! The messenger I sent said that daddy just threw the letter away."

♥

"I REMEMBER so clearly that day of the tornado, Bern. It was very, very hot. You know how hot it could be in Botswana. The sweat ran off of us like a runaway river. We were always mopping up as we served over the counter. If we didn't, then sweat would fall and stain the new materials, or drip into the flour bin and that was not a good thing. We had to be very sure and careful not to bend over too far. The iron roof of the shop used to creak so loudly that we had to shout to be heard. Your father was at Lecheng on the day of the storm. As usual, we shut shop at one o'clock until half past two. As we walked along the road to home, I noticed how black the sky was over to the west. Our rain usually came from the west. I remember thinking: this is going to be a good storm and the heat will be gone for a while. Hell, man, we were about to sit down for the midday meal when I looked out of the window and saw the funnel-cloud coming straight at us. The wind was already very strong but my heart sank when I realised that we were in the path of a tornado. I had only seen such things at the bioscope. I was dead scared.

Do you remember we had the partition going up on the stoep because we had recently moved to the doll's house and we needed more room for you all? There were no windowpanes in the extension. I barely had time to shout to you three, Bern. It was you, Trish and Dorothy. I lost sight of you because the thick red dust came rushing through the house like fire and I was blinded. I ran up the stoep and tried to hold up the partition. It was no good. I got blown along to the end and was nearly crushed against the end wall. The wind just took me and smacked me along, partition and all. You kids were screaming but all I could do was hang on and try to wriggle out of the space between the wall and the partition. Your eyes were as big as saucers and your mouths were as wide as any big cave I have seen. I saw Doll run for the potty and Trish wet her brookies. Your mouth was going and you clung so to Doll's skirt. It was terrible. It didn't last too long though. I remember sweeping up the sand and filling up buckets of it. Then the hail came down. I thought the roof would blow right off or that it would collapse from the weight of the stones. They were as big as ping-pong balls. Your father said that he saw the tornado heading for Palapye and felt very afraid for us, as he knew he would not be able to travel faster than it would.

Everyone's house was damaged by that tornado. Water tanks came rolling down the road as though they were light plastic doing a dance in the street. Sheets of corrugated iron were lying all over the village. Some mud huts collapsed and many trees were uprooted. Our small house remained as it was. That old syringa bent right down to the ground and sheltered us from the full force of the wind. I think that if we had windowpanes in the stoep extension, we would have lost our whole house. I prayed so hard to God and Our Lady to save us and to let me get to you kids in the lounge. That was the only time I remember such a terrible storm. We did have floods once or twice when the river came down in a torrent and the five-mile bridge couldn't be crossed for days but never such a wind or such big hail stones have I ever seen again. Your father was so relieved when he got back and found us all safe and sound. After the storm was over and it was just drizzling, you kids went down to the river to see if it was in flood. There was nothing but a little stream in spite of all the noise and hail. I remember panicking something terrible because about a half an hour after you left the rain came down in buckets again. Lucky there was neither hail nor lightning. You looked half drowned by the time you got home. Your father was angry because your hair was so wet. I don't know why he had such a thing about wet hair. Heaven help you if you got home after sunset and swimming with wet hair. He used to say, 'Lovey, look at the kids' hair! It is late and they still have wet hair. It is dangerous to go to bed with wet hair.' If you didn't dry your hair fast enough you got a hiding. Man, I used to feel so sorry for you."

The Bow End of Rain

This cloud bomb
Wants to burst:
It swarms its mass of menace
Dark and hounding.
High above my head,
It buffs out silver at the edge
But I am bullied into definite steps
And brusquer heartbeats
That run along the road to home.

I am walking behind Dorry from the shop to the house, along the twisty road with the long grass on either side. The grass is sighing and restless and the sky is dark, black with a pink looking tinge to it. I am feeling nervous and I think the trees tossing around their heads are nervous too. Dorry walks with urgency and tells us that it is going to be a good storm and the heat will be gone for a while. She takes Trisha's hand and pulls her along a little faster. Trish can't keep up too well and so Dotty catches up and helps her. She takes her other hand and starts to play one-two-three-up we-go-weeeee. Dorry lifts her at the right moment and Trish swings up in the wind like a heavy parachute that won't open. I am not sure that I want the rain to come. It looks so fierce and there is no gentleness about the way the clouds are scudding like a fury. When we get home the smell of cooking cabbage seems sharper than usual. Dotty and Trish are in the lounge looking at the clouds and the syringa that is moving and groaning like an old woman who can't make up her mind in which direction she wants to go.

The water bag that hangs from a wire around the lowest branch is dangling and propelling itself in a wild sort of circle. It looks as afraid of the wind as the testy branches and the look in Dorry's eyes. She is not telling us that she is afraid of this kind of wind and this kind of sky. She says that our father will be home soon. He will have left the out station, Lecheng, at one. It is only twenty-three miles away. She hopes that he will not be caught in the rain and the heavy mud of the pools that form so quickly. Dorry is about to call Polokwane, our cook, to bring the meal, when she sees the dark pipe-cloud that smokes in an ever-widening circle and fumes towards our home. She runs to the door and shuts it and then to the stoep. She tells us to get under the table but her voice is lost in the shrieking wind that suddenly fills the house. Her face is lost in the red, boiling sand that sweeps and thrashes us.

Dotty fades as she runs into the bedroom and Trish stands wide mouthed next to me. I am screaming, "Our Father who art in heaven." There is no our father and no heaven, just hell and fear and aloneness in a world that has gone deaf and blind. Dotty emerges and lifts Trish and sits her on the potty but it is too late. There is a small pool around her legs and her mouth is still wide. I am still screaming to Our Father. There is no sign of Dorry. She may have been swallowed up in the red swirl. She may be crushed against the wall because the stoep partition has also clamoured along to the far wall. I have no thoughts at all. Just fear. The fear pierces all that I am. It remains there like hot wire in my head until the wind passes and leaves a little less noise behind. It is replaced by another thunder on the roof. Big white balls bang at us and the syringa bends right down to the ground. Its back does not break but the leaves are driven like spikes into the air and fly away with the dust. Then Dorry is with us again. We stand around her in the lounge and cling to her skirt while the hail batters and our tears make more rain down our faces. The floor is a red sand-sea.

When the hail subsides and we can hear ourselves talk, Dorry wipes her forehead and says, "Ye gods, man, that was more than a storm; that was the tail end of a tornado. We are lucky that old syringa is so close to the house. It saved us from damage. The roof is still on and we are all safe. I couldn't hold the partition up and I nearly got squashed against the wall. Come, let me change your brooks, Trish. Doll: you and Bern go and see if the kitchen is still there and if Polokwane is okay." I hang on to Dotty's hand and she takes me away from the red sand-sea into the smell of cooked cabbage. Polokwane still has his head tucked under his arm. He sits in the corner on the wooden chair. He repeats as though it is the first time he has said it, "Metsi aa bela." 'The water boils'. Yes, and so does the wind. When the wind and the rain boil, Dorry disappears and I am thrust into fear like the leaves that are spiked into the air, like leaves that have to leave their tree.

THE walls of our house were once white but the brown earth has splashed up against them so that they are smeared with mud. I get ashamed of the walls. The syringa tree stands close to the walls and protects them from the strong hot winds that sometimes blow. The tap that stands in the back yard drips so that the pool around it supplies water for the fowls; not only for them, but also for the grey doves that gather when my father feeds the chickens. He calls them, "Kip-kip-kippies." They rush to where the corn bowl stands. I watch them flap and squabble. My father says that the fowls are as greedy as people are. They care only for themselves. I do not care only for myself. I care for him, for my mother and my sisters, and for the land's harmony. He says that I should be as careful as the rain. I do not know what he means, but I think that the rain is like a mother that feeds the earth and all the living on it. My father has a favourite hen that settles up on his arm. He feeds it from his hand. It does not fear him. It understands his caring. I wish I could be as sure of my father as the hen is of him. I wish that the rain were always gentle and careful.

When we get home we come through the back door. As we open it, it makes a loud noise, like a cat when you stand on its tail. My father says he will oil it when the cows come home and he has nothing better to do. We are still waiting for the cows and for the day he has nothing better to do. Dorry says he lives on the never-never system and that he will die that way. He is always going to die; every day we hear about the few years that he has left, if God spares him. He says I am going to be his little nun and I am going to be good and make sure God opens the heavenly door for him because my prayers will make sure that he gets up there and that he does not have to go to purgatory. I am not sure where purgatory is nor why people go there but I am sure that I have to be very good and pray every day in case I cause my father to go to the hot place instead of joining the Holy Communion of saints when he dies. I am afraid to do or say anything that might make my prayers less heard and my good behaviour less seen. Dorry says that I should not take any notice of what my father says about my getting him to heaven because he has his own steam, but I worry about it. The trains run out of steam. That is why they have to stand at the water tank at the station for so long. To get more steam. People also run out of steam. My father goes to the pub to get his steam. He gets drunk and becomes angry and we get very afraid of his steam. Dorry is not afraid of it. She says he'll blow his top right off one day and she as sure as hell won't be helping him to put it back.

The back door is made of gauze and the frame is wooden. The air can move shiftily through it and make a song with a thin whistle sound. It cools the house when the days are very hot and the night winds don't blow. We never lock the door because there is no danger from the people of our village. There are just the scorpions and the snakes to be careful of. We never put on our shoes before we have turned them upside down so that if there are scorpions in them, they will crawl or fall out. In the summer, the snakes like to cool themselves on the cement floors. We look under and in our beds before we go to sleep. Sometimes we find a snake sliding along the outside wall trying to get into the house. My father gets his gun and shoots it. I am always afraid of the gun's loud sound and of the death of snakes. They do not seem to harm us but my father says they are like the devil. He tells us that the devil poisons the mind and the soul. It sneaks in while you are not looking and puts bad thoughts into your mind so that if you listen to them, you will do bad things. Snakes put poison into your body and turn your flesh rotten so that you die.

I am now afraid of snakes and the devil. Dorry says the devil is not a snake. It is a fallen angel called Lucifer and that Lucifer can't ever hurt us because we have God's love and a guardian angel to protect us. She says that Lucifer can't hear or see God. When I draw the devil, I make his head very big because it has other people's bad thoughts in it. I make his eyes very small because they can't see God or goodness. Lucifer has no ears because the devil can't hear anything beautiful. His mouth is always wide and screaming because he is alone and nobody loves him; neither does he love anyone. I pray for him but Dorry says he is beyond prayers because he has chosen to lock love out and does not want to be loved. I can't understand how anyone can choose to be miserable and hateful. Dorry tells me not to worry about the devil but to always love and to look at God. Nothing gets impossible or too much for a person that way. She says it makes the human heart very happy to have God in it. When I ride on my bicycle through the bush I sing to God and I know God hears me and loves me. It makes my heart very happy too. I sometimes feel as though I will pop or take off into the sky because God is so beautiful and lives in me. I feel like a house that is too small for the love in it. I think that the birds know God too because they sing their heads off from morning 'til night and never change their tune no matter what happens.

Ruddles lies in the shade of the syringa. When people or goats pass our house he rushes at them. The people do not really fear him. They know he does not bite them. The goats run for their lives and bleat with fear. I feel sorry for the goats. Ruddles teases them but he never catches them. They never learn that he is teasing and so they are always bleating and running. The bells around their necks ring in different tones and rhythms until the shepherds come and save them from the dog disaster. Ruddles hunts with my father. He runs along the bush paths and sniffs the ground. When he smells the spoor of a buck, he gets very excited and runs faster and leaves the path and rumbles through the long grass. If he sees the buck, he stops still and trembles and waits until my father comes to the spot. He sits in silence while my father takes aim. As soon as the shot is fired, Ruddles dashes and yelps and then sits next to the dead buck. My father tells him he is a good dog and gives him a pat for his trouble. If my father shoots guinea fowl, Ruddles does not sit next to them; he fetches them and brings them to my father. His mouth waters and saliva drips from the corners of his jaw but he never takes a bite of bird. Sometimes he gets a reward and my father gives him a piece of dried biltong. He puts it on his nose and Ruddles waits until my father signals that he can eat it.

When it is time to go home, I sit on the back of the truck with Ruddles and the dead buck. Trisha and Kate sit in the front with Dorry. If my other sisters are back from boarding school, we all sit in the back and sing 'Ave Maria, Gratia Plena', in three parts. I do not know why we sing hymns but we just do.

The road that passes our home leads to the river's edge. Often I sit on the bank and watch the water flow. I think of time ticking and running, I think of the river's meaning, its breathing and its ending. I hear my own breathing and I see my own image that is mind-eyed on the brown water's face. I feel at one with the sun, the land and the long grass that whispers around me. I get my head into the clouds that puff and weave above me. My thoughts get thin up there and I can't really think. I just am and I just float. Sometimes I get into Jannie's rowing boat and drift with the river's current. I can watch the mudfish jump and the dragonflies hover and drone above the river's face. I love to be alone with the river. It has life secrets for me. I share its love and its never-failing-to-give-life. I think that is how I will become a saint and a nun for my father's door into heaven, just keep giving and going wherever I must. Sometimes I think that if when the river dies and dries up, I will also die. My father says my mind is full of poetry and I should try also to be practical. He says that one can't live well on poetry. He says the stories he tells me are practical, especially the one about how he was resting under the withaak's shade and a leopard came sniffing at his feet. The leopard did not stop at his feet but began sniffing his knees and even his shirt. He got embarrassed because his trousers were grubby and old. He said from that day on he would never go anywhere without polishing up his veldskoene and wearing decent hunting trousers. He never told me that that was Herman Charles Bosman's story and not my father's. Herman used to live with him on Jimmy Flattery's (my grandfather's) farm in the Groot Marico.

My father tells us many such stories. Sometimes, when he is not so drunk, he tells us to sit on his knees and when the story gets spooky, like the one about 'Ghost Trouble', he speaks very softly and then makes a loud noise so that we jump and scream. It makes my father laugh until he snorts. When he snorts that way, I think it must be like the snorting of the leopard in the withaak's shade. It is sort of low and soft but at the same time it is strange and not a snort that one hears every day. Dorry tells him that he shouldn't frighten us because we'll be calling her for water and we'll be up and down to the toilet all night. He takes no notice and we don't either.

♥

Under beds, there are womb worlds
Where minds waiting for peace can wander
Safe from treacherous, verbal spars
And not negotiated nakedness.

Under beds there are woven webs of care
Which caress the hiding sadness,
Until clear tears can rest their small, lit glories
On cool, solid floors:
There is healing under beds.

Dorry and my father are fighting. They always start the argument on the stoep. When they start depends on which number whiskey my father is on and how anti Dorry feels about it. He always starts up things by blaming us for his behaviour. "Lovey, it's you and the kids that make me drink. I never drank before I married you and had all the kids. You never objected when I started going to the pub and coming home at seven. You used to make my supper and talk to me even when I was late. That's why it became a habit. There were no complaints from you so I drifted into it."

There is always a long silence after this speech. In the silence, terror brews; it seeps into my bones and into my head. When the ructions come, Dorry's voice rises like thick smoke and fire; smoke for the tears and fire for the anger. The fire turns into hot lava and burns down any walls that may protect us from the words. They spit up into the air and batter our ears. My father throws glasses and the bottle with the sick, drunk smell in it. He rages about the liquid wasted on the floor.

Dorry fetches the jug of milk and pours it over his head. "I'll bloody kill you," she screams. I crawl under the bed and press hard against the cold wall and into the cement floor. Dorry's smoke and fire curls and billows around. It sneaks into every corner until my eyes let out their little pools. I whisper, "Our Father, are you in heaven? Hollow is your name." It echoes in the wild thumps of my heart and beats up blood in my brain. I am also hollow, like the bent drainpipe that lets the rain rattle down into the tank. It never moves, no matter how fast and noisy are the water's words. It never leaks, no matter how the rushed rain roars inside it. It remains the drainpipe, solid and still. It permits the running. Dorry's fire still shoots up. "Hugh! I'll box your bloody ears for you, you bastard! Why don't you leave us and get the hell out forever? We will live in peace and quiet without your foul mouth around the place! You can't take responsibility for anything. It's always somebody else's fault. You have never grown up! What do we have to do with your pub-crawling and drinking?" There is the sound of her feet dashing to the kitchen and then plates break against the wall. She runs back. Chairs bounce up the stoep.

My mind runs along the sand path that leads from the village to the bush. The sun is setting and I am thankful for its softer light. It does not spew fire at me but brushes the bush with its beauty. I leave them behind. I feel free of them and their ferocity. Here, there is only the sound of my feet printing a pattern in the silent road. I watch the soil's response. It moulds out my footprints, catches up my churning and my crying. It holds the words that scribble in my thoughts. In its gift of holding there is no spite, no pestilence or pain. It is sacred and safe.

As I walk along, I catch a glimpse of green, a small bush that has struggled to survive in a patch of barren sand. In the shadow that it casts there is movement, a streak of life. I stand and watch for a while. The movement stops. Slowly, I edge towards a little grey mound. Gently I move a twig. I look into the eyes of a terrified rabbit. I hold my breath. It holds its place. I feel the power of its grace. It feels my power to destroy. We keep our space and stare into each other's fear. The small nose twitches uncontrolled and not remembered. Its body shakes. A grunting sound escapes as I bend to touch fur. In touching, I am shocked to find the coarse feel of the coat. It looked so soft upon its back. I draw away my hand. Intrusion frightens me. I have no words to sow my care. I wait and then bend again. I lift up the rabbit from its ground. It trembles still. I stroke the fur beneath its chest. It has a comfort for my loneliness. I have comfort for its fear. The trembling stops. We stand until the shadows stretch in long, thin lines across the road. I free the rabbit of my hold and am thankful for the giving of its world. I turn to home but first I take a time to stare, for friendship such as this comes so rarely in my way.

I am back here, under the bed. My feet are pressing against the wall and my head and shoulders are exposed so that I can see what is going on. I am too afraid to creep right under the bed because I am not sure if it is more frightening to watch the whole battle or to hide completely where nobody will know where I am if hell really arrives. The fire-words prick and pierce. There is no stemming of their tide. "Get the hell out, what are you waiting for?" Dorry's fury knows no bounds. "I will!" my father shouts. "I'll get out of your lives forever! I'll shoot myself!"

Dorry drags the shotgun from the gun-rack. She lifts it into the air above her head. The barrel gleams like a flash of sinister warning as she beats the butt on the hard cement floor. A piece of wood flies through the air and slides along the stoep like a catapulted pebble. She throws it down at my father's feet and then opens the long lid of the rack shelf and takes out a handful of cartridges. My father wobbles on his legs as she thrusts them into his pockets and shouts that he should do a good job of shooting himself. She runs to the stoep door and jerks it open and screams that he should go to the abattoir and make sure he doesn't mess in our house. I do not know where my sisters have gone. I only know where Sally is. She is sitting at the piano and her hands, although they are shaking, are beginning to sweep in the soft tones of 'Silent Persuasion'. The melody sounds strange yet comforting in the violence of the moment. My father is slow to lift the fallen gun and fiddles in his pockets. He tells Dorry he is making sure that they are the right calibre bullets to do a good job. Sally's hands are running along the keys like moon-silver slips over the river waves at night. I see her mouth purse in the half-light. My father begins his stagger to the door. Monica comes running from somewhere and shouts at Dorry and my father. She tells them to stop fighting and to listen to the music. Sally's hands press harder and the music invades the room so that it cannot be ignored. Dorry begins to cry. She says that my father is frightening us and that he should be ashamed that his children have to watch such terrible behaviour. Her tears also gleam as they slide down her cheeks. They linger at the end of her chin like raindrops that do not want to leave the leaves after a storm. My father says he cannot live with us. We are driving him to drink and he will go and end it all. Dorry leaves the door and it screeches shut. She runs to him and begins to pull at his shirt and shouts, "Hurry up then so we can live in peace!" My father lurches to the door and the screech is back like a bad dream.

Sally's hands move more frantically along the keys and the music begins to jerk out a jagged tune that cannot hold the mind and soothe the heart. There are no more trills and flows. There is sudden silence and the sound of the piano lid closing makes a little thud. I crawl back under the bed and press my hands against the wall. My cheek is fed cold cement. We wait for the sound of the gun that will end the nightmare of the fight. It will also begin a new flow of blood. It will seep into our minds and stain our days with unsure futures and sure, unbridled fear. My father's presence flashes before me like a flickering candle flame that will or will not light; like a doubt about life or no life, like a song without a tune.

Dorry's voice calls to us and we emerge from our private places. She surrounds herself with us and tells us that our father will never shoot himself and we need not worry. He will come home and begin a conversation as though there was never a harsh word or a hint of hell broken loose! I go and sit outside under the cool shade of the acacia tree. The bark is rough against my back. The cicadas croon their constant, high-pitched note. My father says that if you are lost in the bush and you are thirsty and anxious, the song of the cicadas can drive you insane. Their voice gets into your mind like a steady screech and no matter what you do it pierces your brain and slowly turns you crazy. I shut off my mind and try to listen for other sounds. I watch the evening dust settle in a thin curtain over the thorn trees. In the distance I see the open door of the abattoir. From its mouth there is only silence. Life hangs like a scarecrow, crooked and forever etched amongst dead heads of grain. The seeds of life only spill when my father's unsteady figure emerges and wobbles its way back home. The gun barrel hangs lamely over his arm. Dorry and he sit on the stoep and brew softer words for their bruises and their pride. Sally's hands move over the keys again. Her left hand crosses over her right, bass to treble, treble to bass as she plays, tenderly, 'Silent Confession'. Dorry says, "It's a pity there is no music for 'Silent Contrition'." My father laughs.

♥

Cut flowers in a vase;
They've forgotten how to grow.
There is no turning back,
My mind cord is severed.
I thought I was a daisy:
Open-closed
So free, so safe in the sun.
Staring into water holes
I see my own face image,
The rains have come.
Mixed up in the clouds,
Whirled and welled within the mud
Lost to touch
In liquid space I slowly sallow,
I have no ideas now, of
How the daisies grow.

JANNIE is very tall. He is so tall that the top half of him stoops forward for fear his head may get lost in the clouds. He says the stoop started when he was very young because people called him 'Oomblik Oom': een oomblik kan ons jou kop sien, die ander, nie! ('Blinking of an eye-uncle': One moment we can see your head, the other, not!). He has blond hair that sometimes looks yellow in the sun. It does not lie on his head but forms another peak like a row of sand dunes after the night winds have visited. He uses Brylcream to keep the dunes more or less in place so that even when he runs or is riding his bicycle they do not rise up and rebel. Jannie's hairy legs and arms seem to go on forever and they also shine yellow in the heat. He carries a white and blue handkerchief in his pocket and wipes away the sweat that wants to drip off his high forehead. He works at the railway goods shed and checks all the boxes and sacks that are off loaded from the trains. I love to help with the unloading of the train trucks. I have a two-wheeled trolley that can be easily pushed and it has a front piece that slides under the heavy boxes and makes moving them simple. Sometimes I climb onto the mealie meal sacks and sit up near the roof of the shed. I watch everyone come and go and Jannie has a stamp and lots of papers that people have to sign. He lets me fill in consignment notes that are put under the metal clips on the side of the trucks to tell people what is in them. He has to be patient because I cannot write quickly yet and I cannot spell words like 'containers of tobacco leaf'. One day I found one of my neatly written notes in the waste paper basket and Jannie said it must have fallen in there. He smiles at me when he tells me, and his green eyes get a look in them that says 'please believe me'. He calls me 'Ou Bern'. I do not know why. It is just the way he talks to his special friends. He says that it is because we have been friends for a long time even though I am still very young. He says 'ou' is short for old. When he speaks his voice is soft and gentle. He does not get cross. He only turns red if he gets into trouble from the stationmaster or if the people complain that their peaches have stood in the shed too long and have begun to rot.

Jannie sits on our stoep with my father and sips tea while my father sips White Horse Whiskey. The more my father sips, the more they laugh about hunting lions up-wind and down-wind and how one has to tread carefully if an animal is wounded and how to get directions from the position of the sun. My father always tells Jannie, as he always tells us, about the leopard under the withaak's shade and Jannie says how lucky my father was not to get eaten. He has a smile in his eyes when he joins in and finishes the story for my father because he knows where it comes from and who was really in the withaak's shade. He knows that Herman Bosman lived with my father on my grandfather's farm, 'Middlerand', in the Groot Marico. My father says Herman was a strange man. He used to teach at the farm school near Tannie Haasbroek's place. He used to walk six miles to and from the school at Heimweeberg every day. He used to go out into the bush late at night when the moon was full and talk to himself. Jannie asks, "Oom, talk about the time that Herman threw the kitchen knife at your sister Maxie and wounded her in the back." I do not know why Jannie calls my father 'Oom Pat' because my father's name is Hugh John. Perhaps it is because he has an Irish surname and people call Irish men Pat or Paddy.

"Ja, nee, that was a close call, man. Maxie was teasing him and he just picked up the paring knife and threw it at her. She was badly wounded and so she had to be taken to the hospital. She still has the scar today and still shows it when she tells the story. Then there was the time Herman got involved in a scuffle between his stepbrother and a man called Pierre. Herman had bought a hunting rifle and Oom Jim Flattery, that is my father, advised him not to take the gun with him to Johannesburg for the July holidays. Oom Jim begged him to leave in the bushveld the things that belong there, but to no avail. During the scuffle that happened in a dark room, Herman fired a shot and then there lay his dead brother David." My father shakes his head and sighs and sips again before he tells of how Herman landed up in jail with a death sentence. He does not say how it happened that Herman got out of jail and was not hanged after all.

Jannie asks my father if he can take me for a ride on his bicycle. I sit on the handlebars or in front of him on the long bar and he rides along the railway line because the path is hard and smooth and he does not have to pedal too hard. His bicycle has three gears: one for level ground, one for getting through the sand, and one for going uphill. He explains to me how to change them and he shows me. He says that when my legs are long enough I can ride his bike and be a proper gear changer. I can reach the pedals if he puts the saddle right down but I still cannot ride properly. I wiggle from side to side to keep the bike from wobbling over. Jannie has taught me to find all the little oil holes and which oil to use so that the wheels turn smoothly and the pedals do not get stiff. I help him to keep his bike clean because the sand gets into everything and jams the breaks and scratches the paintwork. He likes to have a smart looking machine.

Jannie is also building a rowing boat. He says he will show me how to row and how to steer the boat and how to catch fish without overturning it. I go to Jannie's house every evening when the village bell rings at five o'clock. I watch him build the boat and I pass him his hammer and files and the special glue he uses to seal the nails and the joints so that everything is waterproof. He shows me how the boat will float and how it will sink if he does not do things properly. He makes a glug-glug noise when he shows how the boat will sink. He puffs out his cheeks to tell how we would have to save air to get back up through the water if we sink. He says that I am a clever girl because I know how to swim already and so drowning would be out of the question even if the boat sinks. I think of all the weeds under the water and I get afraid that my foot may get tangled in them and then I would not be able to get back up through the water with the saved air. My father says that some cattle drown when they are too thirsty to be careful of the water, and they rush into the mud and get bogged down. They get too tired to struggle, and sink deeper and deeper until their heads are too heavy to hold up.

Jannie's house stands in a row of railway houses along the end of the station. It is a square house built of asbestos. This is because the people who work for the railways can be moved at any time and they just load their houses onto a flat railway truck and ride in the train with their homes to wherever they have to work next. Jannie has been in our village since I was very small and I do not know when he will be taken away on a flat railway truck. He is my friend and I do not want to see him carried away. From the gate to the front door of his house there is a long path made of small white stones that twinkle in the sun. I have to put my hand over my forehead to see where I am going because the twinkling blinds me. The small stones are kept neat by two rows of rocks that are whitewashed. There are two beds of purple flowers growing on each side of the path. There are marigolds along the front walls of the house. Jannie says he cannot grow any other flowers because there is not enough water to keep them alive. Sometimes I water his flowers with the hosepipe that is curled up under the tap. He says, "Ou Bern, you are a good gardener." I take off my shoes when I water the plants and I water my feet as well. I love the feel of the cool water. It makes me peaceful and happy with everything. Jannie gives me a small towel to dry my feet before I go into his house so that I do not get mud on the floors. The floors are brown and smooth. They have a lino covering. In the place where his table stands the lino has worn and there are small holes in it. Jannie makes sure that the table is always in the same place so that the holes do not show. The house smells of 'Sunbeam' floor polish and the lino shines very brightly because Jannie's maid uses clear polish to keep it that way. Sometimes the house also smells of bananas and peaches because Jannie orders his fruit from Mafikeng and it arrives in a box in the goods train. He brings it home from the goods shed. He gives me a peach or a banana when I come to help with the boat.

Sometimes other children from the village come to Jannie's house. They also get excited when they see how the boat is being built. Jannie says he will teach us all how to row and fish. He winks at me so that I know that he will teach me first because I am his special little friend and I am 'Ou Bern'. He doesn't call the other children Ou anything. I am his friend like a secret. We get eager and impatient when he says that the boat will soon be ready. We go to the river every day to check that the water level has not gone down so that the boat can still float and not get stuck in the mud like the cattle. We look at the lines along the dam wall. We bring a very long stick with us and let it down slowly into the water until it touches the bottom. We pull it up carefully to see where the watermark ends. We measure it by standing next to the stick. If the watermark is up to our heads we are very pleased because we know that the boat will sail along and keep afloat. If the water mark gets down to our waists we tell Jannie that he must hurry up because the water is being eaten by the sun and just now there will be no more to keep the boat up. Jannie says that all good things come eventually to those who wait patiently. We have been waiting patiently for a long time. My father says Jannie is slow but thorough and we must be like patience on a monument smiling at grief. I do not understand what my father means but he smiles when he says that so I smile too.

Jannie's boat is finished and it is made of wood and green canvas. It is painted with a special kind of clear varnish so that the water cannot seep into the canvas. The oar is made of wood and green plastic. I am sitting in the boat and Jannie is sitting behind me. He shows me how to hold the oar and how to move the paddles on one side of the boat and then on the other. The boat wobbles a bit but moves forward through the water and makes a beautiful sound as it cuts through the brown river's face and wrinkles it to the bank where the birds sing and dive for the small insects that have been sailed towards them on the waves. It is my first ride in the boat and I am very happy because I am the first child in the village to learn about rowing. Jannie takes me home on his bicycle and tells my father that I am a first class rower and that soon I will be bringing fish home as well. My father says that he is proud of his little rower. At night when I am in bed I think of the warm, brown water. I see my face reflected in it and I hear the sound of the boat cutting through it. In my mind I see the fish push out water rings that ripple out to the bank and I long to catch a fish for supper. I feel happy and peaceful.

It is Sunday afternoon and the sun is very hot. There are no clouds to comfort and the brown water reflects white-light streaks that blind and burn my eyes. Jannie's blue and white handkerchief has been very busy on his forehead. He makes a noise as he rows and pulls the oar. The ripples swell. He steers the boat towards the long shade tunnel made by the thorn tree branches that squat along the bank. When we are in the deepest shade place he digs in the oar close to the boat and it stops its movement and gently rocks and slides along the bank. The weavers sing and chortle. Some young doves squawk and stretch their featherless necks in their nests. Their eyes and beaks look like bruises. I lean back and strain to see them more clearly. My head rests on Jannie's chest. Suddenly he sighs. He breathes more quickly and he says, "Ou Bern, I love you, ek gaan met jou trou. Old Bern, I am going to marry you." He breathes and blows into my ear. I am feeling strange and afraid. I look up into the birds' nests and feel that I have no home, no place of safety, no other to call. Jannie puts his arms firmly around me and I feel a hard lump in the small of my back. He begins to tremble and sweat and murmurs again that he loves me and is going to marry me. He shifts in the boat and it begins to rock heavily from side to side but Jannie lets it do what it wants. He moves his hands down from my waist and feels in between my legs. I am frozen and afraid. I feel lost and alone. He pulls down my panties and puts his fingers on a small spot and begins to rub. My body feels tingling and strange. My mind is terrified and I try to shout but no words come out. I begin to struggle in the boat. Jannie begins a low strange moan and the hard lump goes soft and lame. He breathes in a pant and murmurs my name over and over again. I begin to cry quietly. He says he is sorry if he has made me afraid but that it is love that drove him to feel my secret place.

The shadow tunnel grows very dark and the sun turns cold. I begin to shiver and Jannie starts to row again towards the place that is shallow and safe to leave the boat. He says I must never tell what he has done. I must never tell that I let him love me in my secret place. I must keep our secret until I am old enough to marry him. He says I am six but that I will soon be sweet sixteen and then he will marry me. I do not get on the bicycle bar and ride back home with him. I walk slowly through the bush path and the cold sun hurts in my bones. I do not hear the birds and the goats. The donkeys do not open their mouths and bray in the evening light. They stand very still with their heads low towards the ground. My world has turned silent and I begin again to cry, inside, always inside. I bend my head low towards the ground. I feel like a cut daisy, forgotten how to grow. Jannie is no longer my special friend; he is my special and silent secret. I look down the path along which the thorn bushes squat. It becomes a new tunnel of shadow and offers no relief from the safe, warm sun that has turned so cold.

I do not go to the river with Jannie anymore. I do not help with the consignment notes or the unloading of the trucks. I see Jannie taking another special friend down to the river on his bicycle bars. He calls her 'Ou Poppie' (old doll). My father sits and sips his whiskey on the stoep alone. He says that Jannie does not visit these days. Perhaps he is too interested in his new boat. I say nothing but I know what he is doing.

♥

Love; trust,
Trust love.
Love and trust hold hands
And mingle unobtrusively,
Like leopard-cheetah spots;
Without their facial analysis
Without their subtle difference
And habitats.

But

Our hand holds
Are so full of
Creepy crawly things
That cannot breed
Those full life tokens;
Love; trust,
Trust love.

"So, Bern, let me tell you now about how I met and married your father. Your father, Hugh, was near where I was boarding at the time. I had left the hostel and I found a place to stay. This was in Johannesburg. The woman that owned the house said to me, 'I'll take you to meet somebody nice for you. I'll introduce you to a nice man for you. There's a party on tonight and I'll take you. It is just across the road.' So I was quite happy to go and I walked into this party thing and Daddy was playing the guitar. Henry took me over and introduced me to Daddy and to Uncle Jimmy, and Flo, Joey and Maxi

- his three sisters. I looked at Daddy and thought: what a horrible person, even ugly, you know! Jimmy danced with me, then Daddy danced with me and then he wouldn't let anyone else dance with me but him. I quite liked dancing with him and I got to know him a bit better and thought he's not so bad anyway. Well after that, Daddy had a little car and he used to take me out, not that I liked him all that much although I got involved with him sexually and all but I don't know why because I really didn't like him that much at all. Eventually he got on my nerves because I actually thought that I disliked him more than liked him. After being sexually involved with him I decided I definitely disliked him anyway. He used to come to Tassie's house, you know. I used to shut the damn door in his face. Once I opened the door and was about to shut it in his face and he said, 'I didn't come to see you, I came to see Bobbie.' That was the owner of the house. You know how much of a fool you can feel, Bern! Anyway I still went out with him quite a lot and found that I was pregnant so now what to do? I didn't really want to get married to Daddy at all. When I told him I was pregnant he said that we must get married. It dawdled and dawdled on into the second month and eventually we decided to go and see the priest, just to discover that the priest wouldn't marry us because I wasn't twenty-one! I wrote to my father. You know the mail took time to get there in those days. You wait and you wait and there is no reply and no reply and you think your father is getting his own back, you know. I decided that I had to go back to Durban and tell my daddy all the reasons why I had to get married and all this, you know. It wasn't very pleasant for me. I had to stay at home for over a month. My father wasn't really angry at all. He was quite kind in fact. I think he was disappointed but kind, Bern. They had heard a rumour that I was married already, but they should have known it couldn't be right because of my age.

I came back to Johannesburg. During the time I was away, they had a terrific snowstorm in Johannesburg. I remember being so unhappy because I had missed the snow, you know. Anyway I was back and we had to wait three weeks for banns of marriage to be announced and all that. Eventually we got married. I had already been pregnant for four months. Joey and Flo didn't know I was pregnant; they invited Susie

Vlok to visit and she was one of Daddy's old girlfriends. Man, did she and Daddy have a whale of a time. Daddy was probably teaching me a lesson, you know, teaching me not to be such a snob and so on, because I didn't want him and so on, Bern. They were playing around with her and throwing water over each other and I didn't join in the fun at all. I thought it all bloody disgusting. So I went home, you know, and I stayed home, back to Tossie and them. I just went back and thought: well you can voetsak! That is what you can do now, voetsak! Eventually after a few days Daddy came around again. There was nothing else I could do but accept him. What would I do, you see, Bern? In those days you never had babies without being married. It was disgusting and disgraceful that I had to get married anyway. After I got married everybody knew that it was 'a have to get married'. I was about four months already when we got married. I was very slim and slight so you couldn't see anything. I just looked as though I had put on a bit of weight. You couldn't tell that it was pregnancy weight.

Oh well, and I wasn't good enough for the Flattery family. I was not a Roman Catholic and this was a whole, big thing. I was not fit to marry their brother, who was such a holy Catholic! Ja, true you know, Bern, you laugh but it was true, man. I was no good. Of course once they knew I was pregnant, I was real dirt. So anyway we had a very quiet wedding; it was really not a wedding. You got married in the same church as I did, Bern. Bobbie Fennels gave me away; these were the people I was boarding with at the time. They came to the wedding all those friends of mine but I didn't have a reception. I did have a bit of a one because Aunty Aggie's mother was a very great friend of the Flatterys and she couldn't bear it that I had no reception. You know, my father wouldn't contribute to it at all. There was no way he would have anything to do with it and I don't really blame him. It was my fault and I had run away from home and everything.

Well we got married and Aggie's mother had a little party for me at the house. From there I went to stay back at my lodgings because I told Daddy there was no way I was going to live in the same house with Joey and Flo and him altogether. They were all living in one house and Flo ran the whole household. Not that I wanted to run the whole place but I also did not want to be run and they disliked me.

I thought: I am not going to go and live with them. That was another thing that held back the marriage because I had told Daddy I would not stay with his family in his house and if he didn't find a house, I would not be getting married. He gave up the house and found a room, two rooms in fact. It was a small house in Braamfontein in Melle Street. He rented the two front rooms. He was working then. He was a bricklayer and he got quite good money. We had one room like a bedroom and the other room across the passage. The doors faced each other and you just crossed the passage into the other room, which we had like a dining room. We had a sort of bed-sitter and a table - a deal top kitchen table. I had a primus in there to cook on and so on and rather than live with the Flattery sisters, that is what I had! I was quite happy about that."

> *The tide is in*
> *And above the roaring sound*
> *Your mystery mists*
> *Move in silence.*
> *Caressing, broken waves pull me back*
> *Into oceans of grace*
> *That feed my open soul*
> *With their secret balms.*
> *I see the Sacred One*
> *Transcend your bottled sea*
> *And breathe out love*
> *To heal, to set you free.*

Eventually, who should arrive at our door? Joey! She says she's sorry, she is not going to live with Flo any more; she's coming to live with us! So we had to let her go into the room that we were using as a kitchen! But, I didn't mind, you know, Bern. I liked Joey, so I let her come and we all three got on very well. I cooked for them when they went to work and everything. It was quite all right and I quite enjoyed it. We bought a bedroom suite and Daddy wanted to get me an engagement ring but I said no, I don't want anything from that house, no thank you, I am not having any furniture out of their house. I am not having them say I took their furniture or anything, thank you very much. Instead of getting me the engagement ring, I said to Daddy, you buy a bedroom suite. That's why I never had an engagement ring. After that we never ever had the money to buy one in any case. Not that I cared anyway.

Well, life went on in the rooms in Melle Street and I had to have a coat. There was a shop right next door to the house and I went in there. It was now the Tuesday. I went in there and I bought a coat. It was a check coat, I remember, and with buttons down the front and that, a very nice coat. It was very cold, you know. The woman was very helpful to me and then on the Friday during the night my membranes ruptured and I said to Daddy: I don't know what's the matter but everything is all wet, you know, and there is water all over and so on and Daddy phoned the doctor and the doctor came and said to Daddy, 'Give me some hot water and some sunlight soap.' We had the soap but Daddy couldn't get the primus lighted. We struggled in the kitchen and things got worse and eventually the doctor said, 'What is that man doing?'

I said, 'I think he's trying to light the primus stove.' Doctor went into the other room and said to him, 'A grown up man like you can't even get a primus stove lighted! Just for a little bit of hot water for your wife, for me to examine your wife!' I felt sorry for Daddy; I mean, I had learned to be fond of him already. Anyway, the doctor said, 'Get me cold water!' When it came he washed his hands right up to the elbows and examined me and told Daddy, 'Get your wife to the hospital now.' That was the Queen Victoria Hospital, you know.

Off I went to the Queen Vic and I had Faith. I remember thinking: do I have to lie here forever with these pains? I thought: no way, I am not doing this! I am going to bring it down now, anyway! I am going to press it and get it down myself, because nobody wants me to press down. Of course it was the worst thing I could have done! Being such an ignorant fool, you know. Every time I got a pain, I bore down. They weren't bearing down pains. Faith was born about ten past midnight and your cousin Mercia was born just before midnight on the 5th of February and so Faith was born on the 6th. Man, this child was born and she looked like a little rabbit. Well I suppose in fact I didn't eat properly and that during the pregnancy. You know you vomit and every day at five in the morning I was vomiting and so on and I was off my food. Here was this tiny little mite; she was five and a half pounds. She had bloodshot eyes because of me bearing down at the wrong time, causing the pressure. I will never forgive myself for that.

Anyway, and I breast fed Faith but the little monkey wouldn't suck! Not for anything in the world would she suck my breast. I used to sit in the bed there absolutely exhausted and the Sister sitting on my bed trying to make this baby suck. She just wouldn't suck, so consequently she was starving. She lost weight and she went down to four and a half pounds, poor little mite. It was time for me to come out of the hospital already even though the little girl didn't want to eat. Sister came to me and said that she couldn't let me go home unless little baby put on some weight. She said, 'I can't let you go home on any condition.' So I thought: this is a bloody silly idea this no eating business. I thought: I will make her put on some weight, so I went to the nursery. I got out of my bed and I went to the nursery and I said to the staff nurse that was there, she was feeding the babies, you know. I said, 'Please can I feed my baby?' Actually Faith couldn't suck when she was born. I don't know what it was that caused it but she couldn't suck! So I got this bloody teat that the nurse gave me for the baby and fed her with a few drops at a time and every mealtime I went to the nursery and did that and she put on a half an ounce. I said to Sister, 'Now you can let me go home because my baby has put on an ounce and I am sure she will continue to put on once she is home.' They let me go home. Bernadette! You don't know the agony I had with Faith! Daddy had shifted out of the two rooms and he had got a flat in Yeoville, not in a big building but on other people's ground. He'd got this little flat for me. So we went to the flat and, God, man, I couldn't get this child to eat. I kept on trying to feed her on the breast. They never told me anything about baby's diet in the hospital. I must have been home about three weeks. This little one wouldn't eat. She just cried and cried.

Daddy picked me up and took me to your aunt Maxi. She had one child, Mercia, as I had Faith; babies both the same age. I did not realise that my arrival and problem with Faith was too much for Maxi as well. I thought she was a nasty piece of work. She was so nasty to me, I am telling you! Every time Faith cried I used to feed her on the breast. Uncle Lenny used to bring home monkey nuts because that was good for the milk. Here I was, eating these bloody monkey nuts by the thousand to try and get the milk. I used to squeeze my breast and out would come some drops of white milk. I was so pleased to see that, not knowing that my breasts were empty anyway and that was all there was. I would put Faith on the breast and she would grab the breast. She had started sucking well. She'd grab the breast and she would suck and then scream! She looked like a little skinned rabbit, she was so thin and oh it was a terrible thing to see.

Eventually, I couldn't take Maxi any more. She was damned nasty. She wouldn't come and help me with Faith. Her navel stuck out and Maxi did show me how to sew a penny into flannelette and put it on the navel and bind it with a binder. God, I used to try and bath this child. I didn't know how to hold her properly and I couldn't get this bloody binder on and by the time I did get it on she was freezing cold. Luckily it was summer time. I was there with Maxi for ten solid days. Daddy left me there. From the Monday until the next weekend I had a hell of a life with Maxi and her nastiness. Daddy came that weekend and left me there again for the next week. I said to him I'd rather go home, but he left me there for the weekend again. I decided that if he did not come the next weekend and take me home, I would run away. I packed my case and everything, ready to go out on the Benoni road and thumb a lift home to Yeoville. It was so horrible for me there. Anyway, Daddy did come and I said to him, 'Don't leave me here because if you leave me here again, I'm going to walk home! I'm taking my baby and my suitcase and I am walking home or else I am going to beg a lift on the road. I'm doing it and that is what I am going to do!' Anyway, he brought me home, Bernadette. We went back to the flat and day after day Daddy went to work and I tried to feed this baby on my breast. She sucked my breast but she screamed on it. Maxi said to me that I am over-feeding my baby because every time she cried I put her on the breast. Luckily I did that because she at least got a few drops. Then after about ten days at home with this screaming child I said to Daddy, 'Don't go to work today. If you go to work today, I am going to commit suicide because I can't listen to this baby crying any more. I really will commit suicide.'"

Dear God,
I am grateful for the glimpse of love you gave.
I am so isolated here,
There is no fresh flow,
No peace communion.
My thoughts break at birth.
They leave me listless
In this stoic, limbo land.
I see another's eyes
They stare directly into mine.
They tell no comprehension of my state.
I glass-over freeze and smother
In their closed, half lights that shine.

"Daddy said no he'll stay home so he stayed home and said to me, 'Go and ring the doctor.' This was after a couple of hours at home. He said he would stay at home with baby and I should go and ring the doctor. As I opened the door to go and ring the doctor there was the Sister with her hand up about to knock on the door. 'Thank God I see you here Sister because,' I said, 'I don't know what has happened to my baby, I think I am over-feeding her because every time I put her on the breast she cries all the more.' My own common sense should have told me Faith was starving. So she came in and looked at Faith and said, 'My goodness, she doesn't look overfed.' She sat me on a chair and she made Daddy bring a little stool for my feet so I could be comfortable and she wanted to see me feed the baby. 'My dear,' she said, 'I don't think you have got any milk.' With all the worry and everything, it took every bit of milk away. She squeezed my breasts and - nothing! No milk. She brought in a bottle and gave me a mixture of water and cow's milk and sugar and gave me the measurements and everything. I had to run to the chemist and get a teat for the bottle. Daddy said, 'Let me feed her' and so I gave her to him and she sucked the bottle like she'd never seen food before. Of course, she hadn't! The sister said give her four ounces every four hours but Daddy said five so I did and when Faith finished her bottle she lay there with her little bottom lip over the top one and looked so contented and she slept for five hours. So after that Daddy went to work and I was okay 'cause I knew now how to feed the baby and everything, you know. When Faith was born I was nineteen."

I say, "Shame, Mama, you were a child yourself."

"No," she says, "I must have been twenty because I was twenty-one when Sally was born. Ignorance again, of course. When I knew I was pregnant again I didn't mind, you know. I was going to have another baby; this didn't worry me at all. Anyway, I went to the same nursing home and was sitting in the bed there like a queen and Sister came and asked how we all were. It was Christmas Day and Sally was born on 19th December. The sister wished us a happy Christmas and she said, 'I'll see you all next year,' and everyone shouted no you won't see us for another few years' and so on and I just kept quiet because that was the second time I had been there in the year. She gave us a Christmas present and everything. Sally's birth was a normal birth. You know no birth is easy but it was just a normal birth.

So when it was time to go home Daddy didn't take me back to the flat; he took me to this fort. Daddy had bought five stands of land in Parkhurst. Not down in 4th Avenue where we went to live, but in 15th Street and it was veld and on the property was this old fort. It was used as a fort during the war and we lived in that. It had a big kitchen, big dining room and one big bedroom with another sort of oblong bedroom. It was made of stone and the walls were very thick. The ceilings were all broken and ugly, you know, Bern. There was no bathroom and we had to bring a zinc bathtub into the kitchen and we bathed that way. It was easy to bath the children; we just put a small bath on the table but Daddy and I had to bring in the bloody zinc tub and use that.

I used to stay there on my own when Daddy went to the dog races on a Friday night. Man, I used to sit in front of the stove in the kitchen by myself, don't forget, and I used to get a feeling up my back like my hair was standing up behind me and this cold feeling coming up around at my back, you know. Faith was already then sort of a little bit talky and she would scream out and I would jump from the stove and rush into the bedroom and she would say 'there, there' in her baby way. You know, I used to get ice cold in that one bedroom where the kids were. Sally used to sleep in the pram and Faith in the cot. Eventually I said to Daddy, 'No, I can't stay here by myself at night. If you go to the dog races you have got to get somebody to stay here with me.' Daddy got Aunty Martha's son, he was fourteen, to come and keep me company. He came only once! This creeping feeling and ice-cold feeling, he got it too. The screaming of Faith in the bedroom and so on, you know. When Daddy came home he left and never would come back. No way! I had to learn to stay by myself whether I liked it or not! Daddy didn't believe there were spooks. I never used to get undressed for bed. The races closed at ten at night and it took time for Daddy to get back. I used to sit with the candles burning; there was no electricity at the time."

My hands lie limp,
I have no love gesture,
No evidence of care.
No word sounds
In my fossil soul;
Perhaps, I'm blind?
I walk this tight, tense line.
There is no slack for smiles.
My courage wobbles
The way mirages do.
There is no anchor for your
'I'm with you image'.
Perhaps I'm blind?

"Then old Uncle Frank came to stay with us. He was actually forced to stay with us because he was staying with his son in 1st Street in Parkhurst, quite far from us, you know, and he came down crying one night saying that his son had kicked him out. His son said he had syphilis and so he kicked him out. He had a carbuncle on the back of his neck and he was going up to the general hospital to have treatment. They gave him radium treatment and they must have thought it was cancer. It made it very big and perforated. It got holes in it and so his son kicked him out and told him he had syphilis. He didn't want him in the house. In the meantime it was the radium that had caused the problem. He came down to us and he cried. He had nowhere to go. I said to Daddy, 'You have got to take the old man in; you can't send him away.' So we put him in the other spare room. By then Willie had come to stay with us too and when Uncle Frank moved in he said he was off. He wasn't living with the old man that had garlic in the room! Frank used to soak garlic in water and then drink the liquid. This kept him healthy. Willie couldn't stand it so I said to him there is nothing I can do. I told him he would have to share the room or find a place of his own. The old man can't be kicked out because there is nowhere for him to go. You are working and you can look after yourself.

I used to have these strange feelings when I went into our bedroom. I used to feel there were eyes looking at me. I just could not get undressed for bed. Eventually I told Uncle Frank. I said, 'I can't get undressed in my room because I feel as if there are eyes looking at me from the ceiling, you know, the broken ceiling.' He came with the holy water and he blessed everything and the whole place he blessed and so on. All those strange nasty feelings went away, you know. The old man stayed with us until we lost that property and house and everything. Willie took the car too. He was a property salesman so he needed a car. Daddy lent him the car to get around and Daddy rode a bicycle to work so that Willie could have the car. Eventually one afternoon I was in the kitchen and here comes this big blue car up the driveway.

Willie gets out of it and says, 'Dot, come and look at my new car.'

I said, ' That's nice. Where is ours?'

He says, 'It's wrapped around a bloody pole!' He smashed our car up and got himself a new car. To hell with us, we had no car after that. He took our car somewhere to be repaired and one day this noise comes down the road and I say to Daddy, 'What's that?'

He says, 'Never mind, Lovey, that is our car!' It sounded like a cart of iron junk coming down the road. Anyway that happened; we lost the car. We never ever got another car. We couldn't afford it after that. Willie used to take all Daddy's clothes and wear them all. Eventually I locked the wardrobe door. He just helped himself. When he first started work he never had anything but he need not have worn them to the extent that Daddy had nothing. I got into trouble from Daddy for that, for locking the wardrobe. He said, 'If my brother wants to wear my clothes, he can wear my clothes.' So I thought: well if you want your brother to wear your clothes and have none, then that is okay. Eventually Willie came home with a whole pile of shirts and trousers. Sometimes he would come home and change shirts twice a day. Don't forget I had to do all the washing and ironing. Sometimes I had nine or ten shirts to wash at the end of the week. One day his boss came to the house. When Daddy came home I said, 'They might put your brother in jail. You know what your brother's done? He has taken my name and forged my name and given himself credit up at the gents' outfitters. He signed my name and recommendation to give credit with my name for that.'

His boss said, 'I should put him in jail for that, but he is such a good salesman I can't spare him.' So he got away with that too. Then Willie left us and went on his own, I don't know where. This was all before Uncle Frank moved in. He left after Frank came to us. I was happy he left, Bern. I had a problem with Willie. I used to make scones and put them out to cool and I would hear Willie's car coming up and I would run and put all the scones in the oven and close the oven door so he couldn't see them otherwise he'd eat the whole lot nearly. There was nothing left for Daddy when he came home. Anyway, he left and life went on. It went on well for a while."

Well, there is this thought flash:
(Intermittent, I grant you that)
I see you hung upon a cross,
Your heart and hands
Lie limp too.
Your eye-lights long passed: shone.
Your word breaths silent,
Your love blood gone.
Confined.
Dear God, I had forgotten you.

Dorry does not tap-tap in her chair. Her hands do not feel for safety. She leans and sits in silence. It hangs about us. I say, "Mama, are your memories hurting?"

There is no reply. She sighs, she stares. Her voice is small. "Who knows what life can dish up on our plates, Bern? If you bring me that pumpkin, I'll peel it. We could have it with the stew." We leave her chair to rock new rhythms. We leave her spooks behind.

♥

Dorry's peeling pumpkin.
My mind is full of poetry.
"Some pumpkin's for the deep freeze."
I'm free among the cloud scuds.
In the wind's mellow music.
"It's far too much;
This pumpkin is so big!"
Flutes play through my thoughts.
"The skin's so hard,
My thumb is blistered at the edge!"
I am emptied of all else
But where the poetry has led.
"Pumpkin's good for you."
"What was that you said?"
"I said, pumpkin's poetry."
"You're such a funny one,"
She says...

"BY the time Monica was born, Bern, we had Aunty Mary staying with us as well. I was very fond of her. She used to make this plum duck: she called it that. The whole kitchen, every utensil, was dirtied and everything when this old lady made her plum duck. Frank used to like it but Daddy didn't; he used to complain that it was too heavy. Of course, I had to clean up all the mess she made cooking it and so on.

Aunty Mary was Daddy's father's sister, so his aunt. Frank was his father's brother. But anyway, she came to stay and I was happy to have her. She was old, you know. I was well away pregnant with Monica. When my membranes ruptured, you know I had experienced births before and when they ruptured it was hours before the babies came. I decided I would stay home until it was nearly time to give birth and then I would go into hospital. So, I had no pains, no pains no pains. I didn't worry about it. I thought the birth was still coming and I was having flows of water and flows of water. Eventually I had to go to the toilet and Aunty Mary said to me, 'Dorry, please go to the hospital.'

I said, 'No, I'm not; I have got no pains. I am not going to hospital until I have got a pain. I'm not sitting at the hospital for all that time before I even get a pain.' Eventually she persuaded me to go. So I went and I got one foot into the bath and I said to the Sister, 'You know, I think that the baby's going to be born.' She got me out of the water and rushed me into the labour room and put me on the labour table and Monica was born, no pains at all. Sister said, 'Mrs Flattery, you must have a pain now,' and I said 'no I haven't!' My stomach was contracting and everything but no pain.

Sister said, 'You must have a pain now; the baby is coming.' At the next contraction I bore down and got one pain and Monica was born. It was a wonderful birth but then after that they took Monica from me and I haemorrhaged so badly that it shot out and went all down Sister's clothes. They sent for Professor Black. He came in from the children's hospital. He came in gloved up and everything. He was scrubbed up to do an operation. He had to come to me because I was haemorrhaging to death. They put me under chloroform and I don't know what they did while I was under and when I came to all I could see were two big blue eyes and I started to get up and the doctor gently pushed me back and said, 'You're all right, don't get up now.' When I came to I was saying, 'Oh Lord, Oh Lord.' I don't know what I did, whether I had a confession going or what! Eventually I came right. For that one I stayed at the hospital for the normal time of ten days. I was due to go home and Sister said to me, 'Mrs Flattery, there is somebody who has called for you already.'

I said, 'But it is only eight o'clock in the morning.'

'Yes,' she said, 'But somebody is here. It is a big man with red hair.' It was Willie. He heard I was due to come home and that Daddy was coming to fetch me so he jumped in and fetched me home in his car. So I came home with Willie.

During the time that Monica was a baby, Daddy went on his own in building contracting. Then he went in with his cousin. I said to him, 'Don't go in with Peter Wepener because I don't trust him. He is no partner for you to have.' Behind my back Daddy actually went into partnership. I didn't know. I knew nothing at all. Men came to the front door. By that time Daddy had built us a new house, a proper big house. Eventually after these men kept calling for Daddy, calling for Daddy, I said, 'No, he is not here; he'll be on one of the jobs but I am not sure which one.' One of the men went to the back and I saw him looking through the back window. I thought: that's funny, him looking through the window like that. He went around the front again and knocked again and I opened the front door. He said, 'Are you sure Mr Flattery is not home?'

I said, 'No, he isn't here but come inside.' I sat him in the lounge. I said to him, 'What is the problem? Is there a problem of some kind?' They were looking for Daddy for money. The different sites hadn't been paid. Wepener, the partner, got away with everything. We lost our house and properties in Greenside and Peter got everything because Daddy had stood guarantor for him in everything. Daddy had to pay all the debts. We lost our home and had to shift out to Flo. She put us up.

I had the three children then and I was expecting Veronica. I was well into pregnancy with her and with all the problems I had I couldn't say anything or do anything because it wasn't my home. Flo used to put my three children in the back yard to play. It was like prison because they had a high wall all around the back. All those properties in Benoni had high walls around them. It was a house with steps going down into the garden. They had to play in there and I had to help with the work and all that, you know. I couldn't just sit by and do nothing. The kids used to howl, man, and they'd stand there against the wall with snot all running down their noses. They wanted me, you see, and eventually I used to go and sit in the back yard with them. I just couldn't bear it, Bern; that they were locked up outside like animals. Eventually Veronica was born; I was seven or eight months when I went to Flo. She was born but she died because she had deformed lungs."

Passing through the Valley of Desolation:
Hard tyres turning on hard tar.
The sound of resistance,
The movement forward
Forced by friction.
White thorns on night stemmed bushes
Prod the pain.

But:

Windmills churn the silent water
And little yellow flowers bloom.
The Prickly Pears look dead
And Chopin plays a dream.

"I went back home to the daily routine. Then Daddy was out of work. The war broke out and six months after the war broke out Daddy had no job, no nothing, no property, no nothing. Daddy was quite proud in a way, Bern; he didn't want to go and ask for a job. He had been a boss himself and a contractor. He just couldn't go and ask for a job. I found out afterwards that he would drive around all day to go and ask for a 'brickie' job and not do it. He did one job for the priest who asked him to build the garage at the priest's house and he did that. He got eleven pounds for that and that lasted us for a little while.

I was so worried. I started to make a novena for Daddy to get a job. Then Daddy told me he once worked in Bechuanaland, which is Botswana today, when he was seventeen. He had worked for Chubby Blackbeard. I said would he like to go back there and he said yes he would. He could get a job there and it would be a good way to live. So I decided to make a novena to St Anthony to find him a job in Botswana. Then I used to look through the paper every day and here was a job in Palapye. I said, 'Here's a job for you.' My novena was going to be answered. It was the ninth day of the novena, Bern. Daddy wrote and told that he had worked for Chubby and everything and that he was working for a firm now and wanted to leave and that he would send a reference later. I said they wouldn't ask for a reference. I told him what to say in the letter. There was no reply and no reply. I made another novena to St Anthony to let us get a reply. Then a letter came from Charles Freeman to say that they were waiting for the reference from the last firm he was with. I said he should write and tell them that the firm closed down and that he couldn't get the reference. I said for them to phone Chubby Blackbeard and so on. Eventually they employed Daddy. They sent for him and said for him not to bring his wife and children for three months. He must come down and I must stay behind for three months. I'm telling you, I stayed for a month and a half and I had enough of Flo. Jimmy was keeping us on his army pay and she used to make a few scones and gave the kids a couple of scones and I never had scones at all because I didn't want to eat the food because I was worried about there not being enough food in the house. She used to make bean soup, lovely bean soup. My children used to have that. It wasn't her fault. She couldn't afford to do anything better with the money she got. Eventually I decided I wasn't staying here any longer; Charles Freeman or no Charles Freeman I was not staying, I was going!

So I went to Maxi in Benoni; she stored our furniture in her garage. Flo looked after the kids and I went and packed up everything. I phoned the railways and they came and got the furniture and off it went to Palapye. I had two big oil paintings and I sold them for the train fare to get there. Daddy had no money - the little he did have had to go for food for us. I sold my stove too and I made enough money out of that. I don't remember what the oil paintings were, Bern. They were nice oils. Maxi's mother-in-law actually bought them. I think she bought them because she knew that I was desperate, you know. Off I packed to Palapye. I sent Daddy a message saying: 'arriving such and such a train'. He had to be there to meet me and they had to have a house for me even though the Freemans didn't have an empty house for me. They had to put me in the hotel. I was in the hotel for three weeks. They owned it, anyway. Eventually they got a house for me and put me in there. All of that was done from novenas, Bern. I made them to St Anthony and he did everything in his power to help me in every way. Daddy got his job and I got the fare and we got a house.

Another little incident I forgot to tell you about, Bern, was while we were still in the fort. We were so short of money and it was when

Daddy had already got into trouble but before we had to shift out of the house. There was no food money and no blanket money and the winter was coming on. So I thought: no, now I must make a novena to St Anthony for Daddy to win on the dog races, you know. I had two five shilling pieces and I said to Daddy, 'Go to the dog races and back three and four as a double.' I was standing at the sink on the last day of my novena near the window and a little strip of paper blew into my sink and settled on the water and I picked it up and it had three and four written on it. I had been praying and it was my answer to prayer. I made Daddy back those numbers and he won the double so we were able to get blankets and get some food into the house. So that was the little incident before we lost the house."

Wheels turn.
Sounds rush.
Grass swishes by
So fast that breath forgets.
The eye moves far for comfort.
Statues of cattle life
Lend it.

Illusions flash.
Sight's blind.
Dread, greys the mind
So dark…
Thoughts threaten until
The soul cries deep
For courage:
The gracious God's Love
Gives it.

"Anyway, after three weeks in the hotel the Freemans moved the other couple that only had one child and gave us a house. They shifted the couple into one room and gave us the rest of the house and we stayed like that for quite a while. I had been given a nagapie. This night ape used only to come out in the dark, you know, or when I set the table for lunch every day. I had a tall sugar bowl from an exhibition and the lid used to shoot off. Next thing we sat down for lunch and the lid shot off and who should pop out of the bowl but the nagapie! He was in there eating the sugar. He used to jump around all over the house at night. It once jumped through the fanlight into the Russells' room and they screamed blue murder. They got such a fright. My little nagapie jumped onto their beds and so on, you know. I had to rush and get him out of there. Eventually the nagapie got out and onto the roof and that was that he got eaten by an owl or something because he just disappeared.

Daddy started working in R A Bailey's Number Two Store; they called it that because they had two stores in the village. Number One was not the main store, Number Two was. Daddy was only supposed to be there until a Mr Smith came back from the army. But after the war when Mr Smith came back, R A Bailey didn't want him. So they put him in the store with Daddy and Daddy as the manager, which he used to be, and he left because he didn't like that at all. Then the Russells were there and they lived in the house next to Number One Store. Remember, it was down by the wholesale. We got on very well all of us together. Then of course I decided that I was a tennis fan. I knew nothing about tennis but thought that everybody else plays tennis and why shouldn't I? So, I made myself a nice tennis dress and everything and got takkies and a racquet and all. Above all things, I decided to go and play on a Saturday when all the club people were there. I knew nothing at all but here I was with my racquet and outfit. I was a real what they called 'bunny'. If you were a weak player or a beginner you were called a bunny. You were supposed to miss all the balls and make a fool of yourself. I was quite good, even when I first started. They asked me if I had played before and I said no never and they wouldn't believe me. They thought I must have played at school or something. I did quite well.

Then Mr Morey, he was quite a lot older than me, he took me in hand and took me down to the courts every day and taught me how to hit forehands and backhands and how to serve. He coached me and I became one of the best players at the club. Then I played golf as well. We went around playing that and Daddy used to play tennis as well but then he gave up and just played golf while I was at tennis. He wasn't a very good tennis player so gave up. He used to get upset and sulk if he couldn't have me for a partner. Sometimes when we spun before a game for who was going to play with whom, Daddy would get the other lady in the foursome and he used to plain old sulk the whole game. I used to hit him gentle balls because I was afraid he would sulk if I sent him a hard serve or return because he couldn't get them back, you know! Ye gods, man, what a fuss and sulk that brought on. He gave up tennis as a bad job and he took up golf. Then I took up golf as well. I played quite a good game of golf as well. We used to have tennis parties and people used to come from the other towns as well. They were tournaments, you know.

Every Saturday we had lovely tennis parties. We each took turns in making the cakes and seeing to the tea. We would stop in the middle of the afternoon and have the tea break. You kids always had something good to eat and drink. I baked every Friday because everyone always brought a plate of something. I used to make those Swiss rolls, you know. I used to have that special cloth I used for rolling it up without cracking the cake. I used to boil the cloth first. I made nice Swiss rolls. Every week we also had a dance or a beetle drive or something to raise funds for the war effort. Bingo was very popular. We also had a raffle every week and I used to make a cake for that. It was a rainbow sandwich cake with different layers of colour and I always put pink icing on the top and sprinkled 'hundreds and thousands' on top of that. I used to make cream fillings so they were huge cakes in the end. Everyone bought a ticket and all the funds went for the war.

The Governor General at the time was Jan Smuts. They called him Oupa Smuts. They called his wife Ouma Smuts. Aunty Shaw was very much in with it all and did a lot, more than a lot. Thomas, her son, was sent to the army and we used to make parcels for the army boys. We made twenty-one parcels every week. We had to wrap them and send cigarettes and chocolate and things that were not perishable. It had to weigh eleven pounds. So we used to weigh each parcel. We sewed it into material, you know that unbleached calico; it was cheap. We addressed them and everything and they were sent up North. Thomas's parcel was always special being Aunty Shaw's son and that. We put little extras in for him. I was always so proud of my cake, Bern. But nobody ever thanked me for it or for doing it so this one Saturday

I decided I am not doing this cake. There was a dance on as well that night. I just made little cup cakes and took them down for a change. They had the raffle going and they had nearly all the tickets sold and I came along with these fairy cakes. Aunty Shaw took my tin and said we have all been waiting for your famous tin. I said, 'Oh well, I have made fairy cakes today; I didn't make a big cake.' So they had to raffle Nancy Morey's cake instead, which was a flop because it was just a little flat sandwich cake. After that I used to get a little note from Aunty Shaw saying, 'Dear Mrs Flattery, will you please bake the cake for the raffle tonight?' That was really catty of me, Bern, but I was fed up with being taken for granted.

We had these lovely dances and we even had a band. There was Blackie's Band from Mahalapye. You remember they were just one station down from us and the trains stopped there and everyone got off because Blackie's Band used to play while the engine was filling up and waiting for the other train to cross. Man, people used to dance until the last minute. The conductor always had trouble getting everyone back on board. It broke the monotony of the long train trips up and down the line from Mafikeng to Bulawayo. Sometimes Daddy used to join in with them and play his guitar at the dances. When the war was won, we had the biggest dance we had ever known. Mahalapye came and Serowe came and we had people from Francistown come down and we had a marvellous dance. At the end of the war all our contributions were added up and announced. We in Palapye were second on the list - Gaborone was first. It was the biggest town in those days. We were a small village and our little Palapye came second. We were so proud of ourselves. Old man Freeman, not Charles, A E - he used to double our takings and add it to the funds. If we made two or three hundred pounds, then he used to make it six hundred and things like that, you know. We really got a lot of help. We had the dances in the hotel dining room. They cleared everything away and we put sawdust on the floor. Often the train stopped for over a half an hour and the soldiers used to hop over and have a few drinks and dances before going on with their journey. They were always made very welcome. They used to let the whole country know that there was an army train going up North. Aunty Shaw used to get everything ready on the station. We used to put up tables with tea and cake. We all helped to serve the army boys at the station. You know, Bern, Princess Elizabeth turned twenty-one in Cape Town. She and the Queen Mother, the King and Princess Margaret passed through Palapye. Most of the children were in boarding school and you were the baby. Daddy picked you up as the Princess went past. He said, 'Say hello to the Princess,' and the Princess turned around and spoke to you and patted you. At least you got recognition from the Princess, Bern! They walked up and down the station while the train was filling up with coal and water. We had a better view of the Royal Family than people would have in London and other big cities."

> *When my mind thinks tombs*
> *And my heart is grave and low*
> *I listen, in your quiet word ointments.*
> *They ooze and ease*
> *My slow, awakening soul.*
> *They give me rainbow lights*
> *To see through pools of rain.*

"Daddy didn't really get on with Charley Freeman. Charley was not his boss. A E, Charley's father, was Daddy's boss and he got on well with him. A E liked Daddy because he was a good manager. Charles used to come to Number Two Store and tried to give Daddy orders and so on because he was being trained to take over when the old man retired. Daddy's blood used to boil up so much because this youngster would come and try to boss him around. He used to try and tell Daddy how to cut meat. You know what a good butcher your dad was, Bern. He hunted all his life and knew exactly how to cut up the carcass and what roasts and what stews and fries could come out of where. Daddy made the most wonderful boerewors. He would not give his recipe to anybody and everyone lined up to buy his wors. Daddy ran the shop, the butchery and the bakery.

One day I said to Daddy, 'Tell A E, tell him that you don't like Charles bossing you about. Tell him you don't like the interference!' So he told the old man that he doesn't need Charles coming to tell him what to do. A E told Daddy, 'Well why don't you punch him in the nose? That should shorten it a bit!' After that Daddy used to give Charles the chat back and tell him to get the hell out and so on. Then it was better. Then when of course the old man Freeman retired, Charles became Daddy's boss. Daddy had to bow down a little bit. Ye gods, man, he used to get so wild. At one time, you know, Charles never came to ask Daddy anything or tell him anything. He used to send him a note saying this or that. Daddy got fed up with these notes. Charles had sent one about a mislaid hammer that Daddy had used and they could not find again. The note as much as said that Daddy had pinched the bloody hammer. I said to him, 'Don't let Charles get away with that! Go over there and tell him off. Even if we lose the job we will manage somehow. We can go up North and get another job. Don't you worry about it.' So Daddy went down there and, in the meantime, I saw the way Daddy pulled up his pants when he was in a temper. I rushed into the bedroom and got on my knees and prayed that Daddy wouldn't hit Charles or anything like that. He was going to hit him for sure, Bern. Anyway it ended up that Charles wouldn't come out of his office so Daddy couldn't hit him. Daddy called him outside to come and face him like a man. He said he would give him a thrashing for false accusations so Charles wouldn't come outside and that was an end to that.

Things went quite smoothly after that and at one time Daddy wanted to leave. The old accountant and mechanic left and nobody wanted to work for Charles. This was before the old man retired. Daddy said to him he wanted to go up North to get a job up there. The old man said, 'Well, Flattery, if you want to go, I am not saying don't, but there are advantages for you when I retire. So if you stay, it will be an advantage to yourself.' So we stayed. It ended up that this one store became vacant and the old man told Daddy to apply for a licence. A general dealer's licence, you know. Daddy said no he couldn't do that because Freeman's had applied for the licence and were not granted one because they had too much going on. They had the two stores and the garage and the wholesalers. They had the monopoly of everything. They also had nine out-stations in the bush and farms. The old man insisted and said, 'Put your name in and apply for a licence.' Daddy said no, he could not afford it. A E said, 'Don't worry about it we will put the money in.' So actually the business Daddy had really belonged to the Freeman family. They put the money up. Daddy paid it off slowly but never managed to pay it all off.

We had that business for a long time. That first store eventually fell down. Daddy had built a new shop. He treated the business as his own and bought and sold cattle and all that, you know. It was always bonded to the Freemans and when Daddy died I couldn't cope with that, you know. Daddy had just been shopping with Pat. Sally and Pat were just back from Kenya. Remember they lived there, Bern? They bought a whole lot of stuff and the whole place was full of stock. That was one big debt and before Daddy could benefit from the sale of the stock he died and I was left with it all. I couldn't cope with all the debt and to me it wasn't worth all the worry. The store really did belong to Charles. Charles sort of ruled my life, you know, so I couldn't take it. I just threw in the towel and left and went to Johannesburg."

♥

From whence we come, we go.
We go to from to know
How deep, willed wounds
Break walls
Make ruins of ancient pain.

Let go.

Blue, rivered light-flowers
Flow faith
Through green, visioned life
Into love's full grace
And joy's quiet memory.

"WHEN I became a Catholic, Bern, it was because of a desire to become a Catholic because as a child, Aunty Agnes put us into the convent and as I have told you before about being a Protestant and not knowing what a Protestant was, I decided that I was a Catholic and never ever a Protestant. I was told that I had to be at the cathedral at a certain time and the tram went past the cathedral, a little way past the cathedral and you got off the bus there and all the Catholic children went to Mass from half past eight to nine o'clock. We went to Mass because the convent school started lessons at nine o'clock. So I used to go every day to Mass not knowing anything about it, not knowing anything else about it. I enjoyed that Mass and took it all in. Don't forget, I was only about eight at the time and one day my aunt Edith went to work early and we took the same tram from Umbilo and to town. She saw me getting off the tram at Grey Street near the cathedral. That night when she came home she told my aunt, who was our guardian, don't forget, that Dorry is getting off the bus stop and going to the cathedral. Aunty asked me what I was doing and I said I have to go to Mass because I am a Catholic and so I go to Mass every morning. We Catholics all get off there and then we march down to the cathedral.

Then I was told that I wasn't a Catholic, that I was a Protestant after all and I was stopped going to Mass because I was not a Catholic. I forgot to tell you when I first went home from the hostel, I used to walk a long way from home trying to find a Catholic church. I used to feel bad because I used to make the sign of the cross and I was not a Catholic. Eventually the Finch girls took me to see the priest in Mayville. I never became a Catholic then although I searched all the years for a church and I was never ever satisfied until I got married and became a Catholic then. I became a Catholic because when I went into a Catholic church there was a special feeling of deep peace. I would say it was a calling because I had a desire so strongly to be something, but who was there to go to? There was nobody to talk to about it. I didn't know enough. I was ignorant I suppose otherwise I would have gone to a priest and got the information and that. I was also a shy person, you know. I got the calling being married to Daddy and he was a Catholic and me joining in the prayers and during my first pregnancy I felt closer to God than if I had not been pregnant and had to get married.

It sort of gets hold of you, the Catholic religion. I felt I was called into the Church and I was happy in it, you know. It was a relief to find a place inside where you feel at home and at peace. That is the reason why I got baptised when Faith got baptised. I received instruction all the time I was married to Daddy and then I had instructions after I was baptised as well. I was instructed for about a year before I had first communion. I had my first communion in Yeoville Church. I was the only one on the Sunday. I remember my first confession. I was frightened anyway and I was very pregnant as well, you know - no I wasn't pregnant - I had my baby. I was very frightened of this big confession, you know and you know, my life had been a little bit loose, you know. I had to get married and all that and I knelt there in darkness. The confessional was dark, you know, and when you have been in there a little while suddenly it becomes a bit lighter and the priest didn't have the veil down. He had taken the veil aside and he was talking directly to me and all of a sudden his face was right in front of me and I got such a fright, I nearly fainted in the confessional, you know. But he was so good and kind to me, I sort of overcame that fear.

I remember this incident, Bern. Dorothy must have been about three turning four and I wanted her to have a doll for her birthday. There were no dolls in our village, No one of the shops kept them. I made a novena because I wanted the doll and somehow I was going to get it. It was four days before Dorothy's birthday and a traveller from Jo'burg came to the shop. You know they used to bring samples so that the shopkeepers could see what they were ordering. He had toys and he had this sample of a doll. And I said to him I need to have this doll and he said no I can't sell you this doll but I can send you one. You can order one and I can send it to you. I said no it is too late, I need it before. In four days' time I need this doll and I am going to have it no matter what. This doll is meant for me! And he hummed and haa'd about not having a sample. I said you can explain to them what the doll looks like but I am having the doll. And so I got the doll for Dorothy's birthday. And so Our Lady did send me the doll for Dorothy's birthday. She was so thrilled with her little doll, you know.

After that life just went on in the usual way, tennis and that. Then I had four children and the nursemaid was starched and ironed and the children were starched and ironed before tennis and I went down to the courts at two o'clock and the maid came down with me. I had my tennis while the nursemaid sat down with the baby and fed it. I gave her the bottle wrapped up in a napkin and she sat down on the ground and fed the little one. Everything was perfect and there was no problem with the children. I was very happy in those days. They were very healthy and I had no problem. I had the nursemaid at home too and every morning the children were allowed to make mud pies and get dirty in the sand but in the afternoon they got bathed and clean and were not allowed to play in the mud. They had to wear their afternoon

211

clothes the next morning while the maid washed what they wore the day before."

Blossoms hanging
From rocks off roadways;
Like doggie-paws hurting,
Asking with listless eyes
That the sun shows mercy,
That the rain falls softly,
That the winds blow gently
So that crimson colours
Can reflect an instant's glory
In tired, travelled eyes;
Can give creation's gift of love
That never really dies.

"We went on holiday when Doll was about three. We went on our first holiday. We went to the coast. All of them got measles! Faith was the first one to come down with it. She must have picked it up on the train. I came down to Durban before Daddy. We went to your Aunt May. Faith would not paddle in the sea and she grizzled and cried and she was not well. I didn't think at the time she wasn't well but thought that she just did not want to go and paddle in the sea and so on. Luckily I didn't force her because the spots could have gone inside. Then about the eighth day that we were in Durban, Faith broke out with measles. Then, of course, all the kids got it. Dorothy got it very badly. I don't know if I should say this but it's in the lifetime. May had cleared out a room with four beds in it for my babies and me. It was quite enough space for us. I had Dorothy in my bed and she was restless, and fidgeted and fiddled, fidget, fidget, you know! I thought to myself: she is not well, you know; there is something wrong. I thought she might be getting measles. Eventually I pulled the blankets off of her and there were bugs by the hundred, Bern, baby bugs! May had decided not to use the room before we came. She had not used it for several weeks. She just kept the beds made up and she said she thought the baby bugs that were there had run away and would die from starvation. Meantime they had eggs that hatched out.

Dorothy's legs were covered in bites and she got sores from the knees down and she had measles as well, you know. Uncle Percy and I got rid of the bugs. I got all the kids out of the room and sat up all night with them in the lounge. I couldn't bear the thought of them getting bitten. Percy came through early in the morning and said, 'What are you doing here?'

I said, 'Percy, the beds are full of bugs and look at Dorothy's bites. She is a sight for sore eyes; she is allergic to mosquito bites, and fleas and all insect bites.'

So we got the children wrapped up properly because of the measles and Percy and I cleaned the beds. I took the mattresses off the beds and soaked them with paraffin all around where the bugs go in the seams, you know, everywhere because paraffin does kill them effectively. I treated all the springs of the beds, too. Luckily the beds were iron so the paraffin did no harm to the frames. I also poured methylated spirits on the springs and set it all alight and the eggs were all burned up. Uncle Percy helped me treat all around the skirting boards where the bugs could possibly breed. There were no bugs after that. We made a thoroughly good job of that, you know. Well, I had the kids in bed for about two weeks with the measles and I was also confined to the bedroom because there was no way I would leave them by themselves in the room because they were sick. I only left them to have my meals after I had fed them. They did not eat much, being so sick.

Then, Daddy came for the rest of the holiday. I had arrived before him, three weeks before him. He stayed there too and then after the measles, Monica got an ear problem and her ear was running with yellow, pussy looking liquid. I had to go to the hospital and obviously May took a fancy to Daddy but I had to go to the hospital. He wouldn't leave the kids at the house, he said, but we did have the maid with us to help look after the kids. The whole thing was that he and May were having an affair while I was away. My nursemaid told me, you see, but I didn't make a fuss or anything because what was the object of making it all miserable for the kids and for everyone and so on? When I first took Monica to the hospital Daddy came with me and then I visited her every day and then he decided to stay home after the second visit. When it was time for Monica to come out of the hospital he wouldn't come and fetch her because he would rather stay at home with May and have an affair with her and I went to fetch Monica by myself.

Daddy drank in those days but not like he did later on. He couldn't drink too much because he had a tapeworm in the early days. He just got thinner and thinner and if he drank a beer, he got a terrible burning pain in his stomach. He used to bring me his pay packet home and would not open it. I had to tell him to and to take some money for a beer but he never did. By the time we got to move to Botswana he was well over the tapeworm. We had got rid of it. By the time the children were born he was well on the way with the drinking but he was never cruel to me. I was cruel to him at times, but he never raised a hand to me. He once picked up a candle and came to me. It was late at night when he came home from the pub. I always waited for him and had dinner with him but this time I thought: no I am not waiting and waiting so I had my dinner; it was nearly nine o' clock. The children ate early and went to bed; at seven 'clock they were in bed. Daddy always went from the shop down to the pub. We always had meat at midday and at night it was fried steak and so on. This night he came home so full of drink and sat down at the table and said, 'Where's my food, Lovey?'

I said, 'Get it yourself, it's on the stove in the kitchen and get it yourself!' Then I thought: Ag, don't start a fight, just go and get the dinner. So I went and got the dinner and plonked it in front of him and it slid on the table into his place and he took the plate of food and picked it up. There was a sauce bottle on the table; you know how he loved his sauces. He smashed the plate over the sauce bottle. He got up from the table and started to walk out the door so I wanted to throw the jug of milk at him but I thought; no, I want my milk jug so I threw the milk at him and emptied all of it down his head. It ran all down his neck and shirt. He walked past the candle in the lounge and he picked that up. It was the worst thing he could ever have done. He picked it up and brought it in and put it next to my nose and he said, 'You look out!'

You know, Bern, I just saw red because my feelings rose so badly and I took this exhibition sugar bowl. It was an antique. It was a long, thin bowl, unusual to look at. I took it and I hit him with it and cut his eye open and the sugar bowl got chipped. The sugar went all over him too. He began to look like a half-baked toffee apple. His eye was all bloody and I got more panicky and I broke up a chair. You know we had those globe chairs in those times. I smashed the chair up against the wall and broke it up into splinters. Of course it all calmed down and got sorted out, you know and I saw to his eye. He looked into the mirror and saw the state of his eye and said, 'Lovey, now I know who is boss!' Shame, but, you know, it was sheer temper with me that made me do it. Anyway that was one real set to we had!

Another set to we had was, you know Daddy was always going to commit suicide, he was always having enough and going to do away with himself. It was because he drank so badly, Bern. I used to go off about the drinking. He went to the pub every night and every night he was drunk; not rolling drunk but beyond normal and it became such a habit and I got used to it. One time he came home late and sat on the bed to take off his shoes and fell asleep in the act of taking off his shoe. His hands were resting on the shoelaces and his head was lolled onto his stomach. I went to see what it was with him because he had gone so quiet all of a sudden. I thought: well, you can just stay like that all night. Maybe it will teach you a lesson. He had such a stiff neck in the morning, but I didn't care. He sulked after that, Bern.

When he was drunk he used to beat the kids, when they were little; five, six, seven years old. I used to interfere and then he would hit them harder so it paid me not to do that. I used to run down to the toilet after that and kneel down on the floor and ask our blessed Lady to stop him from beating them. I used to say, 'Please stop him from beating them, don't let him beat them anymore.' It was from the drink that he did it, mostly on a Sunday afternoon when Monica and Sally were such little devils. They would laugh about everything. They were only laughing after all. And playing in their room but he had to sleep after lunch because of the drinking and so they had to go to their rooms and sleep, too. If they laughed and disturbed him, he used to get up and go and beat them. He really beat them and then one day when they went to school Mrs Fordery, the teacher, noticed that they had blue marks on the backs of their legs, like a belt bruise. She came over and asked what the marks were and I told her that Hughie beat the kids when they disturbed his sleep on a Sunday afternoon. She came over when Daddy was home and spoke to him. She told him that she is going to examine the kids every day at school and if she finds any bruises or any marks on then she is going to report him to the police. After that he stopped beating them because he was afraid because Mrs Fordery went off pop and he knew she would do as she said.

So after I got the doll for Doll, she had her party. You know, there were forty-three kids in our village and we had to invite all of them and the mothers as well, don't forget! At all the other parties the mothers used to make all the cakes and stuff for the children and then make eats for the grown ups on top of that. I never did that. I used to make the kids' stuff and say that the grown ups had to have what was over because it was a party for the kids not the adults. Nobody seemed to mind that, you know, Bern. They all used to come just the same, adult eats or no adult eats. I used to make sandwich cakes and Swiss rolls and fairy cakes with hundreds and thousands sprinkled all over the icing. There was always jelly and ice cream and cold drinks. I used to make our own ice cream. I think the mothers all tried to outdo one another with the sausage rolls and savouries and cocktails. Not me, Bern, it was a party for kids not adults. Besides that I had seven kids remember and so seven parties a year. Ye gods, man, I was always baking and making. Not only did the mothers come but the fathers too. They would all arrive after the five o'clock bell and have something to eat and drink. It sometimes turned into a sundowner, not a very big one as they all left before half past six. It was all very enjoyable. I used to love it all, Bern. Daddy was quite sociable in those days. In fact he was very sociable. He could mix with any people, with the blacks and be at home with them. He'd sit on a stone like they did and talk to them in their own language. He could speak several black languages. They called him Baba or Radibatana. They said he was their father. He could mix with the Afrikaans people from the railways and he would be one of them, too. He spoke Afrikaans like an Afrikaner. They called him Oom Pat because of his Irish surname. When he mixed with the society of our village he would be at home with them. He was a very wonderful mixer. At the dances he wasn't a jealous husband. I danced with everyone and so did he. It was a wonderful life for young people and the children had a wonderful life."

I look at the mist this morning
It hangs low but in my heart
There is the hope of rising
Like the sun,
That never really sleeps,
Shines through.

♥

None are lost along the way:
You are all embracing heart with beacon-beats,
Sending constant love signals
For the wanderer to hear.
You are all-seeing eyes in the twilight zones of frailty
Lighting faith-candles that show the wanderer's way.
You are all-mothering spirit breathing
Sweet aromas into crying minds
So that sleeping courage senses hope
In the hunted's hopelessness…

M Y friend Dianne's dog has had seven puppies. My father says dogs don't have puppies, bitches do. He says those seven puppies are for the seven of us children. Dorry says, "Ye gods, man, what next!" but she does not complain when the seven puppies arrive in the back of Pedro the lorry. My father has a lead and a collar for each one and he gives them to us one by one and he tells us to choose a name for ours. He tells us that we are in charge of them and will have to brush their coats and feed them and clean up their mess. We have to keep them out of the hen hok and out of the house. He says that they are hunting dogs and can point to where the ducks or bucks are hiding so that he can get a decent shot. He says that pointers can fetch the ducks from where they fall dead in the water.

My dog's name is Mottle. I call him that because pointers have a mottled coat. Dorry says they are not mottled they are brindled. I like Mottle better so I tell her that my pointer is special and mottled. She says that I am a funny one but she does not argue with me. The other dogs are called Spotty or Sammy and Smudge. I do not want my dog to have an ordinary name. He is so clever. When I throw a stick into the long grass he stands on three legs with his tail straight out and points to where the stick has landed. When I tell him to fetch it, he dives into the grass like a duck into water and he brings me the stick with his tail waving like a whirlwind. If I have something small to give him, I make him sit and tell him to take the tit-bit nicely. Saliva seeps from his mouth as though he is having an epileptic fit but he sits very still even when I put the morsel on his nose. I give a short whistle and he tosses it up into the air and catches it with a snap of his teeth. I always pat him on the head then and tell him that he is a good dog.

Dorry says we must not get to love our dogs too much because my father is going to sell them to his friends as soon as they are older and trained for hunting. She says that two dogs in one family are enough. My heart feels heavy and I do not want to play at all. Mottle is my dog. I walk on the moon because of Mottle. I do not know when I will stop coming here. It is not that I enjoy being here on the moon because it is lonely and barren and my mind empties out like a small bucket of brackish water in a desert. There is no comfort in that for the moon soil or for my mind. When my father says, "Come here, Mottle; let me see your teeth," I get up to the moon very fast. I do not notice how far it is from earth and from being sure of things around me. In front of me is a pit. I can see the bottom of it because it is not very deep. It is as dry as a sandy desert and has nothing in it except a big box wrapped up in shiny yellow paper. The box is tied up and stuck to the bottom of the pit. It has a green ribbon bow on the top. I am afraid to go down into the pit to see it and to touch it. I am afraid that there may be something in it that I do not like. If I open it and see what is in it I cannot be safe from unknowns. I will have to live with the box and what is in it. It is like knowing that Mottle will leave and be somebody else's dog and then I will have nothing to save me from sorrow. I think that perhaps the box holds a beautiful gift for me. Then I can keep it forever and show it to Mottle and play with it and with him and all my worry will be over and the worry I had would be for nothing but a lovely surprise.

Dorry always tells me about surprises. Life is full of them and it makes the days bright and interesting. She says that everything, even the rising of the sun and the rising of the moon, are big surprises that should make us believe in the wonder of creation and the gifts of God's love. I want the gift of Mottle and the gift of his bark and the bright gift of his eyes. I sit at the edge of the pit and stare at the box until I hear Dorry's voice calling and I am back in the yard playing with Mottle and the stick. I do not feel happy or curious. I feel heavy and sad. My father says he is going to train the dogs soon and that the duck pans are full and so there will be plenty of birds to shoot.

We are on our way to the duck pan in Lecheng. My father goes there twice a week because he has a shop along the riverbank. The pan is never dry. There is an underground spring that keeps it full. It is like a green oasis in the middle of the desert. The river sand is deep grey. Sometimes the riverbed is stream streaked and I can wander along the twisty paths from the shop to the duck pan. Sometimes the water cannot flow and there are shallow pools that smell of cattle manure and a green slime floats on the top. If I find a stick I can ruffle the slime and wobble the water to see if there are any catfish swimming under the surface. When the water is shallow they glide along the bottom of the pond and come up for air like flashes of silver lightning in a dark sky. My father says that they can bury themselves under the mud and stay there until the pools are full enough for them to swim again. I do not know if I believe him.

This duck is dead. Its wet, grey neck hangs over my hand like a sad sack of sorrow. Its closed beak and closed eyes loll down onto my lap. The last drop of water that it felt hangs like a diamond, a statement of rich life, from the tip of its beak. It is like a final declaration that is carried on forever. I am alone with its silence; encased in a glass world where all is clear and all is calm, all is bright and I begin the Christmas 'Silent Night'. My dog Mottle is back in the reeds with my father. He quivers with excitement but stands as still as a statue until my father says, "Fetch!" The reeds part and swish and the pan water bursts into pods of sound. The ducks slap and echo in the air and take off in a wild wave of rising. Their honks follow and trail the wave that circles around in a panic pattern. My father's gun barrel gleams through the reeds. Its menacing metal moves along with the wave and the honks. When the wave is directly above his hunting hat he stands up quickly and his gun loads off its deafening language. The airwave sweeps away but one or two of its life links crumble and begin their death fall. As the gun-boom stops its echo a soft, shy splash tells Mottle where to swim. My father shouts, "Come, Mottle, bring the ducks!" His shout echoes over the water like a voice of doom.

I sit still with the wet, dead duck. Mottle and my father have become strangers to me. I cannot feel at ease with them. I cannot think of play and of stick fetching. The duck's dead weight has made a nest in my lap and a dark patch has grown on my dungarees. They are maroon and look like the dark red of the duck's blood. I think that I am bleeding too. My heart is bleeding all the songs of love it knows. I am giving this duck to duck heaven where it will fly and honk again and not be shot from the sky like a lump of grief. I am telling God that ducks should be free and live as long as they are able without gun barrels pointing up at them and pointers fetching them from their watery graves. My father stands over me and tells me that this duck will make a very good dinner. He tells me how Polokwane will cook it and flavour it with his special herbs. He says that his mouth is watering already and that I must put the duck in the hunting bag and leave it in the shade. I move slowly and place the duck in the bag carefully, like a tender treasure.

Dorry is busy with the picnic canvas. She is spreading it out over the grass and weeds. She is walking over it so that the grass and weeds are squashed and we can sit on it easily. Where she has not yet walked, there are bulges and Kate and Trish jump on them and laugh. While they finish the flattening job for Dorry, my father wades through the water pan and Mottle follows him with the last dead duck of the day in his mouth. My father pats Mottle on the head and tells him what a good hunting dog he is. Mottle wags his tail and brings the duck to the hunting bag. My father bends and picks off the leeches that have stuck onto his legs and made blood streams down to his hunting boots that he wears in the water. He says, "Voetsak, you blood sucking little bastards!" He tramps on them and scuffs the ground to bury them so that the flies do not gather around and pester us. Dorry unpacks the picnic basket and puts paper plates out. She puts hard-boiled eggs and sandwiches on them. She has some oranges too and says there are some sweets when we have finished our lunch.

I sit on the edge of the canvas because there is a stain of car grease in the middle of it and the sun heats it and sends its stink to the middle of my brain. It puts the fear of sick into my mind. I do not want sandwiches and hard-boiled eggs. I want the shade of the morula tree and the sound of living ducks and drinking cattle. Mottle stands next to me and shakes himself. All the water drops make brief diamonds and sprinkle across my face. He lies down and puts his head on my lap. He sniffs the duck's blood and tries to lick it up. My father gets a camp chair for himself and Dorry and they sit and eat their sandwiches. Trish and Kate eat theirs too. I sit and watch mine and wish I did not feel sick at picnics. My father says that the flies will eat my lunch and that I had better enjoy it now. I take my plate and walk away to the shade of a mopani tree. I close my eyes and shut out the sight of falling ducks and the smell of growing grease patches. I bite the sandwich and spit out the flavour of bully beef. I heap sand over the bread clod and throw the rest away for the flies, the birds and the lizards. I tell my father that I have had a good lunch. Dorry says that I am a good child and that we will come on a picnic again. I think that I will hide the canvas and never sit on it again.

My father takes his gun and opens the barrel. He folds it over his arm like the dead duck. He takes an oiled cloth and pokes it through the barrels and cleans them. He puts the bullets into his bullet box and carefully places it in the cubby-hole. He says that no small hands should play with guns and bullets. On the way home we sit in the back of Pedro and sing songs. I sing my songs for ducks that fly and fall and become dinner for us. Dorry says that I am a funny one and that nothing is ever lost. She says we are like a chain of life all linked together and we get what we need from one another. Dead ducks help to give us life. God made nature that way. I do not understand God and nature.

♥

I⊤ is a very hot day and I am playing under the big acacia tree in our front yard. Dorry says acacia trees are called thorn trees because of the big white thorns that grow all over them. She says the thorns are modified leaves but I do not know what modified is. I am playing mud pies and my hands are wet and muddy. Lena has gone to do the ironing. I just know that the tree is big and it is cool in the shade. Dorry is sewing. She is making us new dresses and new brookies and new swimming costumes. She uses old school gyms to make the swimming costumes. I like playing mud pies because my hands get cool in the slush and I like the feel of mud. Suddenly I see a white frog jumping near my mud pie. I have never seen a white frog before. All the frogs I have ever caught are grey or brown. I think that I will catch this frog and show Dianne because we often catch frogs in her swimming pool or in the lucerne patch where the swimming pool water flows when we empty it. I want to call Dorry to come and see this frog but I think that perhaps the noise will send it on a very high jump and I will never be able to catch it. I follow it along the stone path that leads to our front door and then it turns and comes back towards the tree. I keep close to it in case I lose it. It jumps all around the tree and I am getting closer and closer to it. Dorry comes out to see what I am doing. She calls me because I have been so quiet. I am following the frog and as it jumps into the fork of the tree I see a large snake curled up and ready to strike.

Dorry is behind me and she whispers that I should not move. She says stand still and keep very quiet. I am so afraid that I am frozen with one foot in the air. If I put down my foot, I will stand on the snake.

Dorry says stay where you are and keep your foot still. I do what I am told because my foot is frozen and will not move. My breath will not relax and I hold it like I do when I am under water in the Freemans' swimming pool. Dorry moves away and she says she will be back very soon. I hear her call Lena. Dorry tells her to empty the kettle's boiling water into a big pot and to bring it to her as quickly as she can. Dorry creeps back very slowly. She says I must move my foot so slowly that nobody will notice that it is moving. When my foot is a bit farther away from the snake she suddenly empties the pot of boiling water over the snake. She tells me to run into the house. The snake coils up and Dorry jumps back from its spitting fangs. Lena runs out with the spade and gives it to Dorry. The snake is dead in two or three strokes of the spade. Dorry says, "Ye gods, man, that was very close and very dangerous!" She says I must never follow white frogs around the garden again. I tell her I will never do that again! Dorry goes back to her sewing and I go back to my mud pies.

I have made many mud pies and I think it is time for lunch. I look at the road to see if my father is coming home. I see him crawling on his knees. I begin to laugh and I shout for Dorry and I tell her that my father is behaving like an animal. He is crawling home for his lunch. She comes running out of the house and she goes to my father. She tries to help him up onto this feet but he cannot stand. I get very afraid because Dorry and my father are not laughing. Dorry runs into the house and she tells Lena to come and help her. Together they help my father into the house. He is very pale and cannot talk. He holds his chest. Dorry sits him in his chair on the stoep. She makes him bend over and tells him to breathe deeply. I get onto the bed on the stoep and I feel afraid like I did when Trisha nearly lost her finger. Dorry says I must stay with my father while she goes and gets the doctor. He is at the clinic because it is Tuesday. I sit and watch my father in silence. The doctor tells Dorry that my father is very ill. He has had a heart attack and he must go to Serowe Hospital. He closes the clinic and drives my father there himself. Dorry follows him in my father's lorry but first she takes Trisha and me to Mrs Freeman.

My father has been in hospital for a long time. He is home now and he sits in the yard with me and eats paw-paw seeds. The doctor says they are good for sick hearts. He does not drink whiskey because the doctor says he can only have one a day. My father says one a day is enough to fill a hollow tooth and he would rather go without.

Trisha and I are on the beach in Durban. Dorry and my father are with us because the doctor said a holiday for a heart attack is a good thing. We sit and make sand pies and we make castles and my father helps us to build them. Dorry takes us to the water's edge and lifts us up when the waves come. Trisha screams and I laugh. My father buys us ice cream and we walk along the shore and eat our cones and are very happy. Dorry says that heart attacks wake people up and do them good sometimes. My father says, "Bliksem se donner se hell!" He says, "To hell with heart attacks!" Dorry tells him that this is the first and last he will ever bloody have if she has anything to do with it.

♥

Dorry looks so serene
Like purple-look mountains:
No evidence of bare boulders,
No treacherous ravines,
No barbs among the peaceful greens.
The black-patch gullies display no depth
Of wound etchings in her mind.
They are so balmed,
So velveted with smiles.

But

I have been on mountain climbs,
Have leaned down thorn-torn gulley cracks,
Have poised their pits with care;
Dorry is not detached
She's just afraid of snare.

"The war years were interesting for us. We used to sew and make Bundles for Britain. Children's clothes came from our own pockets but the dressing gowns for the soldiers came from the Red Cross; they supplied all the material. We did knitting as well. We sent it all to England for children who had been bombed. We got letters from the Queen thanking us for our beautiful work. Aunty Shaw hung all the letters up in the hall so we could all see them. We had no tea on those afternoons. We started at two and stopped at five. We did a lot of work during that time.

"Oh yes, then it was time for boarding school. Mrs Fordery ran the village school. We built the school for the first years of the bigger ones' schooling. The government doubled our funds and the children could go there for school. Monica decided that she had made a mistake in her book. There was one word in the textbook she couldn't say so she decided to rub it out! She made a hole in the book and Mrs Fordery came to see me about it. I said I would get another copy of the book and Mrs F said no, you can't get them and there was such a fuss about the blessed little hole in the book. I said I wouldn't send my kids to the school again. I said I would keep them home; as they were due to go to boarding school the next year anyway. The government wouldn't keep the school open unless I sent the three, as there had to be a certain number of pupils. So the next day I kept them all home. I decided that I wasn't going to buckle to Mrs Fordery. I had offered to get a new book and it was a child's mistake and I was not going to make a huge thing of it. Eventually she came to apologise to me for going off the deep end about it. So I let the children go off to school.

The next year, I decided that the children should go off to boarding school. Monica was turning nine and the government had decided that all schools should be integrated and that there should not be any separation. All children had to go to one school. Mrs Fordery couldn't speak the language so she couldn't teach the black children. She couldn't cope with the different groups. So our children would have had to go to boarding school in any case. It was a terrible thing. I made all the uniforms. I had black serge for the gyms. I made all the uniforms and had to take them to the convent in Mafikeng by train. I took you three little ones with me. After I saw to the bigger ones and got them settled in, we went to my best friend, Helen. We should have stayed with her for two weeks.

Do you remember Mr and Mrs A E Freeman, Bern? They used to own the shops that Charles has now. They helped Daddy to get his own stores. Anyway, Mr A E Freeman had retired and stayed in Jo'burg with his wife. I was at Helen's for a day or two. She called me one morning and said there was a call from Mrs A E. I couldn't believe she would be calling me. Helen said she had invited me to lunch. Somehow I knew something was wrong and when I asked her she said, 'Yes, Dorry, I have had a call from the convent. Monica had an attack of acute appendicitis and has had an operation. She is still in hospital.' I was pregnant with another child at the time and had to get right back to the convent with you three little ones as well. I didn't think to ask if we could stay and sleep overnight at the convent and nobody offered us anything either so we had to take the next train out. It was the mixed goods train. There was no dining car on it so I had to take you somewhere to eat. There was a tearoom at the station.

We arrived home at about two in the morning. The station foreman said he would see us to the house, as it was very dark. He expected another train and said if I could wait for it to arrive, he would be happy to walk with us. I said I would be all right if he could lend us a lamp. You know those station lamps that one had to pump up. They hissed. They provided a good light too. Daddy had arrived home just before that and none of our beds were made; they had been stripped. Daddy was so shocked to see us. I told him about the phone call from Mrs A E and that was that. We were home in three days instead of two weeks.

The older ones used to come home for the holidays. Man, it was a huge tuck-making thing. I used to bake two bins of rusks for the holidays. You kids spent half your lives in the swimming pool at the Freemans' house and you were forever hungry after your swimming. My bins were empty after the first week and then I had to keep you going with biscuits. I used to make ice cream too. You loved it so. Sometimes the fridge, it was paraffin run fridge, did not get cold enough and you would have to wait for the ice cream to set. I found you peeping at it so many times. The poor fridge didn't have time to get cold before the next one opened the door to check. Sometimes you spent so much time in the water that when you got home your skin was wrinkled. Then there was the big going back to school bake. I used to make fairy cakes, sweets, rusks and pack all sorts of goodies from the shops in their tuck box too. Then there came a time that Faith began to cry three days before they were due to go back to school. She would walk behind me and cry. She used to cry because she didn't want to go back; she wanted to stay home. I spoke to her in later years about it. I told her that there was no choice but to send them to boarding school, especially in the later years. You have to have your education and it is a great privilege to go and get educated. She said if I had told her that when she was smaller, she wouldn't have cried.

Then I decided that the clothes for school were getting such a bad colour. The whites were grey so when they came home, I had to bleach everything. They came up all snowy white again. It was a very big job, you know, Bern. I decided no, I am going to speak to the nuns about the washing. I can't take this dirty grey look on the washing. I decided that they should send the washing home by train every week and I could get it clean and white and send it back on the Sunday train. You know, Bechuanaland was so hot, the washing dried so quickly, I could get it back in a day. So of course I had to bake every Friday as well. I put little fairy cakes into the washing. They were not allowed to have any tuck in the dormitories but I used to send them all this in the washing. I hid it in the bottom of the box so that when they had emptied out all the washing, there were the goodies. The children loved that.

Then one time, it was very funny. The children came home and I had to buy new socks. They all came home with huge holes in their socks. They didn't bother to send the ones with holes home so that I could darn them. They only sent the good ones home to be washed. I thought: no, I must darn and bleach all these socks. No good getting rid of them just for a few holes. So I darned them all and put them into the washing tub. You know we used to boil the washing in those days. So, lo and behold, the bleach ate all the wool that I had used to darn the damn things so in the end all was back to normal, socks with holes! They were stiff and hard. Daddy was so cross because I had ruined all the socks and had to send you all new ones. Everything had to be marked as well, you know. I spent my life marking and sewing on labels.

Then eventually Dorothy had to go to boarding school. Then after a couple of months there, Daddy got called to the railway station. It was during the term. He was wanted on the phone. Dorothy had appendicitis and Daddy had to go and see her in hospital. I was pregnant with Trish at the time and could not travel. The doctor wouldn't let me travel. Dorothy was a very weak and scrawny child. She was very pale. She never got fat. She always kept to herself. Once she came home and said that Maureen kept telling her friends at boarding school that our father worked for her father. Well I told her, Bern, 'Next time she does that you take your hand and slap her mouth up good and proper. Smack her right in her face. Nobody is going to worry and I am not going to worry. I will be pleased if you do that.' Dorothy did that, you know, Bern, and nobody ever said a word to me or to Doris about it. There was no tale telling at all. I dare say Maureen would not have dared to tell her parents about it. Things settled down after that. I used to feel so sorry for Hilton, Doris's only son, and Dorothy. They were so young to be going off to boarding school. Hilton used to cry and cry because Faith and the others had to get off the train at Mafikeng while they went on to Cape Town. Faith used to mother him on the journey. He used to cry bitterly. He used to cling to her so pathetically. He was only nine at the time. The train got into our station at about eight at night and all the howling and carrying on went on until it pulled out. I used to suffer for days after the kids left. It was so hard sending them all away when I knew they were crying. Daddy used to say, 'Stop blubbering, the kids are alright. There is nothing wrong with the kids; they will get over it!'"

♥

The crush,
Surge,
Sea, bobbing brown,
Waving,
Weaving, in and out;
The sound of small stone moving;
Some shifting feet with shoes,
Some without.
Forlorn singing,
Parting,
Eyes, tear-bright.
Telling moments;
Children's height?
New blanket?
Rain fallen?
Mama Shaw, still smiling
Warm hands shaking
Kiss
Hug
Welcome back!

IT is seven o'clock in the morning. Aunty Shaw is here at the station with Dorry, my father, Trisha, Kate and me. The stationmaster says the train will arrive at ten minutes past seven. We stand among the many people waiting to greet and part. The white shale stones crunch beneath our feet. It makes music of its own. In my heart is also the music of hello. My sisters are on the train. They are coming home from boarding school. Aunty Shaw holds my hand and Trisha's hand. We stand on either side of her. She says we must sing 'Jump, Jump, Sugar Lump'. It will make the train come faster. We sing and jump but the train smoke is nowhere to be seen. Aunty Shaw says all good things come to those who wait. We wait and no good things come. My father looks at his watch and says donner se hell where's the train? Dorry laughs and says the train is where it is but she stares up the silver lines to where the train bridge ends and the lines disappear into the bush. I go and stand at the big table they put on the station when all the passenger trains pass through. The people sell carvings, drums made of leather, and rugs of animal skins. Some are made up of impala, some of wildebeest and some of Kudu. There is one made of a lion and its head is still on it. The lion has glass eyes and its mouth is wide open. The teeth are clean and its whole mouth is pink and shiny. Dorry says the art of preservation is called a special name when they preserve dead animals. It's like the Egyptian mummies in their tombs. I feel sorry for the mummies and the animals.

I do not have time to feel sorry for long because Aunty Shaw is calling. She and Dorry have seen the thin trail of train smoke in the distance. We try to stand quietly together to see who will first hear the sound of the engine. My father says he can but we know that he is only telling us this because he wants to be first. The smoke gets thicker, we get more excited and we start to 'Jump, Jump' again. When we hear the chuffing of the engine we cheer. The people begin to surge and the whole station looks like a brown, heaving sea. People take out scarves and handkerchiefs. They sing and wave long before the train comes lumbering over the bridge. Aunty Shaw mimics its sound. She says, "I think I can, I think I can, I thought I could, I thought I could." The train's brakes begin to squeal and it slows down. It stops at the end of the train bridge and the stationmaster comes out with a green flag. He gets on his bicycle and rides up the line. He leaves all the surging people behind. He stops and changes the direction of the points. He pulls a steel lever. He waves his green flag and the train starts its churning and slowly comes into the station like a steel giant. We strain to see all the heads leaning out of the windows. When I see my sisters' heads I begin to run along the station but I am swallowed up by grown ups that are taller than I am. Dorry rushes to catch me. My father puts Trisha on his shoulders and Kate in his arms. Aunty Shaw has her blue spotted handkerchief that smells of lavender in her hand. She waves it and I catch the scent in my head. I am filled with peace and laughter. Lavender is a happy smell. It has a happy home in my head. My sisters wave with both hands and struggle at the windows. They lean out as far out as they can. The train takes a long time to stop. The engine drivers make sure it stops exactly beneath the water tank and they pull the tank plug open and guide it into the engine. My father helps my sisters off and he says they must be careful of the steps. He hugs each one as they step down. Dorry's eyes are full of tears but she does not cry. She gives them long hugs. We all hug each other and we all get into Pedro and my father takes us home for breakfast. Polokwane greets us with a smile and he brings a huge dish of eggs, steak, bacon and sausages to the table. My sisters smell of soot and train leather. I love the smell. I am very happy they will be with me for three weeks.

In the back yard stands a huge three-legged pot. Lena, our maid, has all the suitcases lined up under the syringa tree. She is slowly unpacking them and putting the clothes in heaps according to their colours. She will put them all into the big pot when she has washed them in the tub that stands on a wooden block under the tree. She will boil the white shirts and white socks and white broekies. She will put bleach into the water. I sit and watch Lena and play in the sand. I take a cold iron and pretend it is a motorcar and make roads for it and then steer it down and around. Lena gets cross because I scratch the bottom of the iron. It has to be put into the coals under the pot to heat up after the washing has dried so that my sisters do not look like poor hooligans in white shirts that have not been ironed.

We are going swimming. My father will be angry because it is only two o'clock. He says the sun will thrash us and burn us to pieces if we swim before four. We cannot wait so long. We say we will go to Mrs Freeman's pool and sit under the trees and wait until four o'clock. We go and greet Mrs Freeman. She asks my sisters how the school term has been. She tilts her head with interest and smiles at us all. She asks what my sisters have been doing and how is the tennis playing coming along and who is in the hockey team. They tell her all their school stories. Faith says she is the champion tennis player in the school and she is the centre forward in the hockey team. Sally says she is the swimming champion and nobody can beat her, especially in free style. Monica says she has been in trouble with Sister Eta but she is the best at sewing and her embroidery cannot be faulted back or front side. Dorothy says she is just a bookworm and sits by herself on a bench at break times and enjoys the stories she reads. I tell Mrs Freeman that I can now ride my sisters' big bike even though Dorry says she cannot see my face when I peddle. All she sees is the bow on my head, and my eyes above the handlebars. I feel proud and I am proud of my sisters who are champions and embroidery experts and bookworms. Faith asks Mrs Freeman if we may swim in her pool and she says of course we can and that our manners are as good as any champions'. She says Maureen and Hilton will also swim with us. Dianne will swim with me. Maureen and Hilton go to boarding school in Cape Town. Faith looks after Hilton on the train until it gets to Mafikeng. Hilton cries very much when he leaves home and again when Faith gets off the train. Mrs Freeman thanks Faith for looking after Hilton.

I am very pleased with myself. I can stand in the pool and leave go of the rails. I can walk four steps and walk back to them. Sally says I must lie on my stomach on the water and she will help me to swim. I am afraid to get off my feet. I may sink to the bottom of the pool and never come up again. Sally shows me how people float on their backs. She lifts me up and I cling to her. She laughs and says I will drown us both if I do not let go. Slowly she puts me on my back and holds me up from underneath. She tells me to push my head right back and to put arms straight out. I do this even though I am scared. She says, "See, you are floating!" She tells me to turn onto my stomach and shows me how to move my arms and legs and how to move my head from the middle to the side and how to take breaths when I am in the right place. She walks up and down with me and holds me while I try and do what she says. She says I must not be afraid when she lets me go for a second or two. She says this will show me how I can swim by myself. Sally helps me every day with the swimming and then one day she suddenly lets me go and walks away and I swim to the pool wall. I am very pleased with myself and with my sister Sally.

I have been jumping off the wall and into the deep end of the pool. I go right down to the bottom and then shoot up again and nothing happens. I do not drown. Sally says she will teach me to dive. She makes me sit on the side of the pool and puts my head right down and says just topple over without moving your head. When I know how to do this she makes me sit on my haunches and I topple with my head down and my arms straight and pointed together. Sally says I am a star swimmer already and I am also going to be a star diver like Esther Williams. I have seen Esther Williams in the bioscope. She stands on a very high diving board and walks to the end of it and jumps up into the air. She bends her body and touches her toes and then gets very straight with pointed feet and pointed arms and hands before she makes a very neat splash into the water. Sally says I must never lift my head when I dive because I may break my neck or hurt my brain. I know how to dive now and I know how to do racing dives. I race with all my sisters and Sally always wins. Faith does not like swimming and Monica does sitting bomb dives when I am floating on a tube. She hits the side of the tube with her feet and I have to hang on and see how many bombs I can survive. If I fall off I have to let Monica sit in the tube and I have to bomb her until she falls off. Dorothy is a very quiet swimmer. She dives and swims the length of the pool under water and her head only pops up when she is at the other end. I cannot hold my breath for so long.

Sometimes the pool is full of other children. Hilton comes and helps Monica to bomb everyone. Maureen catches us and ducks us. She makes Dianne cry because she holds her under the water for so long. Sometimes we all play catches and we have to dive in to get away from the one that is on. Monica dived across the corner of the pool and cut her leg. She sat on the pipe that fills the pool up with water and cried. Faith and Sally helped her to stop the bleeding and she had to have an injection because she may have got her blood poisoned. Dorry says never jump across the corner of the pool and never swim when it is thundering and there is lightning. Monica is always the last to get out of the water when the rain and thunder comes. She says she is not afraid of a bit of bright light. My father says he will donner the daylights out of her if she gets struck but she says she will be a cinder and how will he do that! My father says she is a little hell se kind and she had better watch how she speaks to her father. She says she is sorry and when she gets away from him she pulls her tongue at him and says voetsak.

The swimming pool has no filter and in the heat the water starts to turn green. We do not tell my father about the green water. He will say, "No more swimming, you will get sick!" Dorry will say: what does not kill fattens. I don't know what Dorry means. Every day the green water gets darker and darker, like the night coming early in the evening after a storm. When we stand on the side of the pool we cannot see the bottom. We do not know what is going on and we do not know what our feet will feel if we jump in. We still jump in and hope for the best. We think we know the floor of the pool and that nothing will happen to our feet or us. When I jump into the green water I hold up my knees and my feet. I do not want to know what is at the bottom and on the floor. What if there are water scorpions? My father says they look scary but they do not bite people. I do not believe him. They have long tails like the scorpions that I find under stones. If we let the water stay green for too long the frogs make it their home. They lay their eggs in it. We fish out the eggs and wind the jelly chain around our hands and wrists. We play 'jewellery, jewellery' and show off our black diamonds in a fashion parade. When there is too much frog jewellery we get sad and Hilton pulls out the plug from the bottom corner in the deep end. The water takes the whole night and the next morning to flow into the beds of lucerne that Mrs Freeman's cattle eat. We get milk from her cattle and I hope it is clean because her cattle eat frogs' eggs and green slime in the lucerne. We do not mind sharing the pool with the frogs. They swim around us or hide under the steps at the shallow end. I do not know where they go when Hilton empties the pool but as soon as the water is green again there is a singsong from the frogs. Sometimes my father shines the torch on the singers and we watch the bullfrogs bubble out under their chins. We laugh and say they look like Satchmo.

When the pool is nearly empty we bring brushes and yard brooms and get dressed in our old clothes. We scrub the walls and the floor until all the slime has gone down the plughole. Hilton puts the stopper back in and we clap and sit and watch the windmill turn and churn and pump water. I sit under the syringa tree and watch the windmill blades cut up the sky. I think the bits of blue between them are like glimpses of heaven. When the water is up to our knees we get in and try and swim again but we can't; we just splash one another and make a huge noise. Hilton puts some stuff called copper sulphate in the water and it turns beautiful blue and I think there is no difference between heaven and swimming.

When we get home from swimming we have to hang up our costumes and towels and dry our hair. Dorry makes a bin full of rusks and we all have one or two when we are dried and dressed because we are starving by then. If our hair is still wet when the sun goes down and my father comes home early from the pub, he gives my sisters a hiding. He makes them lie on the floor or on the couch and he gets his gun-belt with all the pouches for the bullets. He wraps the buckle end around his hand and then thrashes them. When I hear them cry I run to the room and get under the bed and begin a walk up to the moon. I go to a mountain that has a hole in it and I go into the hole where it is all shiny and peaceful and where life is quiet and there are no crying sisters and where I cannot hear Dorry shouting at my father to stop. He shouts back and says if she does not leave him to teach his own kids a lesson, he will donner them even more. Dorry runs to the lavatory outside and prays that my father will not kill my sisters. I shut my ears and I also pray that God is going to help everyone, including my father, because I hate him when he hits my sisters and I hate him when they suffer. After he has hit them enough, he tells them to go and wash their faces and dry their eyes. He makes them stand in a row in front of him and then he tells them why he has given them a hiding. When they have gone to bed Dorry fights with him and tells him he is a bloody bastard and to leave her girls alone. Sometimes Dorry makes him cry because he has hit her girls. I ask God to help me be a saint and a nun because I am supposed to get my father to heaven but he does bad things like hit his own kids. I only come out from under the bed when I know my father is not going to make any more noise. I go and sit on his lap and tell him that I will be a very good girl. I hope that if I am a very good girl he will stop hitting everyone and we will all be happy with wet hair even if the sun has gone down.

Six for a body, five for a head, four for a wing, three for a leg, two for a feeler and one for an eye; this is how we play 'Beetle' at the hotel with my sisters and the other children come home from boarding school. I am never sure why the beetles do not have a mouth but Dorry says there are not enough numbers on the dice to have mouths. My father says beetles keep their mouths closed because they are wise and so never need them. They eat at night when nobody can see them open their mouths and chew. I do not believe him because he says this about beetles with a twinkle in his eye and he winks at Dorry before she can say, "Hugh, you are pulling the kids' legs. Stop it, man, I don't know what next you will tell them about life to confuse the hell out of them!" Thomas Shaw, Barbara Shaw, Aunty Shaw and Dorry arrange the whole evening for us. They put all the chairs and tables in the lounge. They make us sit at the tables and on them are pieces of paper, pencils and a cup with a dice in it. Thomas has a whistle and we sit four at each table. When he blows the whistle we have to throw the dice and we have to throw a six before we can draw a beetle's body. We throw as fast as we can so that we can have a turn quickly and be the first one and the first table to have a whole beetle drawn. We can put legs and wings on the body before we have thrown a five for the head. The first one to finish drawing their beetle stands up and shouts 'BEETLE!' Everyone claps and I feel shy and proud when I am first to have a beetle. Dorry or Aunty Shaw comes to check if the beetle is fully drawn and then Barbara gives a present. Sometimes it is a box of 'Smarties'. Sometimes it is a pencil box with pencils in it and sometimes it is five shillings. If it is a box of Smarties then everyone is your friend for a while and you have to share the sweets with them.

Sometimes when we go and play with Kevin Shaw, Barbara gives us all a box of Smarties and we sit under the mopani tree in her garden and eat them all and then my father gets cross because we do not want our supper. We love to go to the Shaws. Sometimes we sit on Aunty Shaw's stoep and she tells us stories of a very brave man called Livingstone who went through the bush and found the Victoria Falls that rumble along the Zambezi River and then drop over a very high cliff and thunder into the valley on the other side. She says his oxen often got sick and died from the tsetse fly and he had a lot of trouble finding his way. She tells us about Jock of the Bushveld and my father does too. She gives us tea and English scones and butterscotch sweets. We try and see who can suck theirs the longest without biting and chewing them. Aunty Shaw loves Dorothy the most and she calls her 'My Dorothy D'. She gave Dorothy D a very old violin and told her to treasure it because it is very precious. Dorothy D keeps it in its case and she takes it out and looks at it sometimes. She holds it very carefully. After many years, my Uncle Willie stole it for some brandy because he is an alcoholic and needs money and when his is finished he uses other people's. Dorothy D still tells me about her stolen violin.

When we have played enough 'Beetle' at the beetle drive the children at the table that got the most whole beetles get a surprise present. I got a doll and her name is Cynthia. She has a party dress on and Dianne will make me sew more clothes for her because she loves sewing and she makes me sew, too. Mrs Freeman lets us use her Singer machine and we have fun trying to pedal it properly while we turn the wheel and keep the cloth straight. Dorry makes us many dolls' clothes and we are never short of doll fashion.

Dorry is baking biscuits and rusks again because my sisters are going back to school. She has mended all their clothes and darned all their socks and made them tuck from my father's shop. Sally walks behind Dorry and holds onto her dress. She cries and begs Dorry not to send them back to school. Dorry says there are no other schools for them in our village and that they will get used to going again. Dorry looks sad and worried and her eyes get wet. My father tells her not to be silly and that my sisters will be fine at school.

The train comes lumbering into the station. It is a long train and has many children in it. There is no jump, jump, sugar lump when it whistles from the other end of the station. Nobody claps when the stationmaster comes out on his bicycle to change the points and wave his green light at the engine driver. We are all quiet. Hilton and my sisters cry. Mrs Freeman asks Faith to look after her little brood. Faith cries but says she will. My father says, "You girls must be good at school." Dorry says she will write and hide tuck in their washing when she gets it every week. My heart feels heavy and the moon waits for a visit. I stare at the back of the guard's van when the train goes up the line and gives its last whistle. My father goes to the pub and we walk home with Dorry. I think that the next time we wait for the train will be a very long time away.

♥

Sunflowers, bright-smile the earth
In the dark season's drought
Seed your laughter
On brown ground.
The soft rains will sing
And echo it.

WIND wobbles the trees like a foreigner wobbles tradition. I think that I am wobbling too because I am standing at an edge and staring into a mud pool. The rains have been. The dull, brown soil is water sheered and the land's face is bangled bright. I seep and float in and out as life's circles do. My reflected image stares back at me, at one with the brown and the blue of the sky. The thorn trees interrupt my image but I remain seen and I remain tranquil. I am wrapped and bound in the keeping of creation. There is no separation even in my throwing of a small pebble that starts a new wobble and its own echo. What gives substance, receives substance; what waves in, waves out and life pours in the whispers of my mind, as the endless seeding and watering of the ground. I think how odd it is to be eternal. Dorry says that all who have love of the land are part of the land and part of God. Jesus knew how to ask the water to change and become wine: life's wine that was first to fall as water. Mary knew how to ask Jesus to whisper in the water's substance and to make its echo the wine and Joseph knew how to contain and preserve the water and the wine. We are interlinked and inter-gifted to make life whole and beautiful; to fulfil what it is love wants of us. I only know how to ask the rain never to go away for too long and leave the land dry and thirsty. I only know that I will never forget my land roots because they are sacred, like breath.

I am short of breath. I have been short of breath and short of life for six months. I do not live in the village. I live on a corner of hard tar and hard cement. I do not ride my bicycle through the soft songs of the bush. I cannot stand at a mud pool's edge and look at eternity. I have no image in the water, neither the sky. I sit in a bus that smothers me in smoke. Its belly belches out black blaze that leaves a trail of poison behind. Inside the bus people smoke and I am choked by blue, stinking clouds. My eyes water and the clouds creep into my stomach and charge it with the heavy feel of sick. My head's freedom is fettered with thoughts of fainting in a counter cloud that blots out the belching, the reeking cloud and my city survival. My heart swells with tear waves that want to break and splash and find a shore for their falling. I feel the wet of sweat form on my forehead. In my mind I see myself and my sisters standing in front of our village house mantelpiece. We sing like a straight lined choir. My father loves to hear us. He says we are his angels. We sing:

> *"Soft as the voice of an angel,*
> *Breathing a lesson unheard,*
> *Hope, with her gentle persuasion*
> *Whispers her comforting word:*
> *Wait 'til the darkness is over*
> *Wait 'til the tempest is done,*
> *Hope for the sunshine tomorrow*
> *After the shower is gone*
>
> *Whispering hope, whispering hope*
> *Oh how gentle thy voice;*
> *Making my heart, making my heart,*
> *In its sorrow rejoice..."*

I want to cry when I remember the song. We used to sing it in two parts. Sometimes Monica would sing a third part and go off tune because there is no third part that we know about but she would try in any case. I feel that I have lost my sisters and my life.

The bus of bedlam lurches and sways and stops like a hiccup while the people pile off and on. Some people cough and splutter and turn their filtering faces into tight fisted hands to hold in the fort of poison. It leaks around the edges of their mouths and fingers slide to the sides of chins. The man next to me heaves and spits phlegm into his well-washed handkerchief. He rolls the handkerchief into a ball for safety and tucks it into his pocket. I think of seeping phlegm sprawling in the unsafe handkerchiefs waiting for fingers that fidget and fumble until they split and spread to hands that hold and shake good morning to shop people, bakery people, people who serve and save the glut of germs to give away. My stomach squashes at food and a mad rush of ill overwhelms me. I quiver at the bus bell and leap to fresh freedom when the next hiccup comes. I sit on the red bus bench and let the sweat dry and the tears fall and the fever fade.

Dorry says that smoking helps people to calm their nerves. Mine sharpen like spikes that unexpectedly spring off and lash out like fire. When Dorry lights a Rothman's King Size, she settles back in her chair like one who is ready for the rain after drought. She takes a deep breath and the tip of the Rothman's lights up a little red moon. I miss the full shine of the yellow moon that rises above the thorn trees and gives its gold to all. This small, red moon fades as soon as Dorry stops drawing in its fumes. It fades as quickly as my shining, my joy and my hope of return to the land.

Return happens in my head. Thought flashes the smell of cow dung and dust. The scent of ripe morula settles like balm. I feel the mud between my toes and the faint tickle of the tick spiders that I collect and let crawl over my hands after the rain. My memories swell like a sea tide. I open my small suitcase to hide my tears. They drop and spot the brown paper that covers my village reading book. The ink that spells my name begins to creep and obliterate the letters that say that I am a person that sits under the morula tree in our village schoolyard and reads the simple words that help me to grow and bloom. I am now a person that catches city buses where many little red moons shine and fade and breath becomes a struggle for life. I am now a person in a world where people calm their nerves with Rothman's King Size.

Our house in Parkhurst is number 17. It is on the corner of Fourth Avenue and Ninth Street. It sits square on a square piece of ground. It has white walls and a red, corrugated iron roof. The front door is half wooden and half glass. It should have been stained glass but it isn't. The glass is thick and bubbled so that nobody can see through it. If someone stands on the red cement stoep and knocks on the door, only their shape can be seen. It looks like a liquid person, pouring and prying and persuading their presence to be let in. Dorry says we must never just open the front door when somebody knocks because this house is not like our house in the village. Cities are not safe and doors have to be locked because of criminals who break into houses and steal everything.

Monica is the one who does not listen to Dorry. She says she is not afraid of criminals and opens the door before she asks who is there. Sometimes people fight outside our house. They sit on the pavement and begin to drink from milk cartons. What is inside the carton is beer brewed in a special way. Dorry says that the beer is illegal and that in this country black people are not allowed to drink it. They brew it in secret and sell it to one another. When they begin to fight, Monica goes up to them and tells them to stop or else she will phone the police. She stands with her hands on her hips like a sergeant. Her voice cracks across to them and whips them into attention. They shift and try standing. Some fall back on their bums and start the trying again. Some leer and slur in a language that I do not know. We are very afraid that the people who are drunk and fighting will hurt her too.

I do not feel free and safe in my new home. I do not feel happy here. Life here is hard like the cement and tar that surrounds everything. The square that our house is in is too small. The back yard is small and the front garden is a little patch of untidy lawn. There are no flowers in the garden. Dorry says we can plant some in the spring. We can plant zinnias and marigolds and nasturtiums. We grew these in our village garden. They do not need too much water and they do not mind the hot sun. The garden beds lie along the front fence in a straight line and are full of khaki bush. They look like marigolds when they first come up because their leaves are so similar. If you want to tell the difference between them and marigolds you have to squash a leaf and smell it. The khaki bush leaf stinks and the marigolds have a clean, honey scent. Dorry says that she once bought a tray of marigolds from a man who said he was selling at a special price, just for her. When they came up, she was very pleased but they never flowered; they just grew into big weeds. Dorry is now careful about khaki bush and marigolds.

There is hardly any room between the side of our house and the pavement. I think if people bent over the fence, they could touch our kitchen window. I think of our dog, Ruddles. If he had to come and live with us here, he would have to run up and down in a straight line and come to a sudden stop like the end of life. Even the sky here looks interrupted. There are high poles with wires running along the tops of them. The trees that grow on the pavements are also in straight rows and they interrupt the poles. The hills here have houses built right up to the tops of them. All the windows and doors have bars on them. I think that this whole city is barred in squares in straight lines. When people walk in the streets they walk in straight lines. When they catch buses, they wait in straight lines. Some buses that do not belch black fumes have two overhead poles that are attached to straight electric lines. When the bus moves it whines and whooshes along the road and the poles and wires rattle so that there is never silence or softness. When they are served in a shop, people wait to pay in straight lines. This is not a place for village people but for people who do not know the bush and the land. The cars in the streets go along in straight lines, some on the left, and others on the right. Lights on the pavement tell you when to stop walking in a straight line and when to start again. I think that if people had cattle and goats in this city, they too would have to walk and stand in straight lines. Dorry says that we are now living on the straight and narrow road to heaven. She throws back her head and laughs about it. She says her wits have sharpened and streamlined in the city, where life has pace and bustle. I do not want to go to heaven in a straight and narrow line. I will be sick and bored forever. Dorry says we left our village because my sisters are finishing school and they will need to gets jobs or careers. There are no careers or jobs in our village, just cattle and traders and a few shops. It is not a life for young people who want to get on in the world. I do not want to get a career and I do not want to get a job. I do not want to walk in a straight line and to watch lights tell me what to do about the traffic. I want the wind's whisper; the gentle sand dents and I want to feel compliant with all under my bare feet. I do not want to be chained to the end of life.

When I play in our back yard, I have to use the peach tree. It is one of two trees there. The fig tree is near the wall that separates us from the people next door. They are from England and speak with strange words like 'ducky' and 'guv'. I do not play with them because they put on boxing gloves and make me fight with their brother who is bigger than me and hits me in the face so that I see stars behind my eyes. They say it is not real fighting but sport. Dorry plays tennis and darts and that is sport. I play 'Cowboys and Crooks' and I make the peach tree my horse. I call it Trigger like Roy Rogers because I have loved Roy Rogers since I first saw him at the bioscope on the hotel stoep in our village. Dorry still loves him too. She says he makes her knees go weak and she cannot stand it when he has a fight and gets knocked out. I also close my eyes when I know he is riding Trigger near the bush where the crooks are waiting to hold him up and to get rid of him by shooting him. I cannot watch when they tie him up and chase Trigger away and leave him to die in the desert. I remember all the films about him and how he always gets out of trouble and catches the crooks that have to go to jail because he is also the sheriff and has the jail's keys. The films always end with him back on his horse and it stands on its hind legs and he waves at us until the next time.

I have a holster and a gun and I put on my dungarees and use my school hat. I pin up the one side so that I look like a cowboy. I walk like one and talk like one. I like looking in the mirror to make sure that everything is as right as Roy Rogers. When I play in the horse peach tree I forget that the world is square and that everything is in straight lines. I smell the village dust and see in my mind the way the horses gallop and kick up the clouds of earth and how the bushes are covered with it until the rains come and wash them again. I used to gallop on Dianne's horse. I never used a saddle, only a bridle. I used to make the horse gallop on the golf course. Once I galloped to the end of the golf course and went up the hill to cross the railway lines and there was a herd of cattle coming up the other side. My horse went up on its hind legs and I thought I would be thrown off its back but I held the reins and turned its head and it turned right around and galloped down the hill. I could not stop it for a long time but eventually it slowed down and came to rest under a morula tree. I was very afraid and I did not tell my father or Dorry what happened in case they said no more horse riding. 'Cowboys and Crooks' is just sport and a game and not real fighting. Boxing is real fighting and I will not play boxing again even though the children next door call me a scared cat and a coward. I do not like seeing stars in the daytime.

♥

I HAVE to catch two buses to school. One takes me to Parktown North. The other goes to Rosebank. Dorry has been to see Sister Magdalene. She is the principal of the convent. We have to go to school there after the Christmas holidays. Rosebank Convent is in Keyes Avenue. It is a school where nuns teach. I have only seen nuns once before. I went to Mafikeng Convent of Mercy with my father. He calls it Saint Anthony's. He says Saint Anthony always finds lost things if you pray and ask him. I do not think the convent can ever be lost. It is very big and has many classrooms and is in the middle of the town. I could get lost in it and I would have to ask Saint Anthony to find me the way out or to find my sisters. Sister Dominic comes to the big wooden doors of the convent. She greets us and smiles at us. She tells us that Monica is in hospital but we must not worry because she is being cared for by a good doctor. She takes me by the hand and walks along the long corridor with me. Her rosary beads make a special sound. She takes me to a classroom and Thelma is sitting in a desk listening to the teacher. Thelma is shy because I have come into the classroom with Sister Dominic. She walks towards me slowly and holds my other hand. The children in the classroom giggle and Thelma takes me outside before she hugs me hello. Thelma takes me to Faith and to Dorothy and we have a few minutes to talk while everyone is in class. My father comes to fetch me and to say hello to the rest of my sisters. When we leave, I see Thelma wipe her eyes but she waves until we cannot see her any more. My heart beats faster and I feel sad because Thelma weeps.

Monica has had her appendix out and my father takes me to see her in the hospital near the convent. My father says we have an appendix to help our bodies keep pips and seeds from growing in our stomachs. I do not know how the pips and seeds know where to go when we swallow them but my father says he will tell me when the cows come home. If our appendix gets full it begins to ache and then has to be taken out. When I eat the ripe pomegranates from the trees in our village, I think of my appendix. I get nervous because they have many pips and I chew them up after I have swallowed all the juice that surrounds them. Sometimes Dorry gives us a teaspoon of castor oil because she says the pips constipate us. I think the pips get stuck together in a pile and my appendix refuses to let them in, in case it gets too full.

The nuns in Rosebank Convent are the same as the ones in Mafikeng. They wear long black dresses. Dorry says they are not dresses, they are robes and their uniforms are called habits. She says they are not bad habits that we give up for Lent but clothes that they wear every day and they never change fashion. They wear a white bib around their necks and it covers their chests. In France they call the bib a guimpe. My father says they are old-fashioned soup catchers. The nuns also surround their faces with white cloth. It covers their foreheads and fits all around their faces and shows only their cheeks. I do not know if they have hair like other people or if they are special and don't grow it. On top of the cloth that encircles their faces are long, black veils that hang like a half a halo into a point down their backs. When they walk, the tails of the veils flap and shiver. When the wind blows, their veils lift in it and puff out at the back. If we walk behind them in the wind, we try to see underneath the lifted veils to make sure the nuns are like us and just dress in habits so that they become more holy. My father says they are very holy because they marry Jesus. They have no husbands or children because that would distract them from loving God and being able to teach other children all day. They pray when they are not teaching. They do not talk except when they teach. Inside the convent there is silence so that they can hear God's voice.

My father says that God's voice is very quiet and that everyone can hear it if they are silent and listen to the silence. He says I should listen to God's voice because he is sure I am going to be a nun. He says I am his little nun. I think that nuns have to try and be saints. I love the silence. For me, the bush and the soil is silence and the sky moves the silence into my soul. I think I can hear God's voice inside my soul. God makes me feel good and happy, even in the city. I carry God around all day and talk to Him all day. When I talk to people I think that I am including God in the conversation. Dorry says God knows, sees and hears all things, even our most secret thoughts. She says she learned that from the Penny Catechism. I learned it too when I was making my first communion. I think I still want to be a nun and a saint.

I am dressed in a school uniform. My dress is bright blue. My hat is a white panama with a band of black, blue, yellow and white stripes around the crown. My new blazer is striped like the band on the hat. The stripes run in straight lines down to the hem of the blazer. I am with Sally, Monica and Dorothy. We are being taken to the convent by Dorry. She tells us to remember which bus stop we wait at for the bus to Parktown North. We have to cross the road and wait at another stop for the second bus that will take us to Rosebank Convent. Dorry asks a nun where we should go. She tells us that we have to wait on the netball pitch until the bell goes and then we will be shown what to do and where our classrooms are. Dorry kisses us goodbye and tells us that we will soon be happy in this convent. She has to go to work and catch her bus into town. She works at Greatermans. It is a clothes shop.

My stomach is churning and I feel sick because I have never been to such a school before. There are very many children here and they are all in the same uniform. My sisters leave me in a straight line of children who are the same age as I am. I feel alone and afraid. I do not know any of them and they all know one another. They laugh and talk and show what they have got for lunch. They do not talk to me. The netball pitch is made of black tar like the roads. It feels hard under my shoes. My shoes are Jack and Jill's and I wear white socks with them. They come from my father's shop. I remember how they looked all wrapped up in tissue paper with a red balloon tucked into one shoe. My eyes prick for all the other boxes with balloons in them and for my friend Dianne who opened them with me. I think that they are very far away and my sisters are very far away and I am afraid that they will not know where I am. I do not know where their classrooms are and I do not know how to get home again. I am afraid that I will be lost forever in these buildings with straight lines of classrooms and straight paths to everywhere. My head is full of people talking but I do not hear them. I hear the voice of the go-away bird, high in the murmur of thorn trees and the lapping of the river that runs through the bush. I know my way home from there and I feel safe there.

There is a nun at the beginning of each row. They have sheets of paper and are telling one another where the new children will go. I do not know which nun will be in charge of my class. I am very nervous because what if I do not like her or she does not like children from villages?

A nun, who does not have a line of children in front of her, rings a big, brass bell. The child next to me says her name is Sister Magdalene and she is in charge of the whole school and if you are naughty, the other nuns send you to her for punishment. They say she praises when praise is due and punishes when that is due too. When she gets mad with you, she shouts on top of her voice and then the children call her Mad Maggie. I think it will never be a good thing to do wrong things in this place because Mad Maggie has a stern face and I would not like to look into her punishment eyes and tell her that I have not done my homework or lost my book or come late to school. I would like to look into her eyes that praise.

In this school we learn from the Penny Catechism every day. Sr Gertrude teaches us and Sr Imelda teaches us. Every term the Priest, Fr Haskins, comes to examine us to see if we know God any better. He asks me why we make three little crosses: one on our forehead, one on our lips and one on our heart before the Gospel is read during the Mass. I tell him that it is because we are asking that the Word of God be in our minds, in our speech and in our hearts. I think that he is pleased with my answer because he says I am a good child of God. Sister Imelda smiles and nods at me. She has very rosy cheeks and they turn red when she is pleased. They went red.

Sister Imelda has the voice of an angel when she sings. She teaches us hymns and we sing in the choir at Mass. Sr De Padua plays the organ and she takes us up into the choir to practise the hymns. We sing 'Panis Angelicus', which means the Bread for Angels. The song is in Latin and tells us that the bread of angels becomes bread for men. I am not sure why angels have bread because they do not eat up in heaven but we do. Sister Imelda says that we are singing about Jesus our Bread. I do not understand the song but I love to sing it because we sing it in two parts, one following the other until we get to the end and we finish on the same note. We also sing 'Ave Maria': this is Hail Mary but it is not about hail that falls on our roof and makes me afraid. It is another word for 'hello' Mary. Sister Imelda says so. She tells us that virgin means somebody who has never been married and had a child in wedlock. I do not know what wedlock means so I just remember that virgins have no children. Sr Imelda is a virgin because she is not married and never will be having any children. Mary had Jesus but she is still a virgin because the Holy Ghost sent Jesus to her womb. Dorry says wombs let babies grow in them and that is why her tummy got big before Trisha and Kate were born. I am not sure if the womb is in the tummy or not.

We sing 'Ave Maria' by Bach and Gounod. They wrote the song a very long time ago. I also love it because Sally and Faith can play it on the piano and we sing it when they do. Sally sings the second part and I sing the high part. Sally says I am a soprano because I can sing high notes very well. I do not like singing lessons at school because our teacher, who is not a nun, makes us sing scales and 'I Had a Little Nut Tree'. This tree is very special because it only gets a silver nutmeg and a golden pear on it. When we sing the words I can see it standing alone in a garden of light. I can see the sun touching its glossy leaves and I can see the two fruits glinting at me. Sometimes I walk towards the tree and touch the fruit. It is hard and cold and does not feel like the warm morula fruit that hangs its scent over the bush that bends and plays in the wind. I think it is a stupid song and we sing it over and over again because I think the teacher does not know any other songs. She says we have to sing it perfectly before we can go on to sing a new song. We will never sing it perfectly so I do not sing. I open my mouth and pretend that I am singing. Sometimes our class sends messages around to everyone. We nudge one another and watch the nudge being waved along. When it gets to the last girl in the front row, we all sing a wrong note. Our teacher bangs the piano and it also shrieks a strange noise at us. Our teacher's plump round face goes as red as a ripe apple and her pink lips purse like a sour lemon before she punishes us. We have to stand in silence for five minutes before we start the Nut Tree blooming again. We are happy to stand and rest from the song so sometimes we nudge again and have two punishments in the lesson. When we have to leave the hall, we walk in a straight line to the classroom. We are not allowed to talk in the line. The Nut Tree blooms in my head until we get back to class and can think about sums.

I cannot do this sum. I have copied it from the board. I have written a T and a U at the top. I have a number 1 under the T and a 5 under the U. I have a 4 under the 5 and an X next to the 4. Sr Gertrude says we must find the product of 15 and 4. The 'product of' means we must multiply.

I buy sticky buns at the bakery around the corner from our school. I love the smell of them and the look of them. They are covered in icing sugar. The lady that owns the shop puts them in a paper bag for me. I go to the vegetable shop next door to the bakery and I buy a Granny Smith apple. Granny Smiths are big and green and juicy. They have a sweet and sour taste and they make a cracking sound when I bite them.

I want to open my desk now and have a piece of sticky bun because I need energy to think about the product of 15 and 4. I open my desk's lid and begin to unravel the bag. Sister Gertrude starts to walk down the rows of desks and stops to look at me. I have to let my mouth water and pretend that I am doing the sums. When Sister gets to my desk, she stands and watches what I am doing. I put my hand over the sum so that she cannot see that I have made a hole in the space where I am supposed to write the answer. My rubber makes holes when I have a pencil that writes too heavily. I am ashamed of the hole because it spoils my sum book and makes it look ugly. It is like the stain of sin. Sin stains your soul and makes that ugly. My soul has to be clean and bright because I am getting my father to heaven.

Sister Gertrude asks me if I have finished the sums. I do not answer her. I hang my head over my book because I think she will not be able to see that I have made a hole. She bends down over me and moves my hand. The hole stares up at her like eternal silence and I want to cry because I can't multiply and I can't rub out without holes. I hear Sister's rosary beads rattle. She takes my pencil and writes the sum again next to the one I have messed. She tells me to think how she said we must do the sum. I tell her what I remember and she helps me to find the product and I feel better when she makes me write the answer in the space. She puts a red tick next to it and tells me that I will soon know how to do these sums very quickly because we will learn our multiplication tables like parrots and when we say them we will have answers at our fingertips. I want to have the answers at my fingertips so that I can get red ticks and stars all over my book.

When I get a lot of red ticks I show Dorry and she says that I am very clever and that she is proud of me. I get very happy about that. I have not told her about the hole in my sum book. I have put some glue along the edge of that page and have stuck it together so that I do not have to look at it every time I open the book. Sr Gertrude says we should not hide our mistakes because we learn from them. I know that she is telling the truth because I now know how to find the products of many numbers and I know my tables up to the times six. I just do not like the hole. I have not rubbed another hole into my book yet because I write the answers softly first and then see if they have to be changed. Sister Gertrude says we will all learn to write in ink soon. I do not know what I will do because you cannot write softly in ink. You cannot rub out ink sums or ink writing. My book will be a mess and I will have to look at it and show it to Sister Gertrude. She says we will have a special book for writing in ink so that we do not mess all our books before we know how to do it properly.

I am excited about ink. When I go to the CNA I look at all the ink pens and wish that they were mine so that I can practise at home before we try in class. Dorry says I will be blue from head to foot and will have to have a mile of blotting paper to soak up all the extra ink before it runs all over the page. She laughs and says she messed many a book when she wrote in ink. She smiles at me and says she will make ink gloves for my writing fingers so that I do not have to run around with stains on my hands because I am such a fuss pot and want to be perfect in everything. She says ink will teach me a thing or two about human beings.

I keep my ink well at school clean and do not stuff pencil shavings in it because it is getting ready for ink. Some girls in my class are going to be sorry when it's time to fill the ink wells because they have been storing their chewed bubble gum in them. When Sister Gertrude gives us spelling tests and they have their heads down, they chew because she cannot see them but when the spelling test is over, we say the test words and spell them out loud, so they have to get rid of their gum. I store my gum under my desk and sometimes little bits of wood stick to it and make my teeth go edgy. I used to keep it on a morula tree's bark when I lived in the village and sometimes the ants got it before I could rescue it for the next chew. My father told me never to do that because the nagapies widdle on it but I never listened because I did not believe him. I always smelt it before I put it into my mouth and it never tasted of nagapie widdle. Dorry says gum is very unhealthy and I will get polio because all the germs will settle on my spit and stick to the gum and then give the germs back to me when I start chewing again. I am not sure if this is true so I risk getting polio, especially if I have only had a short chew on the gum and its flavour is still there. I think I have had a polio squirt. They make you open your mouth and squirt pink stuff far, back into your throat so that you cannot spit it out and then they say you will not get polio now.

I ask Saint Bernadette to tell God not to send me polio because I like gum. I buy four Chappies and two Wicks gums for two pennies. When I go to Mass I pray about all the people who chew gum and get polio because they become cripples or die. Dorry would have to find some money to buy me crutches if I became a cripple and I would not be able to play netball and I would have to give my new Slazenger tennis racquet to a poor child who does not have one and who does not have polio. I love my racquet and playing netball but I still chew gum. I have stopped blowing big bubbles though because last week I blew such a big bubble, it burst over my head and all my friends had to pick it out of my hair before the bell went. Dorry was cross with me because she had to wash my hair in the middle of the week and comb it all out without pulling it and making my scalp sore. Besides, there is more room for germs to float around and stick.

Today is Saturday and I am chewing my gum very fast because I am very excited. We are going to school for sports day and Dorry is coming with us. I am running in three races and doing high jump. I cannot eat my breakfast because my stomach says, " No! I will throw up all food." I have to listen to my stomach because if I throw up, I will miss the races or come last because I will have to stop in the middle of them. My takkies are very clean and I have put them on my bed in case anyone stands on them before I get to the convent to show my friends how good I am with the Shu-shine. Sr Magdalene says she is not letting any dirty takkies into the school and she will stand at the gate and examine us when we arrive. We are all going to line up at the gate and march onto the sports field behind a Scottish piper. He comes every year to play the bagpipes on sports day. The music makes me sad and I think that I am going to a funeral and not to the races. He plays a song called 'Speed Bonny Boat'. I tell my feet to speed Bonny Bern to the winning line.

We belong to two School Houses: St Mary's and St Aquinas. St Mary's children wear blue ribbons and blue badges. I am in St Mary's and so are my sisters. I am glad they are not in St Aquinas because they would have to wear red and hate me and I would have to wear blue and hate them. We learn songs that make us proud of our Houses; we earn stars for spelling and these get added onto our House points and we have a cup in each classroom to show who won the most points for good behaviour as well. Our song is:

Boomalacka-boomalacka-ba-ba-ba
Chickalacka-chickalacka-cha-cha-cha
Hokus-pokus, Z and D
Who-are-who-are-who-are-we
We are-we-are can't you see
Saint Mary's House for victory

Then we spell S A I N T M A R Y'S and some children hold up placards as we say each letter and jump up when we say St Mary's altogether in our loudest shouts. We sing this song after every race even if we lose the race. Dorry says she loves our song but it will never make the LM hit parade.

I am standing behind the chalk line that has been drawn across the hockey field. There is a man with a gun standing at the side of it. My stomach is not talking to me. It has gone numb. I am bending over because the man is saying 'take your marks'. He is now walking along the line to make sure we have our toes behind it so that we all start from the same distance. My heart is pounding hard because I need more blood to get going. When the man says 'get set', we bend over and touch the starting line with our fingers and put one knee on the ground. It seems to be taking forever for the gun to go off. When it does I start running and forget everything except that long piece of string across the field. My mind has reached it before my body has even reached the first tree. I do not know if I am coming first but I cannot see anybody else in front of me. I can hear feet behind me and to the side of me. I can hear my breath bleat at the air like a lost lamb, and my feet thrashing the ground. Suddenly I feel the string across my chest and another man comes and takes me by the hand and says there was nobody in sight and I am a very good runner and beat everyone by a mile. He gives me a blue ribbon with 'First' written on it and tells me to go to the nuns at the desk. I walk and I look for Dorry and she waves and says, "Well done, Bern!" I do not know why, but I want to cry as well as laugh and be proud. The nuns take my 'First' ribbon and pin it on my tunic and tell me that I may go to my seat now. They write points for St Mary's in a book. They say I will get a prize at Prize Giving for winning the race. My friends clap when I get to my seat and everyone sings the song again. I feel very happy for myself and for St Mary's because I have made some points and I will have a surprise. My stomach is also very pleased with itself and says it's now hungry and will not throw up if I have a sticky bun or a sandwich. Dorry and Faith are coming over with a Cadbury's chocolate. I am pleased and shy. They tell me what a star I am and tell me to have the chocolate before I have to run the next race or do the high jump. Dorry says it is fuel for the fun.

I am very tired and wanted to sleep on the bus coming home. I did not climb the stairs but sat downstairs and held my school jersey over my nose so that I would not be sick with all the smoking going on. I won my other race, I won the high jump and I am so pleased with myself I could pop. I got three prizes; a wooden pencil container with a slide-on ruler and inside, there was a beautiful green pen and a sharpener. It also had an ink rubber in it so I am all ready for my first ink day and can start practising at home. Dotty will show me how to hold the pen and how to dip it and wipe it before I use it on the paper. I will start playing school, school instead of only playing Mass, Mass. My other two prizes are a storybook called 'The Faraway Tree', and 'A Child's Prayer Book'. The prayer book has a mother of pearl cover and the pictures in it are beautiful. They are prayers that the saints said. I will also say them.

I get up at five o'clock every morning so that I can walk to the convent for Mass. I take my children's prayer book with me. The buses do not start running until half past six. If I wait for them I am late for Mass. I go to Mass every day because Sister Imelda says the saints went every day to get very close to God. We receive God in communion and that makes us have God in our souls and hearts. I want to be a saint and a good person. I take my sandwiches with me and have one after Mass so that I can think about sums and also about reading and writing. I have a Radiant Reader. I love the smell of it and the pictures inside it. The stories are about hares and tortoises and foxes and they remind me of the bush.

I am learning Latin. I have to try and read my missal in Mass because the priest says everything in Latin. There are pictures in the missal to tell how the priest is doing the offertory and the consecration. He has his back to us so that we cannot see what is going on up there on the altar. When he says, "Jesus said, 'Take this bread and eat it, this is my body,'" the altar boy rings a bell and Jesus comes into the bread to be with us. When we eat the bread at communion time, Jesus stays in us and is with us. I try to carry Jesus around carefully because he does not like swear-words and lies. He can see the hole in my book and how I glued it up. I am not sure if he wants me to leave my mistakes as they are or if he likes the glued page. I think it makes his heart sad when I do not behave properly. Dorry says Jesus has paid for our sins in full and we do not have to worry about getting to heaven because he has already made a home for us there.

My father says that we will be punished for all our sins. Sister Imelda says God forgives us our sins when we go to confession so we must go every week. We have to try not to sin again after we have said the act of contrition. We can also get indulgences so that all the sins of our whole life are wiped away. I think I have so many indulgences that I can sin and be forgiven for the rest of my life. I still say the prayers for indulgences so I can keep a good stock of them. I try to make sure that my sins do not keep piling up. Sister Imelda says that we should visit Jesus in the church at break times so that he does not get lonely and so that we can get more indulgences.

I also visit Our Lady of the Immaculate Conception. She told Saint Bernadette that she should be called by this name because she is pure and was born without any sin at all, even Original sin - that is the one Adam and Eve passed on to us when they ate that apple in Eden. God was saving that apple for himself. I do not know why because God is a spirit and does not eat apples. My father says that God wanted to know if Adam and Eve loved him more than that apple. Dorry says they were given a test of obedience and that the apple was just a way of doing the test. I get muddled up about all the different sins, like original, mortal and venial. I also get muddled because a snake spoke to Eve and I know that snakes do not speak. They hiss. Perhaps the snake just hissed and Eve made up the story and told lies because she was so hungry and that apple was very juicy. I know that I love God more than apples, even the Granny Smiths.

I sometimes light a candle at the feet of The Immaculate Conception and pray that she will visit me one day when I am holier. I remind her about the times I went behind the boiler in our home's yard in the village and she never came. I also ask her to help me with my sums because they are getting harder every day and I am getting more crosses than ticks. I have to do tests in everything and have to read out aloud in front of the class to get a pass for reading. Sister Imelda writes something on the blackboard for us to copy so that she can give us a mark for handwriting. She also gives us a list of words to spell and then she dictates something for us to write. I get very nervous about all these tests because at the end of them Sister writes out a report card. All the things we learn at school are written down in straight lines going down the report card page and everything we have done is out of one hundred points. If we get less than fifty points we fail. The report card also tells your parents if you have been behaving and doing your homework or if you have been dreaming and wasting their time and their money. In our village we also got a report card but it just said: very good, good or poor and we did not have to sit in a straight line while our names were called out to receive the reports. In this school our marks are read out for all the pupils in our class to hear. I am very afraid to hear my marks in case I have failed and in case Sister tells about my glued page. There are thirty other children in my class. I have made friends with some of them.

I am very quiet in the classroom. Sister Gertrude calls our names out every morning and she sometimes says that I am so quiet she has to check and see if I am still alive. I am afraid to put up my hand and give the answers to all the questions we are asked in case they are the wrong answers and the other children laugh. Carol gets all her answers wrong and some girls whisper that she is stupid and should stay in Standard Two forever. I want to pass and go into Standard Three because they have new desks and their classroom is better than ours. It smells of floor polish and flowers. The children bring flowers to put at Our Lady's statue and sometimes many children bring them and they have to be put on all the bookshelves and on the teacher's desk as well. Sister Imelda makes a list for us and we only have to bring flowers once a month. I am worried about my turn because we have not planted those marigolds and zinnias yet. Dorry says it will be winter before they can bloom. I will have to ask her for some money to buy them when it is my turn. She gets cross when I ask for money because she says she has eight mouths to feed and that my father does not care and does not send us money from the village. She says we are out of sight and out of mind. She calls my father 'the bloody bastard'. She says one day he will be sorry because she will bugger off into the sunset and leave him. I get afraid when she says that because I will never again see the village. I would be afraid if Dorry ran into the sunset, because if I had to live with my father, perhaps he would forget to feed me. I get ashamed to have an out of sight, out of mind father.

Other children's fathers come to the school and fetch them after the sports matches. Dorry does not come to sports matches. She gets home just before suppertime and on Saturdays she has to alter dresses for the shop where she works. She says she will come to watch me play netball when she has turned into two people with four hands. It makes me sad when Dorry says that because, although she sounds angry, I know that she is feeling sad that she has no time to come and see me at school. She has no time on Sundays either. She makes us clothes and takes us to Mass. Dorry is very worried about not having enough money to pay the rent, clothe and feed us all. She is going to the village to see my father and I am afraid because I know that they will fight and that she will cry and come home with less money than she has now. She will have to buy a train ticket and pack food for the journey. She will have to have some money for tea or coffee on the train. She has phoned her sister, my Aunt May, to come and look after us while she is gone. I do not feel safe without Dorry. Aunt May does not know how to do my hair in its big bow. Faith says, "Never mind," she will do my hair and that Dorry should go and see what is what. She has being seeing what is what for two weeks now and I am missing her. I am getting tired of loose bows and no Dorry.

♥

I GOT into trouble at school. I asked Aunt May if I could go to the film at the Perisia Bioscope next to Piccadilly Hairdressers. She said, "Yes, of course." I did not tell her that we are not allowed to go to the bioscope after school in our school uniforms. Sister Magdalene says it's common and a disgrace, especially when the films are terrible with Elvis Presley in them. She says he is a disgrace to society with his hip swings and suggestive jiving. Dorry loves Elvis and so do all my sisters and we are not a disgrace to society.

I have put some home clothes in a bag and taken them to school. My friends Elizabeth, Sandra and Barbara have also brought their home clothes. Most of the other children in our class have also got extra bags at school today. Mrs Wells is going to meet us in the car park outside the school and take us to see 'King Creole'. She says bugger sister Magdalene and other narrow-minded people who think that a bit of jiving is a sin. She says parents are in charge of their children outside of school time. I feel excited and afraid that I am going to see Elvis. He is number one on the LM Hit Parade and when the presenter, David Davies, says his name, he says, "It's Elvis the Pelvis Prrrresley with 'Treat Me Nice'." Sister Magdalene says these radio stations teach children nothing but antisocial behaviour. I am still going to see 'King Creole'.

It is time for our Afrikaans lesson and Mrs Pearson has her lat (cane) on her table. She uses it to tap out sentences and joining words like: Dis, daarom, derhalwe, toe, en tog dan, sowel, as, wat en nog. We have to use these words in sentences and get them right otherwise Mrs Pearson lectures us on stupidity and wisdom. She says it is unwise to try and educate the stupid so she is not bothering with us. And if we fail she will say that to Sister Magdalene. I think Mrs Pearson is afraid of Sister Magdalene because when she says about us being stupid, she takes out her references and reads them to us. They are about what a good teacher she was in her last school and how wonderful the exam results of her old pupils were. I am very stupid today because I have 'King Creole' on my mind and I do not feel like listening to references and doing sentences. I am thinking of how we will get out of the school gates without being seen in our home clothes. I have never done anything wrong at school before and I am afraid Dorry will be angry with me if she finds out that Aunty May has let me get into school trouble.

We are in the toilets at the top end of the school. We are all getting changed into our home clothes and we are all laughing and chatting about Elvis the Pelvis. Carol, who is not daring to come with us, is keeping cavy at the door for us. She says there are no nuns anywhere so we can run for the top gates now. Mrs Wells is waiting in her Morris Minor. When we see her we run and wave. She gets us into a crocodile line and we cross the road and stand in the queue outside the Perisia. We look around for signs of nuns or tattle tale children. We get an ice cream in the foyer and then we are very relieved to be in the dark bioscope waiting for the main picture. We have to sit through the 'African News Reel' and then 'The Phantom Creeps'. We scream when the Phantom appears because he follows people who are alone at home and do not know they are about to be killed. We try and warn them and we remind one another that it is only a picture but we are still scared. At last we see Elvis with his handsome black hair and side burns. He is telling his father that he will not be going to college. He wants to be a singer. He gets into a lot of trouble with bad men and his girlfriend gets shot and dies. He sings many of his hit songs during the film and some people get out of their seats and jive in the aisles. Mrs Wells says we must stay in our seats but we can clap our hands to the beat. She says she will teach us how to jive at home if nobody else in our families will. She says we will have a party for Sandra and Barbara on their birthdays and that is when we can learn to jive. Some other, bigger people are kissing in the back row and a boy has his hand down a girl's blouse. Mrs Wells tells us not to look and not ever to do those things in the bioscope. She says that it leads to sex and babies. I know that I do not want to have sex and babies. I am going to be a nun but I am not sure if they will have me now that I have seen Elvis's pelvis jigging around.

It is Monday morning and Sister Magdalene is in our classroom with her hands on her hips. She is reading out names of people she knows went to see 'King Creole'. She reads my name and stares and shakes her head. She says, "And you, Miss Bernadette, you with your holy talk going to see such disgusting films! I am ashamed of you!" I say nothing and I feel very ashamed of myself. I feel very angry because Elvis is not disgusting. He tried to save his girlfriend from bad company and he became a singer and made a lot of people happy. Most of our class are being told to stand and are getting the sharp end of Maggie's tongue. She tells us that we are to stay in after school from two until five every afternoon for a week and we are to write lines for those three hours. We must write: I must never attend an Elvis film again. There is a prefect in charge of our detention class. She gets tired of sitting around all afternoon and lets us go home at three. Maggie never finds out because she goes to another convent in the afternoons. I still go and see Elvis films.

I am very nervous because Dorry is coming home today and Monica and Sally are no longer in school. Monica works at Piccadilly Hairdressers and Sally works at Velmar Hairdressers. They told Aunt May that they hate school and the nuns and do not want to do Matric and go to college. Aunt May said they could leave school and she helped them to get apprenticeships. Sister Magdalene says that common people go and be hairdressers: ladies do not. They get proper careers and make a success of their lives. Monica says, so what, she and Sally will just have to be common and no good people, but happy ones who do not judge those who will not go to college. Sally says tell the nuns to voetsak, man. There is more to life than Irish snobbery and holier than thou looking down the noses at people. Sally says Mr Velmar is a strange man and is very strict and that is all she needs after the strict nuns. She says the other hairdressers are good to her and teach her how to deal with Mr Velmar. Monica likes Mrs Peters and she says Monica will be a very good hairdresser and is getting on well with all the customers. She gets lots of tips from them when she shampoos their hair and puts in the curlers. It will be a long time before Monica and Sally are qualified so they have a few years to decide if they really want to be hairdressers.

I am glad that I do not have to think about what I am going to be because I know that I will be a nun but not a snob. I am going to be a very holy one who prays all day and talks to people kindly. I do not want to be a teacher, I want to be silent and spend a lot of time in church. I will scrub floors or polish furniture when I am not in church. If I have to go out every day, like some nuns do, it will be to help poor people. I might take a basket full of bread and fruit with me so that I can just give people on the street something to eat. Dorry says wait and see when the boys start coming around and I get to fancy one, then I will change my mind about being a nun. She says I am too young to decide and that my father is putting stuff in my head that should not be there. She says vocations have nothing to do with my father. They have to do with what God wants for me. I do not know how I will know what God wants because He doesn't come and speak to us since Jesus went up to heaven in a cloud. Not even Jesus's mother comes and tells me anything. I often ask her to visit me like Saint Bernadette but she does not turn up when I wait for her in church or at my bedside when I say my prayers.

I am not sure why when we go to Mass with Dorry, we always laugh so hysterically on the buses. It doesn't matter who is travelling with us, Dorry will always look for a chuckle opportunity. The bus is never full. Kate, Trish and I eagerly go to Mass with her. We know what is to come and I think one of the reasons we are faithful to church going is the laugh-episodes. We always race upstairs although I don't know why because the noise of the trolleys connecting with the overhead wires is deafening. Also, if we sit at the front we think our lives will come to an early end. We can't see anything of the bus from there, just the trees and sky. When we go around corners we hold our breath and shut our eyes because we are always sure that the whole thing will topple and land flat on the side of the road. Heaven knows what will be squashed underneath and heaven knows what we will look like as plat as pannekoeke. Dorry tells us that the driver knows what he is doing. We must just relax and trust him. She says that about our father's driving. She says that no matter how much whiskey he has had to drink, he will always get us home because Pedro the truck knows the way home by itself. We never believe her. When we were small and still lived in our village in Botswana, he used to drive us around on the golf course. We always sat in the back of Pedro on top of the food bins or built-in benches for long trips across the desert. When he got to the huge morula tree, he drove in circles around and around it until we got so dizzy we wanted to be sick. We could not relax and trust in getting back home safely. Dorry says he was only playing but we weren't, we were praying for the world to be straightened out again.

Today is a Sunday-bus-to-church day. A man has come up the stairs and has decided to sit opposite us. We are already getting ready for the Dorry chortle. We are looking at him and nudging one another with our elbows. We are squashed into the front seat although there is plenty of room up here. He is very smartly dressed in a grey suit and white shirt. He stands and looks around for a moment and then sits opposite us. He is busy listening to our conversation and begins to stare at Dorry. She is very beautiful, especially when she wears violet. It makes her eyes shine a deep, deep blue. He is staring so shamelessly that Dorry gets the hell in and asks him what he is looking at. He says in a very posh voice, "Nothing much!" You have never heard such a Catherine wheel wind up and weaverbird chortle in your life. In between that we are delivering our own, wild whoops of laughter. We think we will pass out because we run out of breath and hold onto the seat for dear life. Things get so out of hand that the conductor marches up the stairs and asks what is so funny that the whole bus has to be subjected to the terrible commotion and display of uncontrolled behaviour. Among her shrieks, Dorry says, "Nothing much!" and that starts everyone, including the staring man, off again. He snorts between guffaws. This makes him look very stupid in his posh suit because his laugh has no manners. Dorry says he could frighten a bush fire out of burning with a laugh like that, and he could put it to sleep with all the snoring in between. The conductor says please could we try and calm down, although he himself is struggling with an unveiled coughing fit to disguise his own hilarity. Why he can't just let go and screech like the rest of us, I don't know. He could report the fun downstairs and ride a rowdy but happy bus right to the terminus. It could go a long way to lend cheer to others who are going through the solemnity of the Sabbath or the mystery of sung Latin. I say, "Shut up man!" We just can't! We get off the bus like a herd of unruly cattle, pushing one another in the ribs and giggling all the way down the stairs. I think the conductor and the passengers are very relieved to see the last of us.

During the Mass is also an unpredictable time to be with Dorry. Sometimes we all go to Mass together. Sally can never find her hat so arrives with nothing on her head. She nudges Dorry to ask if she can go to communion without her head being covered. Dorry says that the Church rules are the Church rules and have to be obeyed. One can't receive the body and blood of our Lord without the respect of having one's head covered. Sally sighs so deeply that people turn around to see what is happening in our row. I put my head on the bench so as not to be associated with the rest of the rabble. Sally begins a whole ritual of removing her knitting from the shabby old piece of sheeting she uses to carry it around in. It has worn thin and there are little holes all over it. The edges are frayed and strands of cotton hang from them like stray bits of a scarecrow. Sally stretches it over her knee and smoothes it out as best she can. Next thing, she has it perched on her head like a doek or mantilla. She rises with the other people in the bench in front of us and walks up the aisle looking as though she is trying to steady an unusual load on her head. Her nose has that upturned and 'so what' look about it. She whispers to Dorry that no rules and no need for proper hats or doeks are going to keep her from receiving God. I can see Dorry struggling with the laugh pangs. She staggers to her feet and gestures to us to move out of our bench and into the communion queue. I am too ashamed to be associated with Sally so I stand and let everyone else go first. A little way down the aisle, I hear the wind up begin and the trademark chortle being smothered in a handkerchief. It is all so hopeless. Dorry has to push past people and run out of the door as quickly as possible. Sally gets to the front of the line and the priest stares and hesitates before giving her communion. She whispers that she has forgotten her hat. I am never keen to go to church with

Sally any more. She is far too brazen in an awkward situation for me. Her deep blue eyes and vaguely arrogant way of tilting her head can conquer the fiercest opposition and wither the slightest attempt at disapproval.

Sally was always in trouble at school with the nuns because of her way of standing. They said she was openly defiant. She always says she was openly afraid of their Irish eyes that lacked the characteristic smiles. She never answered them when they accused her of this or that and so her silence was a sure passport to a slap across the knuckles. Sally is very talented. When she plays the piano, her long and slender fingers run along the keys with such ease that they make the music feel like soft, clear water flowing over my whole being. I can just sit and watch or close my eyes and let Sally's music transport me to wonderful places where there is total peace and harmony. She sits very straight and tall on the piano stool and tells me that this is correct posture for the classics. Her dark hair falls and folds like skeins of silk when she bends her head and sways her body to meet the crescendos or the allegros of the piece. She can also make us laugh like a hen house full of egg layers. She mimics all the composers and we love her rendering of the Concerto in B Flat Minor by Tchaikovsky. She throws her head about and raises herself off the chair and plonks herself back down and pulls her face up like rubber. She raises her eyes to heaven like those saints in the holy pictures and breathes and sniffs as though she is appreciating the full extent of her expertise. She can switch on her emotions like a professional actor. If we say cry, she sits with her head down for a few minutes and the tears begin to flow. When I ask her how she can just cry like that, she gets a far away look in her eyes and says that there are enough sad things in life to make the whole world cry in a jiffy. I think she should become a famous actor or musician someday.

Musicians can weep over their sad songs and pieces and actors can weep by just pretending to be somebody else. Sally's teacher says she has the talent to be a concert pianist. She has already passed all her Royal Academy of Music exams and merited honours in all of them except the last one which allows you to be a music teacher. Sally only got a merit for it because the nun in charge of the dining room slapped her across the knuckles the night before she played for the exam. She said Sally was talking after the bell. Sally said she had not been talking but the nun did not believe her and called her a cheeky liar. Her hands were swollen the next day and she could not finger the keys with her usual nimbleness and so she passed with merit and not honours. Her music teacher said that she was a disgrace to the school and to her family. Sally did not take music exams after that. Now that she has left the convent school, she takes jazz lessons at Rene Lacy School of Music and she has got very good at playing 'Alligator Crawl'. She slides up and down the piano stool and pulls her face into something as fierce as an alligator. Her neck gets stretched. She swivels it back and forth and from left to right as though she is out to get a dinner from somewhere in the reeds. When she makes a mistake, there is a sudden silence while she says, "Shit!" If Dorry hears that, she says she will wash Sally's mouth out with mustard but Sally takes no notice because she tells Dorry that those days are long gone and that she is seventeen and cannot be subjected to mustard any more. Dorry tells us not to listen to such bloody tripe. When we tell Dorry that bloody is a bad word she says it is what flows in the veins and God made it. I only swear when I am alone or when there is no chance of Dorry hearing because I have learned worse words than shit and bloody.

WHEN we get home from Mass there is always the smell of roast meat. Dorothy goes to early Mass so that she can do the Sunday dinner. She is a very good cook and Dorry says she will be a star mother one day. I call Dorothy, Dotty. She is not mad but I like to call her by that name. She has a special way with me. She makes me feel that Parkhurst is not such a terrible place and that the city has its own way of life and attractions. Dotty is tall. She has light ginger hair and has an egg timer figure. She is very proud of her waist measurement. It is twenty-three inches. Her hips are thirty-six inches and her bust is also thirty-six inches. She hates her nose because it is Roman and she says it is longer than it should be. She says it is not made for flute glasses. She is a quiet person and she is shy. Her blue eyes are calm and they sparkle when she laughs. When she is angry they spit blue flame and you know it is time to run because you get unsure of what she will do if she catches you. Her freckles seem to turn darker brown when she is in a temper. She also goes blood red and sometimes white when she really wants to commit murder. She wanted to strangle me once because I borrowed her best shoes and she only has one best pair. I have no best shoes. I have to wear my school shoes every day. I get ashamed at the bioscope because all the other children have best shoes. Dotty's shoes do not fit me so I stick cotton wool in the toes. Dorry says I look like Daisy Duck but she does not buy me new shoes. She says my bloody father must buy shoes and a few other bloody things in the house. She says she is not a gold mine or a money factory.

Sometimes Dotty takes me with her on a drive with her boyfriend Ian. He is Scottish and has a Morris Minor. It is blue and has leather seats. When Ian drives, he sometimes screams the clutch when we are going down a hill. We always hit the bottom and our stomachs lurch up to the roof and stay there for what seems a long time. He laughs when we squeal at our no stomach feel. Dotty has a group of friends that come home with her from school on Wednesdays. They all teach Catechism and they come home for coffee. Dotty bakes a sandwich cake with jam in the middle on Tuesday because her friends are always hungry after teaching innocent children about the Church and God. Wendy is short and is a champion swimmer. She can dive off the top diving board and hit the water as straight as a pin. She hardly makes any splash and Sister Imelda says that is because she understands diving and will one day be a South African champion. It is nice to have a champion for a friend because it makes you famous too. Wendy has a Vesper scooter and can drive it very well. Sometimes she takes me for a ride. She often sits on her scooter on the pavement and talks to Dotty for hours. She lives near us so she does not have to go home early. Later, Jackie and Allan arrive on their motorbikes. Allan has a BMW. He is very proud of it. He took me for a ride on it once and Dorry was very angry when I got home because I did not tell her or even ask her if I could go. Allan taught me how to sit on a motorbike when it turns a corner. If you don't sit properly, but lean over when the bike is going around a corner, you can cause the bike to skid and fall over onto its side.

Marie Louise, Anne and Gabby arrive like clockwork. Marie Lou is my favourite. She has a blond ponytail and tilts her head to the side when she talks and laughs. She is clever and gets good marks. I think she will be the Head Girl of our school one day. Dotty says so. Her father is an alcoholic and she does not like to talk about him. Anne is Marie Lou's sister and my best friend. She tells me about her father and her brother, who wants to be a priest. She cries about her brother because she says he may become an alcoholic too if he drinks the wine of the consecration and what will happen to an alcoholic priest? She also cries because she is scared she will be an alcoholic one day. Sister Imelda asks me about Anne and says I should tell her why Anne cries when we sit and talk on the bench under the tree on the playing field. I tell her that I promised Anne not to tell and she says I am a good

271

Sally (Thelma) aged approx 18

Faith, 21

Railway water tanks

Mrs Shaw, Dorry

Dad's trading store

Hugh (dad) outside shop

Palapye station

Village road opp Palapye station

Villagers outside hall, Palapye

confidante and friend. I do not know what a confidante is but it sounds nice. Dorry says that confidantes are friends who can keep secrets and do not gossip about others. My father says they are people who are sure of what they can do and can't do. He says he is a confident storekeeper, because he knows buying and selling and his customers' needs.

I think I am a confident confidante. I am sure that I can keep secrets, even my own. I have some secrets that I do not tell anybody. Sometimes I think I am disappearing into my secrets because it is so quiet there and I do not hear anything else except their silence and the birds that sing around them. The songs of the birds make me feel that I belong with the secrets and with the earth but not with any people. I belong only to God who does not speak in a person's voice but in the silence like the birds. I can hear God but I do not understand the language; it is like a singing in my heart not with words or music. Sometimes when I am alone and I hear God, I sing quietly. If it is near Christmas I sing 'Happy Birthday Jesus'. If it is Lent I sing 'O Come and Mourn with Me a While'. The song is about Mary calling us to her side while she stands and watches Jesus die. It makes me cry and I do not like hearing God's voice in Lent. In Easter time, after the very long Mass when people's feet get washed to show that Jesus was a servant, is a servant and always will be one, and always wants us to be one, I hear God's laughing voice and I sing 'Hail Redeemer King Divine'. Sometimes I sing my own songs and ask God to join in because God knows everything, even our most secret thoughts. My father says, "Ja, jong, one day all will be revealed, so our thoughts had better be good and pure."

My thoughts are sometimes good and sometimes bad. My bad thoughts are about giving Monica a slap for smoking in the room we share. I want to squash up all her cigarettes and flush them down the lavvy, but she will find out. She finds out even if we touch the things in her wardrobe. She packs all her clothes in straight rows and in plastic bags and if we move them she knows and shouts until we confess and then she lectures us and tells us she will never speak to us or ever give us anything again. I get miserable when she says that because she buys us, her little sisters, tickey ice creams or wafers for four pence.

Dorry says Monica is a funny one with all her bags and threats. She tells us that it is all hot air and that Monica is as soft as putty. I am afraid of putty because it goes hard if you leave it lying around in lumps. Sometimes, Monica does get as hard and as obstinate as lying around putty. When she is like that, I think her mind windows will never open again and that she will frown and grumble forever. She gets so angry with us, her voice barks like a sergeant straightening up the troops. Sometimes after the barking she gets a dark look and stops talking to us altogether. We have to skirt around her like trackers in the desert trying to find the rain. I feel sad and worried when she pouts and ignores us. I miss her nightly news and her laughter. I like to hear about the clients in Piccadilly Hairdressers and how Monica did their hair and got tips for her trouble. Her boss, Mrs Peters, gets very pleased with her and says she will be a great hairdresser one day. If her clients are not friendly, Monica pulls their hair a bit when she combs it. If they complain, she smiles and says sorry and does it again a few combs later. She says it serves them right for being difficult while she is trying to do a good job.

Sometimes when Monica gets home, her overall is stained with hair dye and she smells of perm lotion. It makes me want to vomit, especially when she lights a cigarette before she bathes and changes into her going out with Tex outfit. When she paints her nails and smokes, I have to leave the room and find some place to sit in the peach tree because I cannot feel like vomiting all day.

When Monica is very furious, she tells Dorry she will commit suicide. She will starve herself to death or commit suicide some other way. She does not really starve; she leaves her sandwiches at home and does not eat her supper but she fills up on hamburgers at work and she eats one before she comes home at night. She sometimes eats it at the bus stop and Sally sees her. She tells Dorry so when Monica misses her supper, Dorry says, "Ah well, all the more for the rest of us, dear!" Monica goes to her room and lies on her bed and stares at the ceiling because nobody cares if she starves. She phones her boyfriend and stares until he fetches her. His name is Tex. He wears black leather trousers, a black shirt and a black leather lumber jacket. He says he is a ducktail. His hair is peroxided blond and combed back like Elvis Presley's hair. He wears bright green socks that you can see in the dark and he rides a BMW motorbike. Even when Monica is in her dark mood, she makes sure she is dressed in her black slacks, her pink blouse, and she wears her cardigan back to front. She talks to Sally long enough to get the buttons done down her back. Dorry worries when she goes off on the back of the bike with Tex. She says: "who can trust ducktails in this world and in this big city?"

Dorry stays up until Monica comes home. She lectures Monica and tells her about all the terrible things that can happen to young girls who go biking at night. Monica says she will commit suicide if Dorry does not leave her alone. She says she will OD and then we will all be very sorry. Dorry says she had better improve her behaviour or she will not have to commit suicide because there will be bloody murder in our home instead. I get frightened of Monica and of Dorry because they encourage each other's impatience until it is hard to tell who is serious and who is not and what will happen next. Sometimes Dotty takes me by the hand and we walk down the road and hold pinkies. She says it will all blow over and life is not a bowl of cherries but even lemons get ripe. Ripe lemons are still sour and you have to purse your lips when you try and eat them. I feel safe with Dotty. She stays calm no matter what is going on.

I think Monica is dying. I am uneasy and very confused because Dorry is angry about it all. She is not weeping and sad like Monica said she and we would be. Dorry shouts and says she should have named Monica, Queen Drama the First because she is so good at causing havoc in the house. She says it is a shame that the job is never done properly and the only lesson anyone has learned is that stomach pumps are not pleasant when you are on the receiving side and that a few aspirins are not going to kill anyone, least of all Monica. She says that passing out on the floor at work with Mrs Peters in attendance is not going to earn Monica any stars here at home. It is not going to get anyone to worship at her royal and dramatic throne. Instead, it is going to get everyone the hell in and not very amused.

Monica is home from the stomach pumping procedures. She is lying on her bed staring at the ceiling. She will not talk to me or to anyone. I ask her if she wants a cup of tea and she says I am the only one who cares. She says no to the tea because she will now be going back to starving. It will be a slow and suffering death but we will see her fading away a little more each day. Dorry hears her and comes into the room with her hands on her hips and says that if Monica does not stop her tripe she will have to phone our father and get him to come and take her to a mental doctor. She says she cannot cope with such nonsense and no kid of hers is going to starve or commit suicide for nothing. She tells Monica to go to sleep and rest her stomach and wake up with a different attitude. Monica phones Tex and tells him all about her family who do not care about her when she commits suicide. He comes and takes her to a party. Her suicidal stomach is suddenly better and able to eat party food. When she comes home, she is cheerful and tells us all about the party and how she jived with Tex and other boys and how he rides his motorbike at full speed with her on the back and how nothing happens to girls who go to parties with ducktails. I love Monica but I do not understand her.

♥

M ARY, our maid, looks after our home when we are out at work and at school. She is very tall and she wears a white doek and a white housecoat. She has black sandals that flap-flap when she walks around the wooden floors of our home. Her slender hands are wrinkled from doing the dishes and the washing. She says we are an army to feed and to wash and iron for every day. She is always cheerful and sings songs while she sweeps and polishes. We ask her what her songs mean and she tells us they are about better times and times of laughter and freedom. She says she sings about mothers and their children and lands with sugar cane and fat cattle. There are songs about the fathers leaving home and going to the City of Gold for work. They never come back to their village homes. They stop sending money to wives for the children. They live in hostels and find new lives and new wives. Dorry says Mary is our saving grace and our pot of gold. She looks after Kate and Trisha and me when we get home and makes us change our uniforms and makes us take off our school shoes and socks so that she can wash them because we only have two pairs. Mary puts my tennis dress in a tub with Jik in it and she leaves it there. She puts mine in with Faith's and we look smart in our tennis clothes and are proud to wear them to tournaments. She cleans our tennis shoes with Shu-shine and an old toothbrush and puts them outside to dry. Sometimes when I put on my tennis shoes, my hands are stained with Shu-shine because Mary fills the holes with it so that I have to poke them open before I can thread the laces and tie them up.

Sometimes Sister Magdalene comes to my classroom and asks me to go home for my tennis dress and racquet because I have to play in the Open A team when somebody is sick. She asks my friend to lend me her bicycle because I do not have any bus fare. I ride home and get there quickly because it is mostly down hill from Rosebank to Parkhurst. I have to wear Faith's tennis skirt and blouse. Mine is in the washing. I have to find clean socks and sometimes I have to take them off the washing line and hang them over the handlebars so that they dry before I get back to school. I have to find a safety pin and make another pleat in Faith's skirt because it is too big for me. I put the blouse over my waist so that nobody can see that I have pinned the skirt. We play at Rhodene Girls School and they are very posh people. I feel ashamed of my skirt and cannot hit the balls properly. Gene Loffell, our captain, tells me to concentrate and not to take any notice of posh girls who peak down their noses. She tells me to give them a good backhand down the tramlines even though I am still a junior. She tells me to show them what I am made of. I feel better when Gene talks to me like that because I feel older and part of the team. I can hit backhands down the tramlines and they fluff up white dust to show that they are still in the court but can never be returned. Sometimes my friends call me Backhand Bern. They say I can beat anybody if I want to and that I will be a tennis champion. I get proud when they say that because I feel good and I am making my school proud too.

Mary has even white teeth and a ready smile. Her face is round and looks a bit like a saucer because her eyes are large and brown. She says she has seen things that would make anybody's eyes large and round. I do not know what Mary means. She says her eyes are always on us so that we do not get up to mischief.

Sometimes Trish and Kate and I do get up to mischief. We wait until Mary goes into her room with the visitors she invites after she has peeled the vegetables. They wait outside our back gate and they look around and up and down the street before they come into the yard and sit in Mary's room. She shuts her door when her room is full.

We can hear the growing conversations in Mary's language. It is not the language of the village. It has clicks and a different rhythm for the tongue. Mary says it is Zulu. She comes from Natal where my Aunt May lives. She says Zulus are brave and have been warriors who have conquered all their enemies. She says they will conquer these enemies too one day. I do not want to be an enemy of brave Zulu warriors. I do not know them like I know the people of my village. I cannot imagine Zulus wandering through the bush with bird songs and long grass playing music to them. They are straight line people. They do no look gentle and happy. They look angry and afraid. Dorry says there is apartheid here and we do not mix with black people. They may not sit on the same benches as us. The benches say: 'Whites Only'. Dorry says bums are bums, black or white, pink or yellow. She says apartheid is not a good thing and no wonder the black people are angry. She says it makes them do things in secret and it will cause a war one day.

Sometimes I dream of the coming war and I always hide under my bed and hope nobody finds me. I see people running from bullets and bombs. People and buildings fall. Huge clouds of dust billow and swallow and then all is silent. Children have wide screaming mouths and run wildly around empty streets. There are no parents any more. Sometimes it is like the dreams I have of the end of the world. I am always under a bed and the world is disappearing until there is nothing left around me. There is a dark hole and I am under an island bed that swings over the hole and I cannot see the rope that stops it from falling down the dark pit into nowhere. When I scream for help, none comes and my voice cannot be heard. I am in a lonely silence and think that I will never see or hear or speak and laugh again. I think that there are no other people in the world. Dorry says I sometimes cry in my sleep and she comes and wakes me and gives me some water.

Trisha, Kate and I are making mud pies. We pack them on an old tin tray and when Mary and her Zulu friends are talking in her room, we climb on the garage roof. The roof is flat and has a little piece of wall jutting up so that we cannot be seen from the street when we lie flat. When people pass the garage we throw a pie and duck down quickly. Sometimes people shout because we have given them a fright and they have mud on their clothes. We also take peach pips up on the roof. We throw them at the cars as they pass and duck before the drivers see us. Once a mud pie went astray and hit the windscreen of a car that was pulling over to park. The driver got a very big fright and we heard him swear and say, "Shit!" We crawled to the end of the roof and peeped around the corner above the gate and saw the man walking around his car with his hands on his hips. He looked up and down the street and up at the trees but he did not see us. We started to giggle and then laugh out loud. We were lucky that the man was already in his car and turning the corner before we began to screech. Mary came out of her room and she saw us on the roof and scolded us. We had to get down very quickly as she said she would tell Dorry that we were very naughty and could hurt ourselves up on the roof. She made us promise never to climb up there again. I still climb on the roof because I use the back yard and the garage wall for tennis practice and sometimes I hit the ball hard and it lands on the roof and sticks in the gutter.

Trisha, Kate and I have a candle and a box of matches because we are going to crawl under our house. There is a small green door around the side of the house that does not face the street. It smells dusty and there are cobwebs hanging from the top of it. We have to take a stick or a duster with us to get rid of any spiders that may be there ready to bite us. Dorry has told us never to go under the house. She says the electricity mains are there and if we play with them, we will set everything including ourselves on fire. We do not listen because we like to play under the house and crawl from one room to another. Sometimes Mary is in the house cooking and we sit and listen to her feet move over the floorboards. Sometimes we tap the boards with a stick to make ghost sounds. She never hears them or stops to listen. We light the candle because we are afraid of the dark and the spiders. We dare each other to crawl away into another room alone and then we blow out the candle.

Today we know Mary is in her room with the people who wait at the back gate. We are under Dorry's room telling ghost stories and getting afraid. We hear the creak of the green door. Dotty's favourite song is 'Green Door'. It is about somebody trying to creep through a green door at midnight. The song says people talk and laugh behind it. Dotty has an LP called 'Shock'. I sometimes listen to it when I am alone and I get scared because it is music with strange voices and footsteps in it and I think there are people in the house waiting to grab me and strangle me. Sometimes there are fog horns that echo and the sound of water lapping at shores. There is one piece that has a gun shot echoing in it and I think of being murdered. Before the gun goes off there is somebody running along a hard pavement and their breath is gasping. Just before the bang of the gun shot the person screams. I do not know why I listen to such scary music. I just do.

We can hear whispers at the entrance of the green door. We sit in the darkness and hold our breaths. We nudge one another and squash together for comfort. We hear men's voices. They are speaking in Afrikaans. We see the flick of torches. We get down onto our stomachs because we are so afraid of being found under the house. We hear the thud and slap of fists. We hear Mary cry, 'Eish, nee my baas!' We hear the men call Mary a kaffir-bitch and they tell her they will donner the hell out of her bloody black body. They will slaan her plat. They are the police and the law and she had better learn that fast. They tell Mary to show them where she has hidden the brew. She cries that it is not here under the house. It is in the pantry between the ceiling and the roof. They tell her to walk. The voices fade. We stay in the dark.

When we come out from under the cellar, Mary is not in the kitchen or in her room. She is in a police van on her way to jail. When Dorry comes home, she is very upset. She swears and tells God that she has had enough trouble and now look what is going on! Can't they leave her Mary alone? Why are there laws for one set of people and other laws for other sets of people? I do not like laws. I do not like the laws of traffic lights and straight lines and straight rows in classrooms. I fear the laws for brewing beer. I fear for Mary. The police come and tell Dorry that they have let Mary go and that she had better never be caught brewing beer again.

These days we go to the cellar when Mary is in the kitchen washing up the dishes. We take our box of matches and our candle with us because we have discovered gold under the floorboards in Faith's room. She drops sixpences and sometimes shillings on the floor and they fall into the cracks and land in the cellar. We save the sixpences and shillings and go to the bioscope on Saturdays. When Dorry gives us money for the tickets, we feel very rich and have two ice creams instead of one. Mary does not give us money any more because she does not make her beer and there are no people in her room these days. We have not thrown mud pies at people and cars because Mary's room is empty of customers and she watches us carefully.

♥

Faith had black hair. These days it is dark brown. Perhaps it is because of the sun and the heat. She keeps her hair curled and uses Drene shampoo because it is best for shine. I think she likes the lady on the Drene shampoo label too because her hair is long and glossy. I go to Tony's Café to buy the sachets of Drene because towards the end of the month Fay runs out of the bottle. She says it's because every-bloody-body-else in our house uses it behind her back. I love going to Tony's for Faith because she always gives me a tickey and I buy a Walls ice cream wafer. You can't imagine the taste of it. It is like taking a bite of heavenly cream and letting it melt slowly in your mouth. I take my time over the ice cream and sometimes when Faith is in a hurry for her hair washing performance, I get a lecture on being as slow as a snail. I get afraid that she will find another shampoo shopper because then I will have to go without my Walls and where will I be then!

We live in Parkhurst now because Faith has finished school and Sally and Monica have nearly finished. My father is still in Botswana in our village with his two stores. We go there during the school holidays. I long for the smell of dung and the soft feel of the sand. I do not feel at home here. I hate going to the convent school. I think city people are strange and very different. They get into their very best clothes to go to town. They spend hours making sure their stocking seams are straight and they spend hours making up their faces with all sorts of eye shadow, foundation powders and lipsticks. You can often see the line where the foundation power stops and their necks look separated from their faces. I often laugh to myself about how so many city people look like over-ripe fruits on sticks. Sometimes I want to use my ice cream stick to scrape off the powder that gathers in the sweat lines of their necks. I am sure all that stuff spoils the taste for their food because it gets mixed up with the lipstick. They can't even cry in peace because their thick mascara that they brush onto their eye lashes runs down their cheeks and makes them look like Tickey the Clown. I expect their eyelids to make a clanking sound when they close their eyes because the mascara is sometimes so thick.

Faith likes to have things perfect; her cupboards and drawers, her clothes and herself. She says she gets the utter hell in with the fact that you can't keep anything private in our house. It's a bloody free for all just to use the bathroom and get your fare share of bath time. She says there is no reward for being the eldest. You get taken advantage of. Dorry tells her to pull her mouth straight and not to be so discontented with everything and everyone. Faith works for lawyers. She is a legal secretary and can type and write shorthand so fast you can never tell where she is in a sentence. I am sure she is a perfect secretary.

On Saturdays Faith takes me to the Odeon to see a film. The Odeon is in Oxford Street and first we go for a milkshake at the Oxford Café. I love being alone with her. I feel like her special little sister and we talk about all sorts of things that she doesn't think to say at home. On Sundays in the winter Faith plays hockey at the Wanderers Club. She is in their team and is the centre forward. She wears her long red coat to Mass and buttons it up so that nobody can see she is going to Mass in sports clothes. I go and watch her play. I am fascinated by how quickly she can say 'bully one, bully two, bully three'. She clashes her stick with the other player and she usually gets the ball out for her team. I know that when I am in standard six, I am going to play hockey like Faith. I get tired on the way to the bus after the hockey or after the film because Faith does not walk anywhere; she runs. She denies this and tells me she is walking but I can't ever keep up so I have to run everywhere with her. Faith is also very good at tennis. She was the school champion and her coach said she should join a tennis club and get a bursary to train professionally. Dorry and my father did not know that our village is listed as a legal club so Faith never got the bursary and never became a Wimbledon champion.

I have also started playing tennis at school and my coach says that I will get very far because I am playing like a much older person already. She says I have the right style for professional tennis and that I should talk to my parents and get special coaching. I am not going to be a tennis star; I have always been very sure that I am going to be a saint and a nun, because my father needs to get to heaven and we need at least one nun in our family. I don't know where Faith gets all her energy. Apart from running everywhere she starts up in the mornings with her trampoline routine. She begins by throwing the blankets off to one side and then lies on her back and bounces until there is enough momentum to give her a trampoline lift off. She somehow lands on her feet and then rushes to the bathroom. When she gets home from work, she runs along the passage to her room and puts her handbag away. She changes into her slippers while she tells whoever will listen that her feet are killing her. She then runs back down the passage and swings around one of the pillars that holds up our lounge. Once she has swung herself and aimed at the right chair she lets the pillar go and flings herself into it. Then there is a wriggling ceremony until the cushion and the chair are just perfect for her and she can begin the evening by telling her news and listening to everyone else as well. Once Faith missed the pillar and landed flat on her stomach in the middle of the lounge. Dorry came running in panic because of the loud cracking sound of the fall. She shouted, "Ye gods, man, what is going on in this house?" Fay was so shocked that it took a full few seconds for her to understand what had happened. There was no stopping the hysteria after that. We still laugh about the fallen acrobat to this day.

Dorry says she doesn't know what she would do without Faith's generosity. My father never sends any money for the rent or for our keep. Faith gives Dorry almost all of her salary for the house. Dorry works too. She gets up at five in the morning and makes sandwiches for the eight of us. We have a choice between fish paste, tomatoes and lettuce, or jam. Sometimes at the end of the month Dorry buys ham or beef and we all choose that. I have mine with hot mustard. My friends at school think I am brave to have hot English mustard on my sandwiches. Sometimes when Dorry is in a hurry I get ashamed to take out my lunch at break time because the slices are thick and then thin and they look like doorsteps that have gone wrong. I try to sit alone with them or I tell my friends that I have to go and see Dorothy before I join in the games.

We play rounders. I love batting or bowling but I hate just standing around in the field in case a ball comes my way. My friends tell me that I am a special person. They say I am holy because I go to Mass every morning and get up at half past five and then walk from Parkhurst to Rosebank. They don't know that I have to be so holy because my father wants to get to heaven without going to purgatory. In any case I love to go to Mass. It is the time when I am alone with Jesus and the time that I know for sure that Jesus is with me because he comes into my heart when I receive communion. I do not know how this happens. Dorry says it is a mystery. I know that it is a true mystery. Sometimes I play priest, priest and Mass, Mass in the back yard. I put a towel around my waist and another one around my head. I tie my gym girdle around my waist. Sometimes I also put my netball team bib over the whole outfit because it looks a bit like the robes the priest wears. I do not know the words that the priest says when the bread changes into Jesus so I just make them up. I cut out round pieces of cardboard and I use a wine glass for the chalice. Trisha and Kate become the congregation and Trisha pretends that Kate is very small and so klaps her every now and again for talking in Mass. Kate complains and says she won't play Mass, Mass again with us. I bribe her into it every time because I say that when I have had my turn being the priest and giving the people communion, she can take my place and I will be the baby who needs klapping. She always believes me but I cheat her in the end because I say she will have to wait until the next day because we are not allowed to take communion twice a day. She cries with fury but I never give in because I feel that being the priest is my job, not hers. I am the one who is going to be a nun and a saint. Trisha says saints do not tell lies and make their little sisters cry. I keep quiet but I do not change the game. I know that I will have to tell the priest next time I go to confession. I am hoping that telling lies is a venial sin and not a mortal sin. I do not think you can be a saint if you commit mortal sins. I know that saints are very upset when they commit venial sins. I am very upset.

Dorry says Faith has the Royal Rose mouth and nose. Her nose is not as big as my father's. Her mouth has thin lips and her cheeks are dimpled. She has hazel eyes and long, black eye lashes. Her skin is smooth and creamy except when she is having an 'Aunt Jane'. 'Aunt Jane' is when women bleed for five or seven days. It is so that they can have babies. I am not sure why they have to bleed and be so uncomfortable and get pimples to have babies. Dorry doesn't tell us younger ones the reasons. She says it's about the birds and the bees and we will know it all when we are older. I have to go to Tony's for little bricks of yeast instead of Drene when Faith gets 'Aunt Jane' because then her skin breaks out in red pimples and she has a fit in front of the mirror. She eats the yeast raw because she says it purifies the blood and gets rid of the pimples. I believe it too because in a day or two they fade and then go away. In fact almost everything goes wrong when 'Aunt Jane' comes to visit. Faith gets out of her bed in a black mood. She hates her hair, no matter how well it curls into the back of her neck. She throws her hairbrush at the wall and shouts about having to put up with this bloody life. If Dorry is making her a new dress and she has to fit it on so that Dorry can get the seams just right, she shouts about her bloody hollow back and her bloody big bum. She thinks life is a cruel business, out to get her at every turn. Dorry says that discontentment will be the death of her and will make her very unhappy on this earth. I can't understand how Faith gets so mad about her figure. She takes a size thirty-four and has an eighteen inch waist so what more can she need to look perfect? When 'Aunt Jane' has finished paying her very unwelcome visit Faith says she is going to send in a photo of herself for the Miss South Africa competition. She has had one taken at a studio and she looks very beautiful. She says she won't get into a swimming costume for the full-length photo because she has developed hockey legs and hates them too. If I were her bum, or back or legs I would be very insulted.

♥

Falling down into far darkness,
Gazing blank at broken hearts,
My stone soul's gone so far,
Dropped deep, deep, down.
The wells of no recovery
Beckon obscurity like a life
Faltering in spent time's pall.

Labyrinths of persistent pain
Lose my memories of joy;
Bind me to truth that cannot
Murmur in the day
Nor cry in night thoughts
That cloak and seal the miseries past.

Yet in the black mist's swirl,
With no sense of dawn proclaimed,
I come upon your silent Being:
Transcendence, breathing prayer
Into aged resistance.
From love beyond my human dream,
Your twilight eyes find me the way
To pure bright grace
Though love may flounder still.

"So, Bern, after we had been in Parkhurst for a year or so, I went down to see your father. He was getting irregular with the rent and we were struggling. You kids were all in school except for Faith. I think Sally was going into Matric and Monica was in Standard

Nine. Dorothy was in Seven or Eight. May came up from Durban to look after all you kids while I was away. When I came back from Botswana, lo and behold, Monica and Sally had left school, my dear, and they were working and earning money and they thought they were queens, I'm telling you. I was very angry with my sister May for doing that but she said: 'Dorry, what is the use of keeping them in school? They are not doing their work, and they don't do their homework. They don't want to be at school; they want to work'. So I got used to the idea and left it at that, you know. So then I had Faith working, Monica and Sally working. The apprentice pay was very small. Faith's salary wasn't wonderful either. But it was more than theirs was. I know that she used to give me twenty-five pounds a month. Daddy promised that if she paid most of her salary into the home because he found it difficult, he would give her the fare to go overseas with Kay Wright, her best friend and her parents. But when the time came for Faith to book the boat and pay the fare, Daddy never had any money for her, so she wasn't able to go anyway.

Then Flo got ill with asthma and couldn't work any more so she was going to go to Palapye to live with Daddy so that he wouldn't be so alone. She did that. I went to see her off at the station and she cried bitterly because she had to leave all her friends and that. But it was good that she went there. The church was nearby and she was a religious woman. And then Daddy used to come up every three months and see us. Actually he and his brothers got down to drinking and it wasn't very pleasant. I would have rather done without them. They used to fight, Daddy, Willie and Jimmy, like proper hooligans. You children used to be afraid and I felt that I could do without all of them and their bloody drunken nonsense. Willie was always so very drunk and he had this gun he used to wave around and shoot off in the back yard. One couldn't do too much about it in case he really fired at one of us or at Daddy and then there would have been such tragedy. He used to upset our lives regularly. I could never find you, Bern. Where did you get to when the fights were going on?"

My father is here. He has come up from our village and he is sitting in the lounge with my uncle Willie and my uncle Jimmy. They are talking about hunting and properties. Jimmy tells them about the war he was in a long time ago. They do not only talk; they drink and their conversation gets louder and they begin to call each other liars and bastards for some reasons that I do not know. Dorry says, "Now, you brothers, stop this nonsense and give the drinking a rest." They take no notice. I know that I will have a trip to the moon behind the pantry door because Willie takes out his gun and begins to shuffle around with the bullets. He flicks the barrel open like a cowboy and spins the drum around like a happy gambler. His face is red and puffy. His hands look swollen. Jimmy gets up to stop him playing with guns. My father says bliksem se donner se hell don't be a bloody fool, man. Willie says he will do as he likes. My father says not in my house. Willie says you are never in your house; this is Dorry's house. My father gets up to klap him and Jimmy gets up to stop him and I get into the pantry and sit behind the door.

There are no tins of sardines and apricot jam on the moon. The moon dust does not rise like a thin sneeze blanket when Dorry takes out her powder puff. I walk along moon paths that stay hard under my feet. They go nowhere. I wander along in grey light and find that my feet get very heavy. My heart feels tired of worrying about people getting klapped and shot. I see a tunnel ahead and so I go into it. There is silence and emptiness here and a fine black mist that hangs about me. A strange wind whistles and the mist begins to swirl. I feel alone and lost. I feel ashamed of my father and his brothers. I feel afraid for Dorry and my sisters. I go deeper into the tunnel. I tell God to find me here because there is nobody else I can talk to. I tell God I will be a nun and a saint but that I will have to start a new life because saints do not sin and I do because I hate my uncles and I swear. I walk slowly down the tunnel and then there are many winding paths in it. I do not know which one to take. I stay where I am and I suddenly realise that I can see in the dark swirling mist. There is a bright light in the distance. I walk towards it but I never get any nearer. The light keeps its distance. It beckons me on and I do not feel afraid and alone any more. I see in my mind the rising sun, a new day and a new life where there are no gunshots, no shouting and no need to hide behind pantry doors.

My Uncle Willie is in the back yard. I hear his voice slurring and swearing. He fires his gun and it echoes in my head. My father shouts "bloody donner se bastard se hell". Dorry is saying, "Give that thing to me before you kill somebody."

Willie says, "Come and take it from me, Dorry, come and help me!" My father says "leave him alone, Lovey". I say "God please help us all". Jimmy says nothing. I do not know where my sisters have gone. I get back on the moon but there is no comfort in going there. I know that from today I will never go to the moon again. I will stay on the earth and listen. I will wait until the words stop and there is peace again. I will wait until my stomach stops swirling like the black mist. I will go quietly from behind this door and find my sisters. I will tell them that I did not know where they were. Dorry says, "Here I am, Willie, now give me that gun!" Willie begins to sob and says that he is sorry. My father says "it is okay, boet". I sit behind the pantry door and watch the tins of apricot jam and think of the sardines that were once in the sea, free and easy. I think that my mind is in a sardine tin in my home in Parkhurst. I long for the sound of the bush and the birds and the San music that whistles through my bicycle wheels when I ride along the bush paths. I stay here in the pantry until Willie and Jimmy go home. My father and Dorry are sitting in the lounge when I feel safe again. My father's head is bent and he is half asleep. Dorry says, "Go to bed, Hugh. You have had enough for one day." I say in my head that I have had enough for one day too. I hear Tex's motorbike rev on the pavement and Monica comes into the lounge. She says she had a 'joll' and where is everyone? Dorothy comes out of her bedroom and says nothing. Dorry says Faith and Sally have gone out with Pat and Ivan. Trish is down the road with Kate at her friend's house. She looks at me and says, "And where have you been?"

I say, "I went to see the man in the moon."

She says, "Don't be cheeky to me do you hear?"

My father says, "These bloody kids need a hiding!" I say nothing. I feel ashamed and alone but I do not go back to the moon. I sit in the lounge with Dorry and I watch my father's head droop lower and lower until he begins to snore in his chair. I bend my head too and I feel as if I am falling down into far darkness.

♥

"THEN Daddy decided that he wouldn't send any maintenance at all. He used to send something every month but then said I would have to find everything but the rent. I had all the seven children to feed and all the friends used to come for tea or lunch. It wasn't easy to cope, you know, Bern. We were reduced to having mostly mincemeat. We learned to cook it in many different ways and so on. Daddy came up once and said to Mary, our housekeeper, that he didn't want mincemeat that night for dinner; he wanted steak. Mary told him off and said that if he could afford steak then he should go and buy it. She told him that the Madam couldn't afford to buy any steak because she doesn't get any money from him. The family never eat steak. They live on mincemeat. That night when I came home from work there was steak for supper. Your father went and bought it. He couldn't cope with Mary's confrontation. He had expected Mary to go and buy steak from the housekeeping money. Things went on for a while. He would come and visit us every three months for a while.

After a time I noticed that I was getting a discharge and the doctor told me that it was a venereal disease that is passed on from a man but that the man has no symptoms. It is nothing to worry about, just not very pleasant. I wasn't going out with anyone at the time but I just sort of brushed it off and didn't really realise that it could be from Daddy at all. And then one time he came up and he had not even gone back to Bots yet and straight after being in bed with him I got such a bad itch. It was terrible and he left to go back home. The itch got worse and worse. I got all swollen and everything. I went to work anyway because he wouldn't pay maintenance and I began to haemorrhage quite badly. I got the doctor. I had a haemorrhaging ulcer. I had to go to hospital and have an operation. In the meantime Daddy was carrying on with black women, which I had no inkling about at all. Later on I got rumours. Auntie Helen said to me that her servant Joseph, he was a very good servant, had gone home for his holidays and he came back with the tale that there was very big talk among the villagers that Daddy had had a child with the maid. I didn't really believe it. I didn't take notice and I never connected it with any of the symptoms I had had, neither with the ulcer. That was the beginning of all my personal problems. I went to Palapye for my holidays. I had to go home with the kids. Alan, your cousin, came and stayed at the house with the big girls to make sure they were safe. I took you little ones with me. I never heard anything down there. You know the wife is the last one to be told. Eventually I decided that I would have to go back to Palapye and stay there. The girls had got married. First Sally was going out with Pat and then fell pregnant. What a hell of a thing that was Bern, you never heard such a fuss and row. Daddy was full of hooey over it. I got a terrible shock just before the wedding as well. What a mess! I will tell you about it after we have our tea!"

SALLY is going to marry Pat. That is what she has been saying every day for a long time now. Pat comes to see her every evening and he stays until late and sometimes only goes home after midnight. She says she loves him and he looks like Van Johnston, the film star. Before they go out in Pat's black car, she ruffles his brown, wavy hair and makes a kiss curl on his forehead like Van Johnston's and says he is 'divine and mine!' I think Pat likes looking like Van Johnston and likes being divine and mine. He opens the car door for Sally and she swishes her skirt before she gets in. Pat has asked my father for Sally's hand in marriage and he says yes, they can marry but when the cows come home. Dorry says my father is looking for trouble and that people have ways and means of making the cows come home early. Sally says she is tired of waiting for those cows and will make things happen very soon. Monica says Sally will be up the spout in no time at all and good for her, with a father like ours. Faith says nothing and Dotty says nothing and I wonder what they are talking about but nobody will tell me. When I walk down the road with Dotty I hold her pinkie and ask her about being up the spout. She says it's what people do when they get married. When I ask Monica what it means she says people have a ball in the back of a car and land up leaning over the toilet heaving their heads off every morning when they begin to think everything is okay. When I ask Dorry she says Monica is full of bull but she thinks it means being pregnant and starting to grow a baby. She says people are supposed to do that when they are married but some people will be far too old to have children if my father carries on forever making people wait until the cows come home. I think things are getting tense and tricky and I am not feeling safe. I feel angry about all the roads that are leading to trouble in our house. I think that I have never been happy here in the straight line city with hard pavements, a hard life. I think that I will never sit in the hen hok with my father and put the fowls to sleep.

Dorry is worried and has been shaking her head a lot. She says she will have to tell my father to come and visit because Pat and Sally have done it! Sally is pregnant. She says, "I just don't know, man!" Monica says she has been telling us that for ages and she told us Sally would be up the spout soon because of the cows never coming home. Dorry says it is not a joke and that all hell will break loose when my father hears about this. My father says he is not coming to visit us. He says he is too busy and the shop is not doing well so he cannot just up and leave things with Aunt Flo. She is staying with him now because she has no husband and nobody to care for her and she has asthma. She is never well. She smokes like an on-going chimney. She lights one from the next and only stops when she is eating and then as soon as she has swallowed her last mouthful of food she fiddles for her lighter and starts the smoke trail again. She coughs in between the smoking and spits into a handkerchief. She puts out her cigarettes in her cup of cold tea or if she is busy drinking the tea she uses the saucer with a little cold tea in it. She wheezes when she talks and cannot walk fast because she loses her breath. My father says she has asthma but will die of emphysema first because she will never listen and never give up the smoking. My father lights up his own cigarettes every few minutes too so he is talking to fresh air and not listening to himself. I do not like Aunt Flo because she makes us darn socks on holiday. Dorry sometimes sends us to my father for the school holidays. Aunt Flo says busy hands keep out of mischief. She thinks darning socks is fun. She blames Trisha for her hens escaping out of the chicken hok and Trisha cries because she has not touched the chickens or the hok. She says I am very cheeky and she will tell my father what a little devil I am because I have told her not to shout at Trisha for nothing and that her hens found the hole in the hok themselves. She has not told my father anything about that. I get a bit nervous before supper when she tells my father what has been happening during the day.

I go to bed relieved about my father's not knowing that I told Aunty Flo off.

On the phone Dorry says that my father is making excuses for not coming up. Flo is a very good shopkeeper and he is being difficult. He says he will come up next week. It is next week and he is not up. Dorry is shaking her head more and more and is taking time off work. She says she will get Pat and Sally to drive her to the Border and meet my father there and tell him what is what. I am pleased that he is not here because I think there will be a great deal of shouting and trouble because people are not supposed to have babies before they are married. Dorry says people will count the months and know what Pat and Sally have been up to because the baby will be born before nine months. She says they had better get married in a big hurry so that they can say the baby is premature. I get ashamed because Sister Magdalene will know and she will tell the other nuns and they will ask me for dates of birth and marriage. They might say that nothing good comes from people who become hairdressers.

When my father does come and see us he grumbles because we have mincemeat every night and he says where is the steak? Dorry says where is the money? He keeps quiet and when Dorry is at work he asks Mary, our housemaid, to get steak but she says no because she only has enough money from Dorry for mincemeat. He gives her money and when Dorry comes home there is steak for supper but she does not say thanks, she just says, "Oh, there is steak tonight; perhaps we have royal visitors!" My father goes red and says nothing but my mouth still gets dry because I think they will start up a fight at the table and the steak is looking good and getting cold. Perhaps I will have to leave the table and hide while the fireworks go on. Monica always has something to say when they are firing up for a fight. She tells them to stop the nonsense and my father says he will box her ears as well. Dorry says she will break my father's bloody neck. Everyone goes quiet because everyone has been looking at steak for some time and cannot resist any longer. My father stops the fighting possibility by making the sign of the cross to begin the grace. Our signs of the cross are very hurried and slap-dash. Sister Imelda would lift her eyes to heaven and ask God to forgive us all for the lack of care and appreciation. In my head I tell God that I will try to be a saint when the steak is finished and that even saints gobble sometimes.

When my father is visiting, we are not allowed to go into Dorry's bedroom at night. She says my father needs his beauty sleep and has travelled a long way in his car that so often gives trouble. He has to fix it every five minutes and has a boot full of wires and a few spare parts in case he breaks down in the bush and cannot get to a garage. His car engine often boils and he has to get a heavy cloth and press onto the radiator cap and jump back when it pops off and shoots up steam like a volcano that I have seen in the bioscope. He says shit and bliksem and bloody rattle trap. Sometimes when he comes to visit it is nearly our holiday time and we travel in the car with him. I think that I am on the moon all the way because I get very afraid of the swerving in the thick sand and the swerving to miss goats and cattle that suddenly rush out of the bush. If we have car trouble then we have to carry on the journey after dark and my father says God help the rabbits and bokkies that stand in the road and stare into the headlights because they are blinded and do not know where to run. Sometimes there is a flock of guinea fowl in the middle of the road. They do not seem to hear the car's rush and drone. My father does not slow down; he puts his foot down and the car rocks and the guinea fowl suddenly lie dead in the road. He says it saves shooting and is a good supper waiting. The car then smells of dead birds and feathers. He puts them on the floor in the back. I have to open my window wide and stick out my head so that my face and hair become the road's colour. Monica says Dorry cannot pull the wool over our eyes and we all know very well why we are not allowed to be in Dorry's bedroom after dark. She says there is nookie-pookie going on and she was not born yesterday. My father says he will donner her. Dorry laughs and says she is looking for it. I have to share a bed with Trish, and Kate has to share a bed with one of my other sisters.

After my father's visit Dorry goes to the doctor because she says she has an infection. She does not know what it is from. She has to go to hospital for an operation. Nobody tells me why. After a while at home she gets better and goes back to work. That is another reason why I am glad my father is not coming to hear what is what about Pat and Sally. Perhaps Dorry will get sick again. Dorry cries when she gets sick and she swears a lot. When she has to stay home from work she gets worried about her pay. She says we will be down to beans on toast. I like beans on toast but not every night because they make you fart and you get shy because you can't help it and it happens in front of everyone. Sometimes people fart in class and we put our hands over our noses while we finish our sums. Sister Gertrude's nose twitches and she takes out her handkerchief and pretends to blow her nose. Sometimes she goes to the vase of roses in front of Our Lady and rearranges them to wave their scent around a bit.

Dorry, Pat and Sally are leaving today. Dorry is taking Kate with her. I am glad that I am not Kate because I am afraid of all the trouble that is going to come because of Sally's wedding. They are going to arrive at the Border at the same time as my father to ask if Pat can marry Sally even if the cows are not home. Dorry says we must pray that he does not get into a rage. I think she is afraid but brave. I pray for Dorry, Sally and Pat every five minutes. I tell God I will be extra good if he makes my father calm about the wedding and if he stops my father from shouting and doing general harm to everyone.

I am running down the road that leads to the river. I have on my takkies and my red shorts and white blouse. I take my school case with me but there are no books in it. It has my clean clothes and wash things in it. I am going to the Gunnings' house in Victory Park. They live on a large plot and have a dairy. Elizabeth is my friend and I am often running down the road because I often stay with Elizabeth at the weekends. Mrs Gunning is a lovely person and she is kind to me. Mr Gunning plays rugby and has a bald head. He says it is good that way because blokes cannot pull his hair in the scrums and rucks. We all go and watch him play and he comes to tell us what is going on at half time. Mrs Gunning gives him extra orange juice. He gets upset when his team is losing and says that the other side are bloody hairy buggers. He is a tall and muscular man and he carries Judy, Elizabeth's little sister, on his shoulders. He plays rugby in the garden with Dickey, who is the youngest. Elizabeth is not Mr Gunning's daughter. Her father is Mr Featherstone. She loves Mr Gunning and their family is happy. We play on the mule carts and feed the mules in the stables.

They do the milk rounds very early in the morning. Sometimes, if Mrs Gunning is not at home, Elizabeth and I take care of the dairy and when someone rings the bell for service we go and fill up their milk cans or give them bottles that have been on the milk feeding machine and have been sealed. If there are no full bottles, we fill them and use the machine to seal the tops. I love the dairy and the farm smell and the mules. They remind me of the bush and the village. Sometimes Mr Gunning takes us to the dairy farm in Little Falls. He shows us all the milk cows and tells us how to check that they are all healthy. He has a very noisy machine that chops up cattle feed and we jump into the pit and get pelted by shooting mealie stalks and pretend we are in a storm. Sometimes we cannot jump into the feed pit because the machine mixes molasses into the chopped food because the cattle need it for their coats and to make them produce more milk. The cows stand in rows in big barns and they are attached to milking machines so that the milk stays clean and pure. In Victory Park the milk is bottled and the cream is separated. Elizabeth knows I love cream and she gives me a whole container when it is time for me to go back home. I drink the cream on the way and I walk home the long way so that I have finished the cream before I have to share it.

Early in the morning all of us go into the dairy field and pick black mushrooms. We know how to tell the real ones because Mrs Gunning has taught us which ones are poisonous. If we find a mushroom that we are not sure of, we do not pick it. When we have a small basketful, we go to Mrs Gunning in the kitchen and she washes the mushrooms and cooks them with eggs and bacon for our breakfast. Sometimes I only have mushrooms on toast and I have cornflakes and cream instead of bacon and eggs. Mrs Gunning makes sure we have fruit salad or paw-paw as well. She says we need healthy foods so that we become good, strong girls. I say thank you and I tell her that I am going to be the best tennis player in our school. Elizabeth is in the netball team with me. She does not like going to the convent so much because she is not a Catholic and she does not understand the Mass and she says it is boring. Mrs Gunning says she goes to the convent because she needs discipline and nuns have that in good measure. Elizabeth rolls her eyes to heaven as though she is a suffering saint.

The Gunnings have a very untidy house. Mr Gunning says it is a home not a house and a happy one where people can be themselves and so what if there are unmade beds and cushions lying crookedly all over the furniture. The bathroom is the most untidy place because the towels lie in heaps on the floor and nobody picks them up. I do and I hang them in neat rows along the towel racks but it does not take long before they are all on the floor again. Mr Gunning says you can't teach old dogs new tricks. I do not know what that means and he says it is an idiom and I don't know what that means either. He says just leave the towels to their fate on the floor.

On Sundays the Gunnings do not get up early and so Judy and Elizabeth and I read stories in our beds before the others wake up. When we hear Dickey and Mrs Gunning talking in their bedroom, we all go and jump on the big bed and Mr Gunning says, "God, is there no peace for a battle worn rugby player?"

We say, "No!" Judy sits on his knees and he suddenly straightens them and she falls flat on the bed. We laugh and screech. We have to fetch the Sunday papers from the post box outside the gate and by the time we get dressed and have breakfast, the room is full of strewn news as well.

I am glad that I am at the Gunnings and not at home because Dorry is not there. I am worried about my father's temper and worried about Dorry and Sally and Pat. I do not know what will happen when my father finds out that Sally is going to have a baby. I do not tell Mrs Gunning about it either. I keep it locked up in my head and when it wants to come out I visit the moon very quickly. I sit by a moon pool and watch the very still water and think that my father will never be still and quiet. He will always lose his temper and shout and thrash and break things or take out the gun and look for bullets. I wish that we could live as happily as the Gunnings. I wish I could be adopted by them and never have to go home and wait for the sight of my father's car parking on the pavement. When his car door opens it is like the opening of a big secret box that may have horrible things in it or it may have presents in it. I never know and while I wait to find out I feel sick and afraid. Sometimes Dorry says, "Here is trouble again!" She smiles when she says that but I believe her. I feel that my father has lost us and he has become somebody strange. When he walks to the gate I get ashamed of his dusty clothes and his dirty hat. He looks like a misfit in the city. He talks like a stranger in our house. There is no warmth and no stories about the withaak and the leopard. There is just the waiting for a fight or no fight. I cannot go to the Gunnings when he is with us because he will get angry and say we do not care about him and we run away when he has come all the way to see us. He does not really see us. He sits in the chair and drinks whiskey and sees nothing but trouble. He sometimes goes into town and sees the trader wholesalers about his shop goods and when he comes back he curses them and their hard bloody line about credit. He says they are all 'bloody donders and bastards'. Dorry says he is not a businessman and that since we have come to the city things have gone down and he is going from bad to worse because he does not know what stock to order and he orders too much of the same thing and too little of the stuff that people really need. If she offers to have a shop talk with him, he says he is the boss of his own shop and thank you for no interference. Dorry says voetsak then, and get the hell back to the shop and ruination. He keeps quiet and the silence stretches into nervous moon mountains that are waiting for me to climb them.

I am walking home with my container of cream. I stop at the river's bridge to take a sip. I feel the rich flow down my throat like soothing silk. I take my time because I do not want to share my cream with anyone. I think Dorry will be home and she will be upset or cheerful. I do not know which.

♥

"So Bern, of course your father blamed me for Sally's pregnancy. He reckoned that I dragged the kids up from the gutter and that was why they did things like get pregnant before they were married. We went to the priest but then had to go and get permission from Daddy. He took so long to say that he would come up to us. He would say this week and next week and never come so we got in the car and met him at the Border. I went and got into his car and Pat and Sally stayed in theirs. I took Cathy with me and Daddy asked why there was such a rush for the wedding. I told him Sally was pregnant. Ye gods, man! There was such a lot of hooey! There were oxen in the road and Daddy was so wild he started up the car and drove full force into them. He was shouting, 'Get out of the way, you bloody bastards!' He was so angry! I don't know how he never hit the cattle and the car and wrote us all off. I told him not to take it out on the poor cattle and just to accept things as they are. He banged his fists on the steering wheel and kept raging. I just sat there and let him have his say because nothing was going to change. I can't remember what else he called everything and everybody. Anyhow, it was all settled and he gave permission for his own good, too, I suppose. He would have hated his brothers and sisters to know. He was such a proud man, Bern. When we came back, I went to Father Bannon to get things arranged. Father said to me, 'But what about Faith?'

I said, 'Oh Father, she is going out with a man by the name of Bernard, and Hugh said they can't get married until February. He hasn't got enough money until then.'

Father said, 'But what if I told you they got married last Saturday?'

I said 'Oh Father, please don't tell me that!' I was struck silent, you know. I just couldn't speak, you know. He said, yes, they got married at the cathedral. Before I went to meet your father, I was looking for Sally's birth certificate and I gave Faith hers too and told her to take responsibility for it now that she was twenty-one and an adult. So she and Bernard went off to the cathedral. She had her certificates to say she was over twenty-one so there was no permission needed. They just got married. They told me nothing about it. They still lived separately so that we would not know anything. So Faith was going to be bridesmaid to Sally and I was still to run up a dress for her. Sally had a lovely dress that I had made for her to go to a party in. We were just going to use that. So I went to Faith and I said, 'So, Faith, I believe you are married.'

She said, 'Yes mommy, but I am not living with Bernard at the moment. I am waiting until Sally's wedding is over and we are having a reception after that.' I said that there was no need to wait. I said if she was already married; why not live with her husband now? I did not dream I was pushing her into a nasty marriage. She stayed home for a while and then eventually went to live with Bernard in Pretoria.

Pat decided to pay for a new wedding dress. It was beautiful and fitted Sally like a glove. Dorothy had to be bridesmaid because Faith was now married. Wendy Anderson's mother made a beautiful cake and decorated it with roses and butterflies. I got Aunt May up from Durban and she did the whole reception; baked and made trifle like you would not believe. Fred and his wife came to take Sally to the church in their beautiful Plymouth. I stayed with Fred and Lilly when I ran away from home so they were more than old friends; they are like family to me. Of course Daddy came to the wedding, Bern, and I dared not tell him about Faith and Bernard. He would have gone mad. Actually he did go mad! The wedding reception was lovely and then after the wedding, it was a Sunday, your father found out about Faith. Faith had gone home to Pretoria with Bernard, unbeknown to your father. Before they arrived back the next day to spend the Sunday with us, Auntie May told him. He went mad! He was going to kill Bernard. He got out a kitchen knife and got ready to do just that. I had to send one of the kids to the bus stop to warn Faith and Bernard not to come to the house because Daddy was going to kill Bernard. He would have, you know Bern. They went back up the road as soon as they got off the bus. Your father couldn't get his hands on them. He cursed them and threw Faith's sewing machine, that she had bought as part of her trousseau, down the steps into the back yard. Ye gods, what a business, I am telling you! He did not see Faith for years after that."

Iᴛ is Sally's wedding day. My father has come and he has on a new blue suit and new brown shoes. He has a new white shirt and a flower in his pin hole. Dorry has on a new dress and gloves and a hat. She looks beautiful. Dotty is Sally's bridesmaid and she is wearing a dress that goes below her knees and halfway to her ankles. She also has on a hat and looks lovely. Dorry has made Trish, Kate and me new dresses. Mine is a candy striped shirt-waister. Faith and Monica have bought their own new dresses. Sally is in her wedding dress. It is pure white and has a train down the back. Dotty will hold the train when she walks down the aisle. My father will have Sally on his arm and then give her to Pat when they get to the front of the church. I am going to sing in the choir at the wedding Mass and Sister De Padua is going to play the organ. We are going to sing Sally's favourite hymn: 'Ave Maria' when she and Pat have said their vows. My Aunt May has come up from Durban and has made many tasty things to eat. She has prepared the lounge with long tables and we will all sit at the decorated tables and have a meal and then trifle. I had to get the cream from Mrs Gunning and not drink any on the way home. Dorry says May's trifles are the best in the world. Dorry says we have to behave very well because Father Bannon is coming to share the meal with us. He will sit between my father and Dorry. My father will behave as well. He will not get drunk in front of the priest. Aunty May says she has arranged things that way.

We are all sitting at the table and Pat and my father have made speeches about being married and Pat said that he will look after Sally and that my father need not worry, he will be a good son-in-law. We all clap and have a small glass of champagne. We stand and say, "To Sally and Pat; to Mr and Mrs Madden!" Faith is sitting next to her boyfriend, Bernard, and they are very quiet and Dorry looks worried. She is not talking very much. I do not know why I am feeling afraid. Perhaps Dorry is nervous in case my father drinks too much and Father Bannon notices. I hear Aunty May tell Dorry not to worry; she will tell my father after the wedding. I am feeling more afraid because Dorry is shaking her head and whispering but I do not know what she is saying. I ask Dotty what is going on and she says I will find out in good time and just enjoy the trifle and the fresh cream.

When the meal is finished, we say grace and thank Aunty May for the meal and Dorry for our dresses. Sally and Pat leave us and they go away in Pat's car for a honeymoon weekend. Faith and Bernard are also going somewhere and they leave too. After they have left my father takes off his suit and says he will never wear another suit until the cows come home. Aunty May says, "Just as well that Faith and Bernard are married already and you will not have to go through that purgatory again until Monica comes along for a wedding." Dorry turns pale and we all stand and stare because we cannot believe what Aunt May has said.

My father is as white as a sheet. Aunty May is saying that he had better calm down and that there is nothing anyone can do about the facts. My father picks up a glass and throws it against the wall. He shouts at Dorry and tells her that she has dragged his kids up in the gutter. He tells her that she is a bloody bitch and that she belongs in the gutter with her kids. He says he curses Faith and her bloody bastard husband and that he will never speak to her again. If she lands up with a bastard who is not good to her she must never come running back to him because he will never answer the door to her again. He says may her marriage be cursed and may the devil look after them both. He goes into Faith's room and takes her sewing machine out of her cupboard and he lifts it up above his head and throws it down the back steps. He bought the machine for her when Faith turned twenty-one. Dorry is crying and shouting at my father and I am running down the road to the river because I do not want to hear any more curses and I do not want to hear my father nor see Dorry weep.

When I have sat at the river for some time I come home again. There is no more shouting. My father is sleeping and snoring and Dorry is helping with the dish washing. Monica is playing the hi-fi that Pat built in the back room and Dotty is drying the dishes. I go and stand close to Dorry and she puts her arm around me and says, "Ye gods, man, the world nearly ended on a wedding day! What have you done to your new dress? It is full of mud. Go and change now and come and help us here."

It is Sunday and my father is sitting in the lounge with a kitchen carving knife in his hand. He says this is the day that he will kill Bernard. He will carve him up for marrying Faith without permission. He swears and swears and Dorry tells him that he had better stop carrying on but he does not listen. Dorry says she has visited one Flattery in jail and she will not be doing that again. She says Willie is a criminal and we do not need another one. Willie sells property to people when he is drunk and keeps their deposit and he never sees them again. The properties he sells are not for sale. I think of Bernard being stabbed to death and of Faith and I get very scared because Dorry says my father is not joking and that he will really do something terrible. She calls Dotty at ten o'clock and says she must take me with her to the bus stop because Faith and Bernard are coming to have lunch here with my father and to speak to him about their marriage. They are going to tell him that they were not prepared to keep begging and keep hearing that they can marry when the cows come home. They are going to say that they are not children and are over twenty-one and that he cannot play games with them any more. Dorry says perhaps my father would not be so very angry if he trusted Bernard but he says Bernard is no good and will never be a kind, faithful husband. Dorry says no men are ever any good for his girls and that you would think he owns them even though they are grown ups. I like Bernard because he plays tennis with me and Faith. He sits and plans his life with Faith in the lounge and we are allowed to hear all about their future budget and how he will build or buy a house and what he will save as well. He works at the hardware shop in our street. He says he was a farm manager in Rhodesia but his mother and his sister told him that he had to be a vet and they sent him to university. He hated it so he left and came to Johannesburg and did nothing for a while and then got this job as a manager. He says he wants to be a farmer in Rhodesia when he has saved enough money to buy a farm.

Dotty and I are walking to the bus stop. Dotty gives me her pinkie and she is silent and walks with heavy feet. I do not talk either. I think of all the things my father has said and I think of the carving knife. I think that life will never be the same again with two of my sisters married so suddenly and I long for my father to go back to our village and come back only when he has forgiven Faith. When the bus comes and Faith and Bernard get off, Dotty tells them what my father has done to her sewing machine and that he has the carving knife waiting for Bernard. Bernard wants to come and talk to my father anyway. He says he is not afraid of an old man. Faith says he does not know how my father can be and they cross the road to the other side and we wait for the bus to return. We wait with them and wave goodbye. My heart feels as heavy as the moon that cannot be lifted into the sky. It hangs around my feet and it takes a long time for us to walk home again and listen to my father swearing with the carving knife next to him. I think that going to school is better than having weddings.

♥

Tree tears
Turn to crystals
In the winter's morning light.
How rich the heart that weeps
In the troubled soul's dark night.

TODAY is the 20th of June. I am at school but I cannot concentrate. Sally is in hospital having her baby. She has been in hospital since yesterday but the baby does not come. Dorry says labour can take time and it is no joke. She says Sally is in good hands at the Marymount. It is a Catholic hospital and the nuns are good nurses. I am trying to think of Sally on the hospital bed having a baby. I do not know how women can be in such pain and still smile when their babies eventually pop out. Sometimes I see babies being born in films at the bioscope. They scream and sweat and then give a loud cry before the baby comes into the world. The doctors hold them up by the feet until they begin to cry. The mothers smile and laugh. Dorry says women forget the pain of the birth and are very happy to see their little treasures. Sally went for a drive with Pat and he took her on a bumpy road and when she got back she broke her water. I was talking to Elizabeth on the telephone and Sally ran past me into her room calling for Dorry. Dorry came to tell me to get off the phone. She phoned the doctor and then Pat took Sally to the hospital. Dorry says she comforted her on the way because Sally was afraid. She has never had babies before and the first one is always the most difficult experience.

It is lunch time. The angelus bell has just finished ringing and I have said mine twice, especially the beginning part where the angel tells Mary she will conceive by the Holy Ghost. I said it once for the new baby and once for Sally. I see Sister Magdalene coming towards me. She stops and then beckons that I should go to her. My best friend Anne is with me and we run. Sister Magdalene tells me that Sally has had a son. She says that the mother and baby are well although it was a long labour. I thank her for the message. Before she walks away she says it is only eight months since Sally and Pat got married. I say it is because the baby is premature but I know that my face has turned red and I know that I do not like Sister Magdalene.

Sally does not work these days. She sits and reads love stories while Dougie crawls all over the floor. He sits in his pram or sits on the floor. Sally puts lounge cushions all around him so that he cannot fall over. When we get home from school, the floor is full of wet nappies and bits of Marie biscuits. Sally says she will kill six birds with one stone by paying us to pick up everything and sweep up the crumbs. She says Mary has enough to do without running after her baby. Dorry says Sally is downright lazy and should do things herself. Sally says there is cheap labour around and why should she when Dougie is very happy crawling and sitting and sucking his Marie biscuits. Sometimes the cheap labour reward themselves with a Marie or two. We sit on the front stoep and chew the edges carefully so that the biscuits become faces with hair fashions around them. We give them names and tell their stories. Sometimes we take Dougie for a walk down the road with the cheap labour money in our pockets and we buy Walls ice creams. Sally gives Trish and Kate extra money for scrubbing her back while she sits in a hot bath reading her love stories. Sometimes I take a pumice stone and scrub her feet. Dorry says Sally will die of laziness. We hope she doesn't because we like the proceeds. We love Dougie too. He has very deep blue eyes and blond hair. Dorry calls him 'Dougs Bugs' and says she is her special grandson because he is the first one.

It is past midnight and Dougs Bugs is fast asleep but Sally is upset and worried and is sitting in the lounge with Dorry. Pat has not come home. He has not phoned or sent a message. He just did not arrive after work. Sally is playing sad songs like 'Wedding Bells are Ringing in the Chapel'. The song says that the bells ring for everyone else but not for me. Connie Francis sings the song and her voice sort of cracks when she sings 'never'. Sally sings the song with her. Dorry says she must not worry so much and that everything will be fine again soon. They make cups of coffee. Dorry phones the hospitals and the police to see if she can find out what has happened to Pat. I tell God that I will become a saint as soon as I can if He keeps Pat safe and sound. Sally weeps.

We hear the key trying to find the keyhole. We hear Pat swear because it cannot. Dorry opens it very quickly. She has her slipper in her hand. Pat stumbles into the lounge and Dorry klaps him with her slipper. She shouts at him and tells him that he is a bloody bugger and a no good father to his son. She says she will teach him a thing or two about being a good husband to her daughter as well. She says how dare he treat his wife this way. Pat slurs and wobbles and tells Dorry he is very sorry. He tells her he will never go drinking after work again. Dorry shouts that he had better say sorry to his wife and klaps him a few more times. Sally comes to rescue Pat and shouts at him while she is busy with the rescue. She drags him by the arm to the back room where they sleep. He follows like a bad dog. I hear Sally's lecture drone until the early hours of morning. I think I will have to take a walk on the moon but I fall asleep instead.

It is Saturday morning. Dougs Bugs is crawling and eating Marie biscuits. Pat is sitting listening to another long lecture. He has his head in his hands and I do not think he hears anything except the throb of a hangover. Dorry comes and asks him how he is feeling after a drunken spree and a klap with her slipper. He laughs and says she is a hard mother-in-law but he would not change her for the world. She says he is an Irish charmer and passop! Sally begins to play the piano and I go to Judy's house for a game of tennis with my friends.

♥

THE Train is starting to move. I hear the wheels begin their grind and the coaches lurch forward in the vast sneeze of the engine as it gathers and grinds into an even pull. In my mind I see the driver release the lever, the bright burn of the coal in the furnace and the stoker with his cap and fire protection goggles and gloves. I have often seen inside the engines when they stop at our village to fill their tanks with water. For an instant there flashes the fear of steam valves bursting and spewing into the air and along the tracks where I cross the lines. Dorry is waving and giving me the 'last touch' and the last lecture on behaviour. She tells me not to forget to lock the compartment door, not to loiter in the corridor and not to talk to strangers. She tells me she has asked the conductor to check on me because I am travelling alone. My father knows all the train drivers and all the conductors. We have been travelling along the line to Bechuanaland for many years. They have been checking on us for many years. I have a letter for my father from Dorry. She says he had better bloody well answer and do what she asks or there will be hell to pay. She says with him there is always such a load of hooey. I am afraid of the 'hell to pay' and hooey because I know my father will not answer nor do what she asks. Dorry will shout and call him a bloody swine and bastard and then tears will fill her eyes and she will get a softer voice and shake her head for want of words to comfort her and us. She will become the desert rain that remains inside, under the ground, and does not spill over and water what is above and in need of replenishment. She will sink inside. I am sinking inside.

We have travelled the tangle of lines through the city. I have put my suitcase under the bunk and have settled next to the window. Every so often a train whizzes past and for a moment I am not sure if I am moving forwards or backwards and I am caught in a whirl of sound that rushes me into a frozen world of muddle. Later, there is just the steady clacking of steel wheels on the lines. The gentle rocking and the smell of leather and smoke lull me into a half daze where hard tar and straight streets have no influence and the wind urges the veld to sing its soft songs. The low thorn trees wave in scattered freedom. In my mind I begin to sing of the village, of cattle and of corn.

By the time the sun begins to set we are in the heart of the Groot Marico. I think of my father and of the many tales he has told of the time when Herman Bosman lived with him on his farm. I think how it would be if I were on the wagon of spooks that ate up the cattle-whip and left my father and his friends running through the bush to home. I wonder how the cattle arrived without a herdsman and what awaited them along the moonlit paths that seem to go to nowhere and to come from nowhere. My father says that in those days he was afraid of the dark, especially in the bush, because when he was a small boy and cried in the dark, his father made him sleep on the doorstep outside the farm house so that he would learn to be brave and learn to be a man. I feel sorry for my father when he tells me about the cold, the sounds of night and the dark. I do not understand how children can be grown ups when they are children. My father was also a sickly child and was told that only sissies get sick. Dorry says when she first came with him to our village he was very weak and very thin and often got dizzy. She took him to the doctor, who discovered that he had a tapeworm. Dorry says the worm filled a bucket. My father soon got strong and well again. I never knew my grandfather and I have never seen my grandmother. My father says she was a midwife and was well known for delivering babies in the Groot Marico.

While the train fills up with water at Groot Marico station, I get off and walk along the platform. I go to the station café and buy some koeksisters and sweets. Dorry gave me ten shillings for the journey and I have already eaten her sandwiches and hard-boiled eggs. Later I will order dinner and the steward will bring it to my coupe. I will not have to feel shy or offer some to anybody because I am alone and I do not have to talk to strangers. At seven o'clock the bedding steward will rattle on my door and come and make my bed on the bunk. The sheets are very clean and white. The blankets are royal blue. They have SAR woven into them, in case people want to steal them. Everyone will know that they really belong to the Railways and one would have to sleep with theft on the mind. I love to snuggle up in bed on the train. It rocks me to sleep. The conductor will wake me at six in the morning because we will get into Palapye station at seven and I will be in the village again. I will ride my bicycle through the quiet bush and listen to the birds. I will be at home.

I am not at home in my home. I am ashamed of the shabby furniture, the half dusted tables, the cobwebs in every corner and the stale stoep polish that does not shine. The brass tray that stands so proudly on the dresser is dull and there are patches of green invading it. My father has a long pole leaning against the lounge wall outside. He says the wall will fall down at any time now. He says no amount of patching will save it. If I stand in the doorway, I can see the weeds in the overgrown yard through the crack. My life feels like the wall that cannot be patched. There is a vase of stale water and dead flowers on the windowsill. It stinks. There is a musty smell in every room. It is as though nobody has been living here. When my aunt Flo lived here with my father, she kept everything clean and tidy. She died from smoking. The lion skin rugs puff up dust when I walk over them. I feel dirty and itchy and unwelcome. When I fold down the bed cover, dust rises and I sneeze. I take out the sheets and blankets and hang them on the washing line. I wash the pillowcases and leave the pillows on the cement slab under the syringa tree. I think of my train bed and long to be going back to Parkhurst and the straight-line life. I miss Dorry and my sisters. I am lonely here and my father is like a stranger that I do not know and to whom I cannot speak.

My bicycle tyres are flat and my bicycle is full of dust. It stands forgotten in the shed, which is full of old wood. Rat droppings and fallen dove feathers cover everything. I take my bicycle to the tap and wash it. I oil the wheels and the chain. I pump up the tyres and polish the leather saddle. I raise the saddle to suit my height because I have grown since last I rode and listened to the gentle harmony of the bush. I make sure the spokes are clean and I shine them with 'Silvo'.

I ride around the yard where there is a path among the weeds to see if the tyres will stay pumped. I feel heavy and I want to cry. I think that I have no place that is my home. My father has become a foreigner. He asks questions about Dorry. He wants to know where she goes at the weekends and who visits our house and how long they stay and how often they come. He sneers at her letter and calls her a bloody bitch that wants, wants, and wants. He swears to God that Dorry will get nothing from him. He says she can struggle until the cows come home. I keep quiet. My head wants to grow into a balloon and float to the moon.

There is no sound here, on the moon. There is no bloody this and bloody that. There are no cows that do not come home. There is a shaft of golden light in the dark. It shines on a liquid lake that does not flow but shines its lit gold back at the sky. Outside of the light shaft is the inky dark of eternity. The stars are very bright and I see the Seven Sisters clearly. I feel as though I can reach out and touch them. They bring a warm and comforting glow into my head so that it does not want to be a balloon. It wants to contain the light. I begin to sing a silent song that creates itself in my mind. It is about the go-away bird that calls in the bush when there is danger. It frees itself from harm and keeps the other creatures informed so that they too can escape harm. Around the moon lake grow white arum lilies. Their leaves are green and glossy and they shine in the dark. I sit on a moon rock and place my hand in a lily's cup. It lights my fingers and they become soft and beautiful. I think I will stay on the moon and in the lily garden. There is no desert and no rain here, just quiet and light that shines me out of worry and sadness.

I have not been to visit my friend Dianne because her school has not broken up yet and she will only get home next week nearer to Christmas time. I have seen her mother and she has asked me to come and have tea with her. When I have tea with Mrs Freeman she lets me watch her make scones or flapjacks. Sometimes I pour in the little doses of milk while she mixes and gets the dough right. She whips the cream when the scones are baked and then we sit on the veranda and she serves me tea in a white china cup and she puts a blob of cream on the strawberry jam. It sits beautifully on top of the scone and my

321

mouth waters until I take the first delicious bite. I feel very special and she tells me all that has happened in the village and asks me about Parkhurst and the nuns and Dorry. She says I should come and spend a night when Dianne is home. She says all the tennis players in the village will be pleased that I am home because I am so good at serving aces and hitting backhands and getting the ball to drop just over the net where nobody can get to it. She calls me Berna and says, "Well, well, now, Berna, you have grown so much."

I tell her that I have been working hard and have been in Standard Six this year. I am hoping to go to Standard Seven when I get back. I say that I am in the Open A tennis team and that my coach says I must go professional as soon as I am older. She says she is proud of me; a village child doing so well on the courts and showing everyone what village children can do in the cities. I say that I cannot become professional because I am going to be a nun and will leave for the convent as soon as I leave school. She laughs and says we will see! In my heart I know that I will be a nun. I know that I am trying to be a saint.

♥

The baby's lips are closed:
Plaster pulls.
I feel the eye fluids well and flow.
I stand beside the crib,
With fearfulness exposed.
I watch the little hands
Reach up and touch
A plaster mother's breast.
Plaster father's hands are closed.
Plaster baby's being looks stressed;
There is no one to protect.
This Christmas gift is closed.

MY cousins are here. They have come with my uncle. It is nearly Christmas time and they are excited because they know that they will get presents. I am excited too because I do not know what I will get either. There are many things in my father's shop that I could have. There is a new and bigger bicycle for ladies. There are new tennis shoes and white socks. There are smart shoes and dress materials that Dorry can sew up for me. I could take them to boarding school. My father says nothing and my uncle says wait and see. I watch my father every evening when he comes home after he has been to the hotel. He sits under the syringa tree and mumbles. I stand in the dark and listen to him swear. He says life is a bloody bastard and donder se hell. He says God forgive us sinners. I want to go and sit next to my father but I am afraid. I want to talk to him about the stars and the Seven Sisters but I know that he will send me away.

I feel lost and alone. I think of Dorry and of my sisters. I think that I am going to ask my father to send me back to them before it is time. I cannot stay here with my uncle and my cousins. Somehow the land has lost its gentleness; the bush has new secrets that are not easy on the ear. The hoopoe bird's hollow sound seems to echo in my soul and I cannot seem to answer with my own bush songs. I return to the house and leave my father with his thoughts and with his words, with his wounds.

They sing and the drums beat their joy. They tell of the star and the stable; they show with their hands how God cares for us. They lift up their eyes and praise the new birth. The priest tells the Christmas story. He says we are saved by love and that we should keep singing and loving the way God does. I sit next to my father. He does not smile, nor does he sing. He sighs and remains silent. In my head I sing 'Silent Night' even though it is early in the day. I think of Jesus in the cold stable. The sheep bleat and he smells the smell of wet manure. Mary and Joseph try to keep him dry and warm. I think how strange it is to have God in a stable when he is the king of all the earth and all the people. I think God is hidden and strange.

We greet the priest and the people and we walk from the church to the shop. My cousins and my uncle talk and laugh. My father begins to talk and laugh, too. He shuffles the shop keys and finds the right one for the door. He lets us in and opens the shop shutters so that we can see. He tells my uncle and my cousins to choose a gift. They try on trousers and shirts and shoes. They look in the mirror and are pleased with themselves. My father says Christmas is a time for giving and celebration. His voice is flat and he does not smile. I stand in the shop. He says that everyone must have a happy Christmas. He does not look at me. He does not tell me to choose a gift. I feel ashamed and hurt. I do not know what to do or what to say. I remain silent. My father shuts the shop and my cousins take their new clothes home. I lag behind. My father does not call me. He walks with them into the house.

I sit beneath the morula tree's shade. My hands move slowly over the soil as if to wipe out the hurt and the shame. I make little graves and watch the sand slide away from the heaps. I think life is like a sand heap that drains away and does not return. Life gets lost like sorrow seeping into the secret places of the soul. It does not find its way back to joy and to laughter. It plods on to places where everything is withered and dead. It leaves no trace of past presents of love and light. I do not know why my father does not wish me a happy Christmas, and why he gives me no gift. I begin to talk to God. I tell of my confusion and pain. I say that perhaps I have been a bad person so that my father cannot love me as he does my cousins. My hand begins to sweep away the graves and I leave the soil smooth and flat. I leave no evidence of life draining and joy dying. I am about to return to home when a car's sound creeps along the road. It stops beside the tree. My friend Dianne calls to me and asks why I am sitting here alone. I smile and say I am waiting for my father and my cousins. I say we are going on a picnic for Christmas Day. I say happy Christmas to them. They tell me to come and visit Dianne on Boxing Day. I smile and thank them and they wave while the car moves away.

I begin to weep and watch my tears plop into the soil. I carefully cover the small, dark holes. It does not cover my anger or my shame. After I have sat for some time, my cousins call to me. It is Christmas dinner time. I walk along the path that leads to home. I do not want Christmas dinner. I want to be in Parkhurst. I wonder what Dorry and my sisters are doing on Christmas Day. Are they having roast turkey and has Dotty made them fruit salad and is there Walls ice cream with its heavenly creamy taste? Has Dorry made a pudding with sixpences in it? My stomach shrinks at the thought of guinea fowl and venison. I can see in my head the packet of SRV cigarettes at the side of my father's plate. I drag my feet like sleighs in the far off land of snow. The heat makes my clothes prickle and I enter the house with dread.

We sit at the table and my father says grace. He thanks God for food and for families. I try to eat the heavy lumps of lunch that barb at my throat. I try to smile with my cousins. I look at the plaster figures of the Christmas Crib. I feel ashamed that a baby was born in a stable. I feel ashamed that I was born and that my father's heart is as unyielding as the moulded plaster family that stare from worlds so close to one another but so far from contact and from comfort. My uncle and my father tell of how the guinea fowl was shot and how the impala was hunted and what a good shot my father is because the bullet made such a neat hole between its eyes. The buck dropped straight down and did not even have time to bleat before it died. My uncle says he will treat the skin and make a rug to remind my father of his perfect aim. I get up from the table and run down the passage and through the door. My father has no time to shout me back. I heave up the bars in my throat. I run to the river and sit beside its bank. The thin wind makes quiet music in the trees. I sit still and Christmas passes like a gift that has never been opened.

I walk slowly down the path that leads to home. My father sleeps and snores. My uncle and my cousins have gone. When he awakes, my father asks me where I have been. I say I have listened to the wind. He says his hand will make wind where I do not want it. I stand still and say nothing but the anger fire-pierces my mind like sharp knife stabs and neat holes between eyes. He moves through the back door and sits under the syringa and begins to mumble. He says Dorry is a bloody bitch and he will show her what is Christmas and what is not and to hell with her and her kids. I think that I hate my father and I do not understand him. When I get back to Parkhurst I will tell Dotty about hating him but she will say that he is hard on the outside and has a heart of gold. I think he has a heart of stone.

♥

"I AM going back a bit now, Bern. You know Daddy never sent any other money except the rent. We had to cope as best we could with Faith and the other two working. I got a job with Edgar's as a fitter. I had to see to all the alterations etc. I loved my job. The little ones were left with Mary during the day and she did the cooking as well. Little did I know that our wonderful Mary was busy making beer and hiding it in the cellar! She used to make it in the house and sell it on the quiet. She used to pay the children not to tell me. I used to think to myself: this girl is always giving the little ones sixpences. It never dawned on me that she was busy bribing you all. I thought what a nice kind type of person she was. In the meantime it was to keep all the little mouths closed about the brewing. You know it was illegal.

Anyway, after the wedding, Pat and Sally moved into the back room. I had a door put into it so that they could get in and out of the house from the stoep. Pat was working then as a rep for Randal Brothers, so they sort of paid their way. I was working at Troy Street at the time. I moved from there too to Rosebank, just around the corner from your school. I became the alterationist for Jonas Dress Shop. Pat came to the shop to tell me that Sally was having rather a bad time in labour. In fact her muscles were not working and would not contract properly. She was supposed to have had a doctor and a caesarean baby. She went into the Marymount and the sisters there decided that she should have a normal birth. They were going to force the labour and why shouldn't she have a normal birth? They did not realise that her muscles were not working. Eventually they almost dragged the child from her. She almost died.

327

Then I left the job because you know I had to let Sally finish her apprenticeship. I was not going to leave her half way through her apprenticeship. She needed her qualifications. At that time I had heard rumours about Daddy and the black woman. I did not believe it. Helen's brother used to phone me daily to go out with him and I used to refuse daily. I thought it is not right because I am a married woman. I was a Roman Catholic and I had no right to out with anybody else. In the end, when I found out that he had really had this black baby, I decided: to hell with the husband and the church and I started going out with Don. I never approached Daddy about what he was doing but decided I would teach him and so on and do the same and see how he would like it.

One time Daddy came up for Christmas and was deciding to stay over for New Year. I was so worried he would stay over because I was going dancing over New Year with Don and another couple. We were going to the Diamond Horse Shoe. I was not very nice to Daddy and so eventually he decided to have New Year in Palapye. To my relief he went home, you know. We were not very good friends anyway. When the news about the black woman and her child came out, I decided I wasn't going to sleep with him anyway. I discovered that that ulcer I had came from him. I never connected it at the time. The doctor told me I caught it from a man and I said I didn't because I knew I had not been with a man other than Daddy at that time. One can be so stupid, Bern. I stayed out the whole night and we had breakfast at the club. Sally got panicky, as I had not come home. By the time I got home it was eight o'clock in the morning. I was in my evening dress and everything. I was a bit ashamed coming home in my evening things like that. When I got home Sally had phoned her mother-in-law to say she was worried about me because I had not come home. Just as she put the phone down, I walked in. So she phoned her in-laws back and said I had arrived. Her mother-in-law said to tell me I was very naughty.

Eventually, I told daddy I was going out with Don. I said he could carry on with all the blacks and I would carry on up here with whom I pleased. He told the Bishop all about it. They already knew all about Daddy and his child and Monsane. I only found out that they knew when I went back to him for good after all the kids had left home. That was after Monica got married. I put the little ones into boarding school and I went home. Ag, now I have forgotten my train of thought; now I have forgotten my own thoughts. Oh ja, he told the Bishop all about it, the cheeky thing. The Bishop must have phoned the priest in Rosebank, Fr Bannon, because I stopped going to church because I was not the type to carry on and commit adultery and then go to confession so that I could go to communion and then carry on again. I just cut it all out and finished. Fr Bannon phoned me about it and I said, 'Yes, Father, that's right, I'm going out with somebody, he's going out with black women, I'm going out with someone.' He phoned me every morning to ask me if I had decided to give up this man and come back to church. Every day I would say, no father I have not decided to give him up. I am not going to Mass anymore. I am not going to communion again. I am going out with this man so don't phone me again. But every morning he phoned and asked the same question and got the same answer back. I told him every day; I have decided to do what I think is right not what he or the church think is right, and too bad!"

♥

I LOOK along the rail track. The lines shimmer in the sun. My eyes hurt; the lines merge and become a silver shaft. I sneeze because of the dust and the smell of dung hangs in the air. I hear the cattle being prodded into the dipping troughs. Their lowing tells of fear. I watch the silver shaft. I cannot tell if the merging is real or not.

I turn my gaze from the lines to the small boy. He turns a bicycle wheel. He rolls it along with a thin piece of wire. Its high sound on the shale makes music for his singing. I cannot tell which the song is and which the music is.

The 'Lion Beer' sign reflects and spasms its message. The group of youths make dust and merriment. They bang bottles, shake tins and clap sticks together. Froth creeps around the corners of their mouths. Here is a hand waving with the rhythm of the drum. There is a bead of sweat falling to the ground. Their voices sparkle out the warmth that comes from within. They are satisfied with the heat, with the beer, with the music and with the dry soil. I know their song, I see their dance but I do not share their warmth. I do not feel their peace. I begin to play with a pebble. My dirty toes draw aimless patterns in the sand. I notice the shape of my feet but I do not really see them. I become conscious of the train's whistle and stare vacantly towards its sound. The roar subsides. The steam swirls into nowhere. Only the creaking of the tracks can be picked out of the new silence. This silence is oppressive. It comes from within.

I drop the pebble, leave the sand patterns and walk away from the lines. I pick my way with care lest I tramp on the goat droppings or the little star shaped thorns that irritate the feet. I clear a shady patch.

330

The shadow cools my feet; they throb and tingle. In one hand I place some dry goat dung. I examine it like one that tries to think freely, like one who does not know fear, like one who is not burdened. There is no soothing for my fear. There is no breaking of the silence.

I put my ear against the tree. From deep inside I hear the low groan. Perhaps it is the wind? I recall the woman's moaning. I hear the man's grunts of pleasure. I see the wet body shaped along the sand. It shines because of the sweat that flows so freely. There is no cloud across the moon to hide their nakedness. The sand clings to the woman's skin. Its leprosy spreads and imprints a pattern; little pits, little lumps. The woman cries like one who is mad with joy. He murmurs urgently. Their writhing spreads the leprosy until their skin is caked and cracked and ugly.

I stand motionlessly. My body floats and is strangely aroused. I am stricken with shame. My fear knows no bounds. I cry with eyes that have no tears. The man is my father. The woman is our servant. She washes and irons our clothes. She chops the wood and lights the fire. She tends to the house and feeds the chickens. My mind cannot bring back these images of her. She is my father's lover. She serves him in another way. I try to gather up the fragments of my new world and run back the way I came. My fear runs too, like quicksilver darting through my veins. It withers up my thoughts like the drought withers up the land. It weights my soul like the backs of donkeys are weighted with what is not their own. It burdens me like heavy, wet clay heaped upon the dead. I creep into my bed and feel the heaviness of dread inside my head. My heart becomes a smother shell for all the life that was yesterday's joy.

The sun rises from the night like a great fire that waves a wand across the sky. The land becomes inflamed and the hills blush their welcome back. I stare at the streak of green across my windowpane. I listen to the birds chatter. I smell the dust that hangs about like yesterday. I feel no urge to move and greet the day. I think of Dorry. She prods and shouts at us in the mornings. She laughs at my reluctance to get up for school. She heaves and hisses and shrieks at my stubbornness. She does not know my darkness. She does not yet know her own. She is making sandwiches in Parkhurst. I hear the woman-servant in the kitchen. She sings a song for the day, for the sun, for the corn.

Like a foreigner, I walk along the path that leads to the church. Perhaps I will find mending for my mind there. I sit in the quiet and try to ponder the problem. I did not deliberately come upon their lovemaking. My father said he would walk and pray. He showed me his book of prayer. I followed at a distance. I would wait for him to find his place at the river's edge. I would come from the darkness and share it with him, like the star that can and cannot be seen. We would hear the crickets talk and join in the worship of the sleeping river. Perhaps he would tell me how the stars were born and how the world became dressed in such beauty. But then, the woman came.

I hear the beating of beads and the priest sits beside me. He smiles his peace and I ask for a blessing. I bend my head. I am afraid to look into his face. I feel ashamed and filthy. He asks, "Are you troubled, child?" I tell him of my fear and of my filth. He tells of the Christ, afraid and filthy on the cross. He soothes me and tries to bring me back to light. I tell him of the morula tree that stands among the goat droppings. I say that the moaning is in its bark. He guides me through my mind storm until I speak freely of my father and the woman and their leprosy. I speak with a stranger's voice. It echoes beyond old, known hills into new unknown valleys.

The priest is still. He does not hurry with words. Silence hangs between us like a dark cloud ready to spill the rain. I shuffle my feet. He plays with beads. He begins to speak calmly and softly. He tells of weariness and weakness. It sometimes takes love's gift and squanders it. He tells how the weaverbird builds nests that are destroyed. He says that people are like the birds trapped in striving and never finding home here. God sees their endeavour more than their failing. God loves their trying more than the sadness of their blindness. God sees the promise of their future more than their present searching. He says my father's searching is our suffering. He says I must use suffering so that I can have eyes that see the truth and a heart that cares for it. I do not understand. I fear. He asks that I love the earth and its people trapped in striving. I must grow to God like the flowers to the sun, open and beautiful in its light. I must nurture peace because its gift is rare and strong. "Be gentle with yourself, with your father, with the servant and with Dorry."

I walk back to where the morula stands. The moaning is in its bark. I sit in its shade and play with the goat droppings. I weep for land that waits for rain, for birds that weave and lose their nests, for fathers who betray mothers and children. I weep for Dorry and for myself. When I return home, the back door screeches like a cat when you stand on its tail. The woman sings and irons. Dorry sits at her machine and sews. My father sits in the syringa's shade. He whispers to himself. His hands that are huge and rough cover up his face. I watch his hair cling to his head. It keeps its place even though the wind blows. He whispers to himself. I cannot hear the words but I know that his mind is heavy. I cannot go and sit beside him and listen to the stories of the stars that are optimists. He senses my presence and lifts his head to speak. With his movement, comes the dark movement of the woman who serves. She says that the meal is ready. She speaks with the voice of a stranger, not with the voice of a lover. Perhaps the leprosy has gone. Perhaps it is like the seventh star that blinks and bewitches until it cannot and can be seen. Perhaps tomorrow the weaverbird will build a perfect nest and the morula tree will not moan. Perhaps people will no longer be trapped in striving. Perhaps Dorry will not weep. Perhaps the rain will wash the whole earth clean.

When the world became too dark
For the sun to show its face,
When the rose was still too young and shy
To give me of its grace
I stood lonely, in my barren soul-garden and cried my need.
There was no answer;
I wandered on.
And then there came
A Hollyhock's colour
That blushed and smiled
Into a young girl's face:
I felt a gentle thought.
I prayed a simple dream.
I longed for love again.

I AM sitting on the stoep wall doing nothing. I stare at the Hollyhock that stands pink and tall against the stoep pillar. It sways gently and bends its head in the hot breeze. I think it is an eternal optimist bobbing and bending and bearing the sun and the lack of care in our front garden that nobody weeds or waters except me when I feel ashamed of the state of it. Dorry says she does not have time for luxuries like gardening. My sisters say we were born in a desert and so they know nothing about planting and weeding. From time to time, Dotty and I have planted zinnias and cut the grass but then it seems that the gardenia tree sends its strong, sweet smell into the house and we forget that everything else needs care. I feel ashamed of our house and our garden. The lounge carpets are frayed and the furniture is worn. Dorry says money does not grow on trees and my father does not send manna in the desert. In fact he does nothing for us at all. She says he is a bloody old bastard and she will also do as she pleases. She says she doesn't see why she should behave like a saint while he is messing around much better and getting away with it all. I say nothing because I know what my father is getting away with. I keep it in silence in my head and I walk on the moon with it because I do not know what will happen if Dorry finds out what he is doing while she is struggling to make ends meet here. I found out because I went to my father for the last holiday and I followed him along the path that leads to the river. He said he was going to pray where it is peaceful.

My thoughts are cut off because I do not want to think about that time. I am afraid of this time. I am afraid of Dorry and of Don who phones her every day. She has begun to say yes to going out with him. She goes to dances and she goes to her best friend's house for the weekend with him. She tells us not to worry about her because she is now happy and has had enough of my father.

I am not a good person any more. I am fighting with my sisters and I am very insolent. When Dorry wants me to do something I have a lot to say. I grumble and I am stubborn. When Dorry is out with Don and it is time for me to go to bed, I refuse. Monica says I am a brat and I spoil her smooching time with Rex. Rex is her new boyfriend. She met him at Zoo Lake swimming pool. She goes talent hunting there every weekend. I have never seen Monica get into the pool. She sunbathes. She puts on her cat-eyed dark glasses and lies in a pose on her towel under the trees so that her freckles do not burn and show up. She does not go brown when she gets sunburnt. She goes bright red and gets very sore and if she is not careful she gets blisters. Rex gets cross with me too and he says he will not take me to the Zoo Lake tennis club to play with the A Team adults. I say bugger off and leave me alone. Sally has reported my behaviour to Dorry and she has tried to talk to me kindly but I say nothing and behave badly anyway.

Pat, Sally's husband, has talked to me, too. He told me to listen carefully because he is the only father I have around these days. He said I am changing into somebody that nobody recognises anymore. He tells me what a kind and sweet girl I was and what a bad tempered one I am now. He says he will tell Dorry to send me to the new boarding school at Venterspost. The sisters of Notre Dame are there, not the sisters of Mercy. I tell him that he is not my bloody father and that he cannot give orders to me or talk to me as though he is in charge of everyone. I say I do not care about the sisters of Mercy or the sisters of Notre Dame and that I do not care about anything any more. These days Pat does not lecture me. He tells me to come and sit with him near his home-built Hi-fi. He plays classical music and he says I must close my eyes and listen while he tells me the story of the music or the opera. He says there is nothing better for the mind or soul than classical music. He says he is sorry Sally has been playing jazz these days because it has ruined her classical touch. I have learned about Beethoven and all his symphonies. When everybody goes out I stay at home and I lie on the floor and listen to Chopin's etudes. I let the music enfold me and I feel less miserable. I remember the quiet sounds of the bush before I followed my father and before the weddings and Don.

I am sitting here in the peach tree. My sisters have run down the road to look for me. I have taken a brick and thrown it through the glass windows on the back stoep and I have smashed them. It is because of Don and Dorry. I am feeling cold and very angry and very afraid. I always feel cold and afraid inside. Sister Imelda has told Dorry that I do not pay attention at school and that I will fail if I do not start doing some homework and getting my work up to date. I do not care about school or about passing or failing. I just play tennis and netball. I am in the Open A tennis team although I am still only in Standard Six. When I feel angry I can hit the tennis balls into the tramline corners and nobody can get them back. My tennis teacher says she has played at Wimbledon and I can too if I put my mind to it. My mind will not be put to anything. It wanders all day and gets onto the moon and stays there.

My father's car has just parked on the pavement. I get off the stoep wall very quickly and go and tell Dorry. It is Saturday and I am lucky that she is not out with Don already. Dorry runs to her bag and gets out a sixpence She gives me her little notebook and tells me to find Don's number in it and to go down to Tony's café and phone Don because he is coming to visit her later. I put the little notebook in my pocket with the sixpence. I go to my father and greet him. He smells of whiskey, stale tobacco and dust. He asks if my mother is home and I say yes and that I am going to the shop for her. He takes his old leather suitcase and goes inside.

I run to Tony's and ask the woman who is using the phone there to hurry because I have an emergency. She carries on talking and ignores me. I run down the road to Tenth Street and that phone booth is empty. I dial Don's number. I am relieved to hear his voice because I am afraid he may have left to visit Dorry. He asks me if I am okay these days and tells me that he has not seen me around. He asks if have I been playing tennis a lot. He says he has heard that I am doing very well in the 'A Team'. I say nothing. He asks if there is something wrong at home. I say, "Yes, there is a lot wrong. You are wrong and Dorry is wrong and my father is wrong." He is silent and then I say, "Listen, you bloody bastard, the other bloody bastard from the bush has arrived, so do not come around until Dorry phones you again. I hate all Bastards!" I do not hear what Don says because I slam the phone down and then I pick it up and slam it down again until I have broken it. I leave it dangling and screeching and run back home. My father is sitting in the chair in the lounge. Dorry is looking at his hands and chest. They are full of sores and pussy blisters. She says she will have to phone the doctor. She asks what he has been doing to get these sores. He says he has done nothing but had a rash and the doctor injected him with penicillin. Dorry tells him to go and bath and then they will go to the doctor. My father has to stay here for at least a week because the doctor says he is allergic to penicillin. Faith does not come to the house to visit my father. She stays with Bernard in Pretoria.

My father is better but he says he will not go back to our village until Monday. He tells Pat to buy two tickets for the cricket. South Africa is playing England. He says the other ticket is for the cricket crazy girl. We catch the buses to Wanderers and I sit in the stadium all day with my father and we watch and cheer when the runs are made and the wickets fall. I can hardly believe I am watching Hugh Tayfield, Trevor Goddard and Roy Mclean; I have only heard their names on the radio. My father says, "Bloody donders se hell!" a lot and he stands and takes off his hat and waves at the fours and the sixes a lot. I laugh with my father again and I forget what he and Dorry are doing and I long for life to be as it was.

♥

"THEN, Bern, Monica got married. Of course Monica didn't give us a chance to get on our feet. She went and made her own arrangements. She went with Rex to fix it all up. She came and said to me she wants to get married. I said well give me a chance to get things in order, I can't even pay for the cake yet! She took me by my shoulders and shook me and pushed me out of the door and said that I get on her nerves. She banged the door closed so quickly that it hit me on the back of my head. I couldn't get out of the way fast enough. Well that was that! She made her own arrangements. Her mother-in-law had a reception for her and Rex at her house and Mrs Peters, her boss, gave her the two top tiers of her own wedding cake. So this cake must have been at least 20 years old. Anyway, it looked very nice. I couldn't afford to pay for another cake just then. It was just too much money. I was not getting any help from Daddy. I told Rex, I said, 'I'm not going to tell Monica's father that you want to get married because it's too soon. We have had two marriages. I just can't do it.' And he took a train and went down to Palapye and told Daddy. Funny enough Daddy liked Rex. He thought Rex was great and so on.

So Daddy came up for the wedding and for the reception Mrs Tucker had for them. Aunty Molly came. It was a very nice show and Monica bought her own dress. Monica said she would do it herself and she did it herself! She went back to work after her wedding and so did Rex. Rex moved in with us in Parkhurst. So they had their own bedroom because Faith had moved. Of course, nobody could have refused Monica permission to get married because she got pregnant. She was not going to put up with Daddy's nonsense like Pat and Sally did. One minute yes, one minute no and then next year and then when the cows come home. Anyhow, they moved in. My goodness me did they fight. How they would fight! Ye gods, Bern, I'm telling you. Then Rex decided they would move. I would interfere because, after all, they were in my house, you know. I couldn't put up with the nonsense. So Rex decided to take a flat. He got a job on the mines and he took a flat in De Villiers Street near the station in Johannesburg. Monica had her baby and they were in the flat. Rex was not going to have his mother-in-law interfere with his baby. They were quite capable of bringing up their own child. So they did not need any help from his mother- in-law. So I kept myself out of it all. And eventually the phone rang and it was Monica on the phone. I did try to go once a few days before this and the lifts weren't working. I couldn't walk up all that flight of stairs so I went home and thought: well maybe it's for a reason and I shouldn't go. Then a few days after that the phone rang: 'Mommy, Dennis keeps crying. The baby's crying and Rex is crying too. I don't know what to do. Please come and help me.'

'Well, all right,' I said. 'You can shift back here. Bring your baby, pack a few things and that and let Rex bring you home.' He brought her home. I think it was tension that affected the little one, as he quietened down. He was not getting the right food and so on. I showed them how to do it and Rex decided to give up the flat and shift into the house where I was. He decided it was better to have mother-in-law around than not. I helped them with the child and that. One time, they were busy fighting, I'm telling you, Bern. They were carrying on so badly that I opened the door and walked in and here was the net from the cot, the baby's cot. It was alight from the candle on the stool next to the bed! Here they were dragging at each other and dragging the poor child between them. In the meantime the net was on fire; Monica trying to take Dennis and Rex hanging on to him. I raised Cain, I'm telling you. I gave them hell! Rex had to put out the fire. He poured water all over the net and made a terrible mess on the floor.

Things quietened down, you know, and the baby was seen to. Monica never worked when she had the baby. She stayed at home. Then Rex got a job on the mines quite near. They got a mine house and got their furniture on hire purchase and settled down. We used to go and visit them and they would come to us. Eventually Rex got a job in Evander and they got a lovely house. Monica had all her other children in Evander."

Nobody feels like going to another wedding. I have on a new dress that Dorry has made. It is nylon and has a flared skirt and it is full of little blue flowers. I have no new shoes and so I am in my school shoes and socks. I feel sad and angry that I have no new shoes. Dorry has been complaining about Monica's wedding. She is very angry too because Monica gave nobody time to save up and prepare at all. When she told Dorry she wants to get married and Dorry said she should wait and give my father some time before she starts asking, Monica slammed the door in her face. She shook Dorry's shoulders and Dorry was afraid of her violence. We never know when Monica will fly off the handle into a rage for nothing. She has been doing this for as long as I can remember. Once she gets into a temper we all scatter because she does not care what she says or does. She fights with Rex as well. He has to do what she says or else there is a huge row. I am tired of rows and upheavals. I am not going to sing in the choir for this wedding because Monica has asked somebody to sing solos. I am glad about that because I do not want any of my friends to see that I have to wear school shoes to weddings. Dotty, Trish, Kate and I have to catch the buses to the wedding because there are not enough cars to take us to the church. We can only get a lift when we get back home and go to the reception at Mrs Tucker's house. I have not seen Monica in her wedding dress. My father has on the blue suit he wore to Sally's wedding. Faith is not coming to Monica's wedding. She has moved to Cape Town with Bernard. My father does not ask Dorry how she is. He does not say anything about Faith. When Faith phones she says she is well and fine. She and Bernard are working. They are not having babies yet.

The organist is playing the wedding march and my father walks Monica down the aisle. Rex is standing at the front and is looking back to see his new wife. I am standing in the middle of a bench so that nobody can see my school shoes at a wedding. The Mass is dragging along like a slow bush road that winds its way and goes nowhere special. I am not really here in the church or with the people.

I am lost somewhere that is hard to find and hard to leave. I think about the moon but my head will not go there. I hear the soloist sing 'Ave Maria' and I think she has a screechy voice and that she should have singing lessons. Dotty nudges me and says how well the lady up there sings. I say nothing. I watch Monica and Rex come down the aisle and after the mass they stand at the back of the church and we kiss them and say God bless you both and be happy together and a lot of things but I cannot mean them because I cannot feel them. I think I am dead and this is my other world body smiling and saying bless you both.

Mrs Tucker has made many lovely decorations for the table and the food is good. There is no trifle but there is other pudding with cream so I cannot complain. My father sits with Dorry and Monica and Rex and with Mrs Tucker. She has no husband because she is divorced. Her husband used to carry on with other women. Monica told us. I look at my father and at Dorry and I think they will get divorced when the one knows what the other one is doing. I think of Don and the way I swore at him and I do not feel sorry. I feel angry all over again. I want this wedding to end so that I can go home and get into bed and go to sleep. Sometimes I wish I would sleep forever the way some people in the operas do. They get shot or stabbed or take poison. I think how Carmen flirted with Don Jose and how weak he was with her charms. She was unfair. Monica is also unfair. She gets her way with everyone through being violent. My father is the same. When he gets angry, he thrashes whoever is near or he gets out his gun and bullets and threatens murder or suicide. I think that in the end people have enough of unfair treatment and they do things to stop it. Don Jose stabbed Carmen through her heart. I think that perhaps Dorry and my father will end in a tragic murder. Dotty offers me more pudding.

♥

Light footed on the high plains
I tread:
The light's so clear
Its brightness hides my fear.
On my safe, high ground
You suddenly appear.
You beckon me to follow
Deep, deep down
Into a dawn of dark marshes:
I dread.
Why are simple tears
So terrible to shed?

I AM in my father's car going back to our village for the holidays. I do not know why I am going because I know I am ashamed of my father's house. I know how he was when I went on the train to our village the last holiday. None of my sisters want to come with me. I am also afraid of the way my father drives this car. It swerves around in the sand and sometimes he gets into skids but he says it is safe because he knows what he is doing. He tells me never to put my foot on the brake when I get into a skid one day. I am too young to drive but one day I will drive my own car if I am not a nun. Even if I am a nun they will teach me to drive cars because they do missionary work and have to get around the small towns and big cities. We have stopped several times because the engine keeps overheating. My father says the car hates the city and the altitude and it misbehaves. I say the car is a crock, like my father. He says

343

I must watch out what I say to crocks because they can turn into crocodiles and then what?

I walk through the door and fleas rise like a black cloud in front of me. I feel sick and itchy and ashamed that my father has let his house go to such an extent. I go to the bathroom. There is rust where the taps drip and there is a black line around the bath where nobody has cleaned. There is a stale smell of sweaty feet and a pair of shoes lies on the floor. I cannot see any signs of Polokwane or of any other help in the house. I go to the room my aunt Flo used to use and it looks dusty and when I lift the bed covers, my eyes sting from the dust. I do not unpack my clothes because I am afraid of flea invasion. I begin sweeping and cleaning the room and then the house. I spray the lion skin mat and hope that the fleas are dead. Polokwane comes to the kitchen at five o'clock to cook the supper. I ask him where the maid is and he says there is no maid, only on a Monday.

I wait for my father to come home but he does not arrive. He has gone to the pub after work. I have my supper and then I go to bed. I sleep through the night until I wake to itchiness. I scratch and when I get up in the morning my legs are raw and blood has dried on the bites. I tell my father that the house is dirty and there are fleas in it. He says he cannot see them and I am fussy like my mother. I am very sorry I have come to visit my father again.

My cousins are here again and my uncle has come with them. They sleep on the stoep with my father. My cousins do not help clean the house so my father has got a maid to help. I feel a little happier. Lerato cleans well and soon the floors are shining and the windows are clear. There is a new smell of floor and furniture polish. The bathroom is also clean and the bed linen is washed and ironed. I feel that I can go and visit Mrs Freeman without feeling ashamed to talk about my father's house.

Dianne is home from boarding school. She says I must go to the bioscope with her on Friday night. I ask my father and he says yes but I must take the spotlight torch so that I can see in the dark because there is no moonlight at the moment. The film was called 'Casablanca'. Lauren Bacall and Humphrey Bogart were the stars. There was a Gene Autrey short film before interval so Dianne was very pleased and teased me about Roy Rogers. I am happy that I went to the film and that Dianne is here. We can play tennis with Hilton, Nancy and Mr Morey. Perhaps my father will give me golf lessons when he plays on Sundays. My uncle says he will show me a thing or two about darts and cards but not about sports. He plays poker and he is good at cheating. He is very quick to flip cards and if you do not watch carefully, you do not see him hide an Ace for when it is handy. My cousins help me to watch him and we laugh when we catch him. I like my uncle when he is not drunk. Dorry says he was a good young man until he went to the war in North Africa. He came back a different person and began to drink. He used to wake up in his sleep and shout and duck under his arms. He used to have shell shock. My father never went to war because he was not healthy enough. I do not know what was wrong with him. Dorry says he used to have asthma and could not breathe properly.

I am walking down the road that leads to our house. It is very dark because this is the third night of no moon. I am not afraid because there is nothing that can harm me here in the village. I feel at home and the night owl's hollow hoot, and the silent plovers tell me that there is no danger. When I reach our yard, I turn the light onto the tin toilet house. My uncle is sitting on the cement block under the syringa tree. There is a bottle of brandy next to him. He turns because of the bright light. He tells me to come and talk to him. He says I must switch off the torch so that we can see the fireflies. I stand next to him and begin to tell him about the film but he says I must be quiet to give the glow-worms time to feel safe after being in the light. We stay in silence until we see the fireflies make small, moving stars around us.

My uncle gets up. He is not steady on his feet. He lopes towards me to balance himself. He puts his hands on my shoulders and moves behind me. He tells me to look at the fireflies. They set him on fire, too. He says I am a lovely young girl and I must save myself for a good young man. I say I am going to be a nun and I will never get married. He says he will show me a thing or two about love. He pulls me against his body and grips me so that I cannot move. He wiggles and I feel his hard penis press into me. He moves so that his hand is under my breast that has hardly had time to grow. He slurs love words into my ear. My cousin comes out of the house and watches. I want to call my father but I can hear him snoring beneath the open stoep window. I know that he is so drunk that he will never hear me. I tell my uncle to leave me alone. He tightens his grip and says I must turn around and feel how hard his penis has got. He says it is because I am so attractive. I say okay and he lets me turn around. I slap him through the face and call him a bloody drunk and a bloody sick bastard. I kick up my knee and he bends and groans. My cousin runs inside. I leave my uncle under the syringa with his drunken thoughts. I go to my room and close the door.

I walk on the high plains of the moon. There is no shadow here. Just the light before my uncle's darkness came. There are no words here. No enticements away from trust. I feel no threats. I feel no fear of frantic hands and hardening body parts that mar my innocent image of my uncle sitting on a cement block to watch the fireflies. There is calm and clarity and comfort. There is the world I own. Privacy and peace are mine. I do not want ever to come back down.

The dawn is like a dark marsh where the sun only flitters with uncertainty. I get out of my bed and kneel for a while. I tell God to take my uncle away to where I will not have to speak or listen or yield or run. I do not want to see my silent cousin who has watched his father wound what was innocent and free. I think of Jannie and the boat and the bicycle I thought was free. I think that life has no real place for me. There is no free laughter or real light. I can only contain the dark and live in its silence. I feel filthy and afraid. Perhaps my uncle will tell my father that I am the one who misbehaves. Perhaps he fears the consequences of my resistance. I tell God I will be a nun and a saint and that I will never marry because men cannot be trusted.

I walk slowly down the road that leads to my father's shop. He is sitting on the counter doing nothing. There are no customers in the shop. His yellow fingers play with his cigarette. He flicks the ash that is not there. He asks what the film was about. I say it was too romantic and sad and there was too much kissing in the mists. He laughs and says that love is strange and beautiful and that it is the oldest story in the world. He says I will understand it when the cows come home because he is still struggling with love and look how old he is already. He says it is a donders se ding!

I say nothing. I do not know where Dorry's love has gone. I do not know where my father's love has been.

My uncle is coming down the path that leads to home. There is nowhere I can hide and nowhere for me to run. We stop. We stand. My uncle smells of brandy and sweat and his lips are pink and caked with dust. He has stale saliva in the corners of his mouth. I want to be sick in the road right at his feet. He does not look at me. He looks down at the ground and his face goes red. He says that last night was a test for me. He was finding out if I am a good, clean girl or not. I say he is a filthy bastard and that I hate him. He asks my forgiveness and asks that I pray for him. He says the drink eats him up. I tell him to forgive himself and to ask God to help him. I say that I do not help worms crawl. They have their own bellies that belong low on the ground and crawl their way around life. My uncle's eyes are full of tears. He says he hopes that one day I will respect him again. I say when the cows come home. I say I hope that his son can respect him one day again because he saw what his father did. He says nothing. I tell him to get out of my way and to go back to his own home because I will tell my father and then somebody will be dead.

My uncle leaves our village on the train. My father says something has happened to make him leave so suddenly. He says perhaps it is the heat. Perhaps it is his wife that needs him in Johannesburg. I say nothing. I know that I will not come back here again and when I leave on the train, my village will never be the same or my own again.

I sat beside the river's edge.
It was quiet but for the bleating and the birds.
I watched him climb the river's bank;
He did not choose the road
But bent and braved the bush and hill.
He chose a stone beside my chair,
To share my presence;
To settle in my silence there.

He said, "Hello."
I said that too.
We watched the goats and cattle chew.
I rose.
My smile, prim-pressed.
I walked with care.
He sat upon that hard, cold stone
With wounded soul
And solemn stare.

I am at the river's edge saying goodbye to its peace and to its long flow of history. I am transfixed by its deep brown that glows the sun back. I do not have to go to the moon when I am with the river. I can sit in its sounds and hear its music. I know that I will not come here again. My village time had come to an end. I see Tsalala's hat rising like a small brown moon. He walks slowly and surely towards me. I sigh because my silence is severed. I cannot respond like the child I was under the water tank for trains. My life has changed and I have reached another river's bank.

I have arrived home on the train from our village. I have been scratching the flea bites and my legs are covered in sores that have gone septic. They are all over and scabby. I am very ashamed. Dorry says, "Ye gods, what have you been doing to your legs?" I tell her about the fleas. She says my father is a dirty bastard and she will never let any of us go home with him again. She asks if he sent the money he promised. I say he did not give me anything. She begins her swearing ritual and says she has had enough of my father and she will leave him and marry Don. I do not think she will marry him because he knows how much I do not like him. Dotty does not like him either. She says he is a slime ball. When Dorry was not in the room with him, he tried to kiss Dotty. I think he is like my uncle and I hate him. The only thing we like is his fish and chips that he brings from his fish and chips shop.

Dorry says I am going to boarding school. She says I am getting right out of hand with my temper and the way I speak to people. I know which person she is talking about. He comes around here almost every evening. And she goes out every weekend. I am very unhappy at home and in our village and I am very unhappy that I am being sent to boarding school. I feel that Dorry is getting rid of me so that she can have peace and quiet with Don. I feel that life is shifting into places that I cannot understand or feel at ease with. I think of the night winds that blow up the sand dunes and heap them into shapes they have never been and will never be again. I think of the moon and know that there is no place of peace there for me. My mind stays here, cold and lonely and unwilling to move.

♥

The tarred roads turn and shift direction.
They straight line out of known home
Into dust roads along the rows of mealies
Making music in the winds of change.
My tired fury peters out into depression.
It deepens in the journey; unconfirmed
In attitudes that will belie the valley's depth
And mountains that are too high to climb.

Pᴀᴛ has told Dorry about the convent in Venterspost near Westonaria where he works. He is a salesman in a shop there and he says they stock the uniforms for the convent school. He brings them home for me to see. The dress is sunflower yellow and the blazer is almost blue. The badge has some red roses on it and the motto is: 'How Good is the Good God'. It is written in French. It is the motto of the sisters of Notre Dame. They were founded by somebody called Blessed Julie Billiart. Pat says they are very kind and cheerful sisters and the school is newly opened for white children. It was a school for black boarders but the Government has sent them away to another area and now Venterspost is for whites. He says I will love it there. I do not think I will love it. I will hate being away from my sisters and from Dorry. I say I do not want to go but Dorry says she will not hear any more from me. The months drag on and I do not do well in the exams. I have failed Standard Seven and Dorry says it is a very good thing that I am going to a new school because I will have to repeat the year.

I have on my new school uniform. I look good in it but I can still see my legs that are covered in sores. I am ashamed and afraid to appear in public. Pat and Sally and Dorry are taking me to Venterspost. Before I leave, I say goodbye to my sisters. They wave and encourage me to be good and to do well. I have torn an old sheet into strips and put it in my suitcase. I will bind it around my legs so that the sores cannot be seen. Inside I cry like desert rain that does not reach the ground. My tears are withered up by constant chat and cheerful comment, about new futures and new chances to change. I am silent and block out the buzz that seems to ring in my head and cut off any thoughts. I watch the road go by like long stares at life that has no more meaning. I feel cold, afraid and alone. I watch the back of Dorry's head. It turns and twists for answers to her questions. Have I got my tuck? Have I got my pocket money? Have I read the list of rules? I nod but I do not answer because I cannot dare my voice to utter words I fear will turn to rain.

Pat turns the car into a soft sand road. On either side are fields of mealies, high and straight and green. Dust rises and sheds its filters onto leaves that wave a welcome that I cannot contemplate. In my heart is hatred for Dorry and for Don. There is hatred for my father and for my uncle and for Jannie. There is hollowed existence that was once life. I think of Dotty's pinkie that will no longer let me find stability.

The tyres crunch the driveway stones and we park. My sick legs stumble out and I am exposed to eyes that do not look at me. They fall below my knees and linger into stares. A sister comes to shake Dorry's hand. She takes mine and says, "So this is Bernadette. We have heard so much about you. You want to be a nun?" She looks at my legs. She says, "What happened?" I tell her they are veld sores from the bush. She says that they will soon be cured of that. She says that Sister Therese knows about these things. She is a teacher and a nurse.

I have been in Notre Dame Convent for a week and I have cried every night. I do not cry in the day because I do not want people to know that I am very homesick. I miss my sisters and Dorry even though she is still going out with Don. I feel lost and alone in my new class. There are only twenty girls in Standard Eight. Some come from the mines in Carltonville and some come from Johannesburg and one comes from Windhoek. Everyone in my class has been here before so I am the only new pupil. A girl called Joey sits in front of me and Donna sits behind me. Donna is not pleased to be in boarding school. She says she has a boyfriend who belongs to the 'Wandering Hand Society' and she misses his hands' travel route. She says her parents put her in here because they found out about the wandering hands. They caught them in action on the couch when Donna thought she and her boyfriend had the whole evening together. Her parents came home early from their friends and that was the end of freedom for Donna. She sighs when she tells me this story. She asks if I have a boyfriend. I tell her about Ralph. He comes to the house because he is Bunny Scullard's brother. Monica told him to come and see me. He is a good looking boy with brown eyes and brown curly hair. He is tall and well built. He wears blue shirts and a black leather jacket like his brother. Bunny is a Ducktail and belongs to a gang but Ralph is not wild. He is quiet and says I will be Mrs Scullard one day. When he walks me down the road he tries to hold my hand. I put my handbag in the hand he is trying to hold and he runs around me to the other side where my other hand is free and so I change the bag to that hand. When we go to the movies, I wear Dotty's high heeled shoes. I do not have any of my own. I put cotton wool in the toes because they are too big for me. I also wear Dotty's lipstick because if Ralph tries to kiss me in the movies I can say that my lipstick will smudge and Dorry will find out. I am too afraid to kiss boys in case they get like my uncle or Jannie. Dorry says I look like Mini Mouse in Dotty's shoes but I think I look smart and very grown up.

Joey is Afrikaans but she speaks English very well. She says she will be my friend. She never looks at my legs. She is kind and gentle. Annette is very clever and she says she will help me because she has heard that I did not pass Standard Seven. I do not know who told her. Sister Patricia has put her in charge of my study time and says that with Annette behind my revision efforts I will do very well. I believe her because today I got full marks for my Geography test. Annette drew a map on the board and made me learn where all the capital cities of the world are. I did not forget any. It is the first time in my whole school life that I have got full marks so I am very proud of myself. Sister Patricia says do I see what a bit of work can achieve?

It is Friday and all the girls in my class are going home for the weekend. Dorry says I can only come home one weekend every month. I watch all the cars arrive and all the hugs and waves. I feel hollow and alone. I think that the world is a dark and cruel place. Sister Patricia comes and stands next to me. She puts her arm around my shoulders and I begin to sob. She says I will be all right but I do not think so. The tears keep on running and the more Sister Patricia holds me the more I sob. I have cried for so long that I cannot see. My eyes look like Chinese slits and my cheeks are so red they look as if they are bleeding. I have no more tissues left. Sister Patricia has gone to phone Dorry. She says perhaps I should go home this weekend and then I will be fine next weekend.

I am in Pat's car going home. Sister Patricia took me to Randfontein station and the train took an hour to get to Johannesburg. There is silence in this car. Sally says Dorry is not pleased about me coming home after one week. She says I will have to do better than this. She says they had to go to boarding school and never come home for three months and do I think I am somebody very special or what? I say nothing. I have a sore nose and sore eyes and I do not want to start crying again.

Dorry says hello but she does not kiss me or hug me. She says I must not think this is going to be the order of the day. She has put me in boarding school for a good reason and I will have to 'ruk reg' and grin and bear it because I will only be coming home once a month from now on. I do not know if I am more miserable at home or at boarding school.

We have to put our names down if we want to get up early in the mornings to go to Mass. I put my name down every day. I go and sit with the sisters long before the bell goes to warn us that Mass is about to begin. I find it a comfort to be with the sisters and with God. It is the only time I feel that life is good and that I do not have a lonely, hollow feeling inside. When I see the sisters talking to one another, they seem always to be happy and they laugh a lot. I think that they are happy serving God and people. I think that more than ever I want to be a nun. I want to be a sister of Notre Dame.

Every Friday we have assembly in the hall. The hall is really two classrooms with a partition between them. We open the partition and it serves as a hall. Sister St John is the sister Superior of the Convent. She does not teach us because she is busy doing everything Sister Superiors have to do to like the accounts and giving spiritual guidance to everyone. We listen to her for a half an hour in the hall. She tells us that the minute we are born we begin to die. We laugh but she says that this is true. We can never have the same moment back because the present dies all the time. She says that there is a different kind of dying. There is the dying that we do when our life ends and the dying that we do every time we are kind or every time we do things that we do not like doing for the good of others. She says it is the death of selfishness and the birth of self tenderness. She says God is all about self tenderness and self giving and that is why God is infinitely joyful and happy and that there are no tears in heaven.

She tells us a bit more about Blessed Julie Billiart every Friday and says she knew about joy even in her most difficult and sorrowful times. Julie could always say, "How good is the good God!" She said this during the French Revolution when the priests were being hunted and had their heads chopped off if they did not belong to the Revolution. Julie hid them in her home. She was always on the run because the people said she was a witch and they wanted to burn her at the stake. Somebody tried to shoot her father while she was talking to him in her home and she got such a shock that she became completely paralysed. One day her priest friend asked her to pray for somebody who was very ill and sick but who he thought had a lot of God's work to do. She said a novena like Dorry does and at the end her friend told her that the prayer was for her own healing. He told her to stand up and walk and do God's work. She did stand up and walk and worked for God until she died. She founded the order of Notre Dame and sent missionaries all over the world to educate poor children and to tell people that God is so very good. I love to listen to Sister St John and to hear about Julie.

I have been in boarding school for a year. I like my friends and the sisters but every time I come home for a weekend and it is time to go back, I get very homesick. I get taken to Donna's house and her father drives us back. I do not talk on the way. I watch the grasslands and mealie fields and the birds dart in and out of them. I remember the weaverbirds and their songs. I think of the smell of rain when it falls on the dust. I think of my father before I found him with the black woman. I long for a life that I will never have again. There seems to be no end to loneliness. Dorry hardly ever writes to me. She never phones or leaves messages. She never sends me extra tuck or pocket money. It seems as though she has left me here without a care.

I am writing to Dorry. I am telling her that I am the Head Girl of this school. I am telling her that the pupils voted for me and the sisters voted for me because I have grown into a very responsible person and my marks have improved so much that Sister Patricia says she can hardly recognise the girl who arrived with sores on her legs and a poor report. I tell her that I have been in the school play about Blessed Julie Billiart. When the curtain came down and I went to take my bow, everyone stood and clapped because I was such a good actress. Sister Patricia says she is amazed at my acting talent and I am a packet of real surprises. Sister St John said she was moved to tears. I am moved to tears because Dorry was not here to see the play.

Father Augustine is very tall. He has very deeply set eyes and very black hair. His Adam's apple sticks out like a broken bone and it moves up and down like an engine pump when he speaks. He is speaking now. He is showing us books that Sister Patricia has found under Donna's bed. He is saying that these are filthy books and the people who read them will get filthy too. We are all shocked and silent because we have never seen Father Augustine so angry. Sister St John and Sister Patricia are sitting next to him. Their faces are very white. They are also very angry. When Father is finished telling us about filthy books, he talks more quietly about holy purity. Donna sits next to me and she sighs and whispers without moving her lips that they belong in Noah's Ark. She says romance never killed anybody. I do not move in case Sister Patricia sees me. It is very hard to be the Head Girl because my duties are to make sure the school rules are kept and that if they are broken to take proper action even against my friends. When we go to the shops on a Saturday morning we walk along the sandy road through the mealie fields to Venterspost. Sister Mary Therese, a new nun from England who has very long and dark eyelashes and a peaches and cream complexion, has to take us. Donna buys cigarettes and smokes them behind the shop while we are waiting for everyone to finish buying sweets. I cannot buy anything because I have no pocket money. I get very ashamed to tell my friends that my mother has not sent me any money even though they share their sweets with me.

Donna says I must never tell on her about the cigarettes. I tell her that I am the Head Girl and that it is my duty to report when the rules are broken. She gets very angry with me and says I am not a good friend and that she will tell her father never to give me a lift again. I say I am sorry that I am not her friend but that I cannot betray my duty. I think of Faith and how hard she must have found it to report all the nonsense that happened in her boarding school, especially when Sally and Monica were guilty of doing wrong things. Faith also wrote to Dorry when the nuns locked up Sally in the dark corridor under the statue of Our Lady because they said Sally stole that sixpence and Faith knew that she did not do it. She gave her letter to a friend to post but it never arrived. Dorry said she never got it. I do not know what will happen when I report that Donna is smoking behind the shop. I feel sick and sad that I am the Head Girl.

I am feeling terrible because Donna has been expelled from our school. Her father came to fetch her today. Sister Patricia says it is not because of the smoking but that Donna has done something else that cannot be allowed to happen in boarding school. I know what she did because I heard Sister Patricia talking to her in our classroom when we were at lunch. She caught Donna stealing money from the tuck shop money tin that is kept in Sister Patricia's cupboard. I feel very bad because I stole a shilling out of the tin when there was a movie at school and I had no money to pay for the ticket. I am the Head Girl and I stole a shilling. I do not know what Blessed Julie would say or what God thinks. I will put back the shilling when Dorry sends me some pocket money or the next time I go home and bring some back.

I have chickenpox. I have sores all over me again. I am not ashamed of these sores because they are not there because of fleas. Sister Patricia does not want to send me home because it is near exam time and she says I need to stay here and study even with chickenpox. She moves me from my dormitory cubicle to a room in the nuns' side of the convent. The room overlooks the courtyard and when the sisters are at supper and the pupils have finished their meal they gather under the window in the courtyard and call me. I go to the window and give them a royal wave. They ask what it is like in the convent where the nuns are. I tell them it is quiet and peaceful and there are long corridors. I know that one day I will live in this section of the convent. Every day I get surer of that.

I have to go home by train now that Donna is not here. I miss her because she is a rebel and I am not. I tell Dorry and my sisters that I am in another school play. It is called, 'Cabbages and the Cook' and it is a comedy. I have to light a cigarette and pretend to smoke it in the play. I feel sick when I strike the match and put the cigarette into my mouth. Dorry says good acting takes care of our personal likes and dislikes. She says she will see if she can come to the play. I have to have high heeled shoes and a dress that is calf length. I take Dotty's shoes and dress even though she has said she cannot spare them. I am ashamed that I cannot bring any of my own clothes and shoes because I do not have any others, only the ones I wear at the weekends at school.

It is Saturday afternoon and Sister Patricia calls me and says I have visitors. I get very excited but then I get afraid when I see Ian's car because I know it is Dotty and she has come for her clothes. When I get to the car Dotty unwinds the window and says, "Where are my clothes and shoes?" I say that I had none to bring for the play. I say that I am sorry. She says I am a bloody little bugger and that she has nothing to wear either. I beg her not to take them back home because I will have to tell Sister Patricia that I have no costume for the play. In the end Dotty says I can keep them and she will make do. I love Dotty very much.

Pat and Sally have brought Dorry to see me in the play. Dotty is here as well. I am very nervous now and very excited because Dorry has never seen me do anything at school. I am afraid that I will forget my lines or that Penny, who is the Cook, will start screaming and shouting and losing control like she has done in the rehearsals. She is supposed to get cross but not hysterical.

The curtain goes up and I feel that I am in another world. I forget about Dorry and everyone who is watching. I feel only that I am the

Madam of the house in charge of Cook, who cannot cook cabbage to my satisfaction. When I light the cigarette, I hear somebody say, "I bet she has done that before!" At the end everyone claps very loudly and some people whistle. I feel wonderful and proud. Dorry says I am a star, and I feel like one!

I am in Sister Patricia's office and she is reading an official Notre Dame form to me. It says that if I want to be a sister, I must sign it. It says that I will have to teach or nurse or scrub floors if I am asked. I do not care because I want to be a nun so much. I sign the form and Sister Patricia hugs me and says she knows I am doing the right thing. I will make a very good nun.

It is the end of the year and I have passed Standard Nine. Sister St John has presented me with a new missal for the Religious Education Prize. She tells the pupils that I am leaving the school and I will be going to England in February to be a sister of Notre Dame. Everyone is silent. They look at me with wonder. When they see me after the prize giving, they say they cannot believe that I am going so soon. They say they will miss me and that I was a good Head Girl. Some of them cry because I am leaving. I do not cry because in my heart I know that I should be a nun.

♥

Sorrow seeps deep
Beneath the soul's surface,
Like sea edges that creep along the shore
After the violent tide has pushed and gutted them.
The water wells within
And quietly tells its grief
In silent suffering.

My father is here with us again. He has come, not for another wedding, but to see me off to the convent. I am still going to be a nun but I am not sure about a saint. I have said my goodbyes to my school friends and the sisters at Venterspost. They had welcomed me. Sister Patricia is very proud and pleased with me. I have passed my Standard Nine. She says I can do my Matric when I return as a sister of Notre Dame.

Bishop Murphy in Botswana is very disappointed that I am becoming a sister of Notre Dame. He had wanted me to be a sister of the Cross and Passion and enter the convent in Francistown. They would have sent me to Ireland but the SND novitiate is Ashdown in Sussex, England. I am very nervous because I have to fly by jet plane. I have never been on a plane, only on the trains up and down from Botswana to Johannesburg. My father says I am widening my horizons. Dorry says I am far too young to enter now. She says I should go out more with Ralph and his friends and enjoy my teenage years and then if I am still keen to be a nun after I have my Matric, she would be very pleased. My father tells Dorry to leave his little nun alone. God is calling her and I will be his way of getting to heaven.

I do not know if God is calling me. I think he is because I have had it in my heart to be a nun since I can remember. Sister Therese at school says I should be careful and think about it deeply because when I saw 'The Nun's Story' I told her it made me want to enter straight away. She says I am not Audrey Hepburn and the convent life is very hard and there is no romance attached. I tell him not to worry; I will never get married and I am not looking for an easy romantic life.

My father is sitting in his chair. I have been dressing up in my best clothes because he is taking me to town. He has to buy me all the winter clothes that I need. I have to have Wellington boots and long socks. I need a warm suit to travel to England in. It is winter there and snowing. I have never seen snow so I am excited. I go to my father with my best clothes on and tell him that I am ready. He sighs and says he cannot take me to town today. He will do it tomorrow. He says there is still plenty of time. We have the whole week. I say nothing but I think that my father is unfair. I have had to get dressed up for nothing. He says yesterday that we should go today and get things done. Dorry has gone to work thinking that when she comes back she can start helping me with the labels that have to be sewn on everything. She has already made me two black dresses with white collars. The collars are detachable because they are not washed in the same lot with the dresses. My sisters are also at work and Trisha and Kate are down the road playing with their friends.

I go and change into my shorts and sit on the stoep and do nothing. I worry about the long way England is from home. I think about the snow and flying on a jet. It will fly to Cairo and then to Rome and then to London. The sisters say they will meet the plane at a place called Heathrow. I am not going to enter the convent alone. A girl called Anne Holiday is coming with me. She is arriving from Cape Town by train on Friday and we will fly together on Saturday. She is going to spend the night here in our house. Dorry says we can share a bedroom and talk about being nuns all night if we want. I am worried about Anne coming to my house. It is untidy and Sally's little boy Douglas sits on the carpet and eats Marie biscuits and messes crumbs everywhere. Sally leaves his nappies everywhere and he spills his milk everywhere. I am ashamed of this house. I am afraid that Anne will see my father drunk and Dorry may fight with him. They may fight about Don and the black woman my father has in our village. I feel very tense but I feel glad that I am leaving this house because I have never been happy in it.

It is Tuesday and my father is sitting in the lounge in his chair. He tells me we will go to town for my clothes today. He says I should hurry up because he wants to get out and get back early. I ask him if he is sure we are going today. He says I must not be cheeky and I am not a nun yet so he can still give me a klap if he feels like it. I laugh and he laughs. I bath and get dressed in my best clothes again. I go to my father and he has a glass of whiskey beside his chair. He says it will be better to go tomorrow. I am angry but I say nothing. I go and change and I go and see Elizabeth for the last time.

Mrs Gunning says I am mad becoming a nun. She says they are funny people and who knows what goes on when they lock themselves away from the wide world. I tell her they keep silence, they read and study, do the cleaning and cooking and they pray for many hours a day. I tell her that when they have finished their training in the novitiate, they get trained to nurse or teach or if they are not going to do that, they run the accounts for the convents and they cook or look after the sick sisters. Elizabeth says how will I live without tennis and hockey and netball? I shrug my shoulders and say God will make sure I am happy enough without them. Mr Gunning shakes his head and says that a pretty young girl like me should be out enjoying life and not be thinking of convents. He says my old tennis coach will be very sad to hear of a good Wimbledon possible going off into the sunset with a long habit and blinkers on. I laugh because I know that they are not Catholics and they will never understand nuns. Elizabeth asks me if I will come back to Venterspost so that she will at least be able to visit me there sometimes. I tell her that I may be sent anywhere in the world and that I will make vows of obedience and go anywhere and do anything that I am asked. She shakes her head as if to say she thinks I am mad. Elizabeth is still in Rosebank Convent with the Sisters of Mercy. She tells me that she causes trouble because the boys that work at the garage opposite the school whistle at her and my other friends when they leave the school in the afternoons and Sister Magdalene stands at the gate to make sure that is all the boys do. She says she cannot wait to do her Matric and get the hell out of there.

I am feeling very sad because I have said goodbye to the Gunning family. They are like my family and I have always felt safe and welcome with them. I am walking home with my last pint of Gunning's Dairy cream. I am sipping it very slowly because I do not want it to finish and I do not want to get home because I know my father will be drunk in his chair and the lounge will be messy with Douglas and his crumbs and nappies. I think I will be glad to leave my father and his whiskey. I will be going to people that have never heard of him or of anyone in my family. I will never have to talk about what has been going on. I will never have to tell about Dorry or my father or about Jannie and my Uncle.

It is Thursday and I am in my best clothes again. There is only one day left to go to town because we have to go to the station and meet Anne tomorrow. I am standing in the lounge asking my father when we will go and get my clothes. He is drunk and he slurs. He says, "When the cows come home!" I am very angry. Pat's brother, Sydney, is here with my father. He is helping him to drink up all the whiskey. He smiles and begins to say hello and I explode. I tell my father that he is a bloody drunken bastard and he is a useless father and that I hate him. I call him names like dog and swine. My father's eyes are very wide and he is trying to get out of his chair. Sydney's mouth is shocked open and he does not know where to look. He shifts in his chair. My father is wobbling before me. He is raising his hand to klap me. I shout at him. I tell him he can now prove what a good man he is by slapping young women. I tell him he is a drunken coward as well and that I will be pleased never to see him again. I say that I am ashamed of him and of his behaviour. He lurches forward and I step back. He falls back into his chair and I run from the lounge onto the stoep and through the front gate. I leave two red faced men behind.

I run to the river at the end of our road. I take off my stockings and I sit on a tree stump and rip them up. I am very angry and very worried. I want to cry but the tears will not come. They dry up in my throat and I clench my teeth to stop them. I am ashamed of crying and I do not know why. I hear my breathing and my heart's heavy pounding. I think that the world is a hateful place and that there is no peace for me in it. I wish the river would come down in a flood and wash me away to a place where I can just be myself. I think of the moon and the times I have walked on it. There is no moonwalk now, just the fear and the anger of not knowing if I will leave for England or if I will have to stay at home and wave goodbye to Anne. I sit here at the river all day and when the sun is ready to go down, I walk slowly up the hill to home.

Sally is in the kitchen. She says, "Where have you been all day? Daddy is furious and is out looking for you. He and Pat have been riding around Johannesburg. They have been to all the churches to see if you ran there! You will be murdered when Daddy gets home. You had better run and wait until Mom gets here. God knows what will happen now!" I tell Sally that I do not care if today is the day I die. I will not run any more. I will face my father and see this matter to its end. I will not be played with every day and then told: 'when the cows come home!' I have had enough of drunken men who make promises and never keep them. I have had enough of men who cannot keep their promises because they are too drunk to think or stand or walk to anywhere.

We hear the car engine and Sally urges me to run. I say I am going to the gate to meet my father. I stand on the stoep with my arms folded and watch my father pull up his trousers. Dorry says we must know this dangerous language. When my father pulls up his trousers it means he is very angry and about to do something violent. I wait for my father and his violence. I am cold with fear but I do not move. I wait. He opens the gate like one who does not want to go through it because once through there is no going back. His face is red and his lips are white. He does not wobble anymore. I think I have woken him up with a shock. He stops in front of me. He says, "You had better get down on your knees and apologise to me for your behaviour. You had better ask God's forgiveness as well. I am going to donner you!"

I stand with my arms folded. I say; "Do you think you are God? Do you think I am going to kneel before a drunk who makes promises every day and does not keep them? I will not say I am sorry for the things I said because they are true. You are a drunkard. I am only sorry for shouting the truth at you; not for the truth!" My father's eyes are very blue and very huge. He says nothing. He passes me and goes into the lounge quietly. He sits in his chair. His shoulders begin to shake. He puts his hands over his face. He weeps. Pat follows him and goes for the bottle of whiskey. He pours one for himself and shakes his head. He says nothing. Sally comes and stands at the entrance to the lounge. She sees my father weeping. She says nothing and goes back into the kitchen. I hear her chopping beans. She begins to hum a song. I leave my weeping father and go and sit in my room. I feel drained and afraid and very empty of all thought. I ask God to help me and my father and family. I think of the moon but I do not go for a walk. I stay on the earth and in my room where life is very hard.

My father calls me. He looks at me with red eyes that have still got tears in them. I stand very still. He asks me to come to his chair. I walk there in silence. He says I must sit on his knee like I used to when I was small. I sit on the edge of his knees. They feel frail and cannot stand the weight so they shift a bit until they are steady. My father tells me in a very tired and subdued voice that I will never see him drunk again. He will never raise another glass of whiskey to his lips. He will never break any more promises. He will always be my father and I will always be proud of him. He tells Pat to put the bottle of whiskey in Dorry's cupboard. He says he will leave it there like a monument to this moment. He says he is proud of his nun and that he loves her very much. I say that I am his daughter and that I love him too.

When Dorry comes home she says she will take me to town very early in the morning. We will go to the wholesalers my father deals with and ask them to open their storerooms to see if there is any winter stock that I can have for my journey. She says, "Ye gods, Hugh, what a bloody business, man, just to get this girl a suit to travel in!" My father says nothing.

We are in a wholesaler's storeroom. She is a Jewish woman. I know by her hair and nose. She has a kind face and asks Dorry what I need winter clothes for at this time of year. Dorry tells her that we are Catholics and that I am going to the convent. The woman says I am going to be a bride of Christ. She says she can see that I am a good girl. She says because I am leaving the world to be a bride of

Christ, she will give me the suit for nothing because she wants to make the bride of Christ happy. We leave with a pale blue suit. I look good in it. I feel happy and Dorry and I laugh on the bus and say that it is a good thing that my father never took me to town. He would have had to pay and he has paid in a different way. Dorry says, "Ye gods, I just don't know, man! Let's hope he keeps his promise not to drink again!" Dorry says if he keeps his promise, she will stop seeing Don. I say that I will pray for them both. We are silent for the rest of the way home. I get off the bus for the last time. I have no regrets.

Anne is here. I like her very much. She is kind and laughs a lot. She does not look at our house with critical eyes. She feels at home with nappies and crumbs. She keeps saying that we are two young and crazy girls for going off to the convent to be nuns. I say God is the crazy one who calls us. She says how do I know I have a vocation? I say I don't, I just feel it in my heart. Later, Pat and Sally take us to the drive-in. We go to the 'Top Star'. It is built on top of a mine dump. Anne and I sit on the floor outside the car. Sally gives us a blanket and says we can yak our heads off there and not disturb them watching the show. It is very late when we get back home. Dorry has folded our bed quilts down and puffed our pillows. We talk until we hear the first birds call. There is a bunch of zinnias on the dressing table. I think of our garden in the village. It makes me want to cry. I think that tomorrow I will leave both homes forever.

We are at the airport. A lady from the travel agent is talking to us about the flight and tells us about Heathrow. We are hearing her but we cannot listen because we are too afraid and excited. She tells Dorry and my father not to worry about us; we will be cared for on the flight. We hear the announcement and the lady shows us where to go. I hold Dorry and she weeps. I hold my father and he weeps. I hold my tears that seep beneath my soul surfaces and let them well in there. We walk onto the plane and I wonder if I will ever see Dorry and my father and family again. We hear the engines whine and we see the world streak by before we rise into the air. I think I am flying to the moon.

The plane has landed and we are taken to a huge building. We have never seen such a building before. It has taken us ten minutes to get to it from the plane. The bus hostess says we are at the terminal. The lady at the airport in Johannesburg says we should go to the terminal in London and the sisters of Notre Dame would meet us there. We do not see any nuns. We sit on our suitcases and wait. We are nervous. We sit for more than an hour. I say that I will try and phone the sisters. I go to the booth and the phone is strange. Besides numbers on the dial it has the letters of the alphabet. I pick up the receiver and I dial 0. I do not know what else to do.

A voice says, " Can I help you, ducky?" I say we are lost at the airport terminal. The lady tells me to go to a desk and tell them there that we are lost and they will tell us what to do. I go to the desk. Anne stays with our suitcases. At the desk they tell us we are not at the terminal. We are still at Heathrow and they give us instructions. We take our luggage and we get on another bus. It is a BEA bus and it drives us through a lot of traffic and we see some of London. We arrive at the terminal but there are no sisters there either. We sit on our suitcases. I go to the desk and ask if there are any sisters of Notre Dame waiting to meet two girls from South Africa. We hear them announce our message. We sit and we wait. There is no reply. The lady at the desk asks us which flight we came to London on. I give her our plane tickets and she says we are at the wrong terminal. She asks us where we are going and we tell her. She phones the convent in Ashdown for us and they tell her that we must go to St George's Notre Dame Convent in Southwark. They tell the lady to get us in a taxi. We are very tired and very afraid but very relieved. The taxi driver is kind and he drives a long way through grey streets and bellowing traffic. I cannot believe I am on the other side of the world. Dorry and my father seem lost to me even in my mind. I cannot think of mud pools or river banks or the soft sound of the wind. My feet cannot imagine the feel of thick sand or the feel of mud. The hooting cars echo strange noise into the air, like doom.

The taxi stops. We see the grey building that the driver points towards. He says, "Here we are loves, this is Bedlam! I don't know what two young loves like you are going here for. This is the mad house in London!" We are lost. We are afraid. We say we want to go to St George's Convent in Southwark. The driver laughs and says, "That's better! That is just around the corner. A world apart though!"

The taxi stops in front of the convent. There are nuns in a row on the sidewalk. They wave at us as though we are the Queen. The Sister Superior comes and opens the taxi door and says we are welcome to Notre Dame. We will spend the night in London and we will leave for Ashdown in the morning. She says that they expected people from Africa to be black and look at us; we are white! We are led down long corridors to our rooms. We are left to wash and freshen ourselves and then we are given a meal. We feel very strange and uncomfortable in London. We are already homesick and the bleak London sky makes us want to cry. There is no snow, just ice cold rain. Sister Superior tells us to write to our families and tell them all about our adventure at the airport and terminals. She gives us Notre Dame letter headed paper. I feel like a nun already! I begin: 'Dearest Mama. I was lost in London…'

♥

"So, eventually I gave up the house. You, Bernadette, decided you wanted to be a nun and go overseas. At fifteen and a half off you went overseas. Then Dorothy went off to New Zealand to marry Ronny and then I had Trish, Catherine and myself. I didn't see any point in staying in the house. I had to support the kids and myself and there was no help from anybody. Pat got a job in Nairobi and Sally shifted out into a hotel so she would not have any expenses except the hotel and she would join Pat as soon as he got things settled there. All had their own lives to live so I decided to tell Daddy I would go back. He came up at the July holidays and I said to him, 'Now I am going to have to come back to Palapye.' Cathy was late starting school as I did not want her to go to any other school except the convent in Kroonstad and they had no place for her so she had to wait a year and started late.

I put Trisha into boarding school at Venterspost, where you went to school, Bern. Daddy said to me, 'No you are not; you wanted to come to Jo'burg, so now you stay here.'

I said, 'There's no way I am staying here. I'm afraid I am coming home whether you like it or whether you don't like it! I am packing up the house and letting it and I am coming home.' He had this child and the black woman was already very pregnant with the second one and your father did not know that I had been told about them but that I did not believe the story. I went home anyway and she was working in the shop with Daddy; very, very pregnant and I still couldn't think that it was his baby. In the meantime it was, of course, his and she left work and went and had the child at Moeng. It was named Lebang. God

368

knows why. I said to Daddy, 'I can't understand you; you're carrying on with black women.' I am at home now and Father Murphy, not yet a bishop, at least I am not sure if he was a bishop by then, came and spoke to me and then to Daddy. He said we should leave the village and go somewhere, perhaps to the coast, and start over again. Pat and Sally were going to come up here from Kenya and run the shops. You see, Bern, I nearly went right off my head with all this business with your father and the black women and children. The Bishop kept speaking to me and eventually my mind was set on staying with Daddy. I never slept with him. I ran my home like my own home and this black woman used to come into the kitchen and do whatever she pleased. She cooked for herself and everything. I eventually got home one day and said, 'This is my kitchen, not yours, and so you can just get out. Take your things and get out!' Daddy was so nervous that there would be a hells-balloo explosion but there wasn't.

A few years later, Lebang was already a little boy, I said to Daddy, 'Hugh, you have got these two children. It's no good; you have to support them.' So each month I used to give the black woman money for the two kids, you know. He said he wouldn't carry on with her any more. But he did it all the time behind my back. The reason I gave him money to support the kids was because I found out about his continuing to carry on. I caught him. I know that he used to send a box on the truck when it went to Bobanong and I suspected that it was for this black woman. She was a schoolteacher, you know. I thought: I am going to catch this one out so I put a double carbon in the writing pad and he wrote to her. 'My dearest love, I'm sending you a few things.' He used to write to me like that: My dearest love, and he signed it: love Hugh. So I starved for a few days over that. I got into my bed and I didn't get out of it and I cried and cried. Your father said, 'Cry, you bugger you; cry, you bastard you!' I stayed in my bed and I wouldn't have him come into my room and the only one who came in was our cook, Moremi, and he brought me tea. I had no kids at home at the time. They were at boarding school. Eventually your uncle Jimmy came up from the farm he was working on and came and told me that I must stop all this and start eating again. I showed him the letter. He said that perhaps Daddy hadn't written it, that perhaps

I was mistaken. I said to him, 'Whose writing is this?' Jimmy agreed that it was Daddy's handwriting. He said, 'Don't you want something to eat?'

I said, 'Just leave me alone, just get out, I don't want you here. I don't want to see anybody; my little cook, Moremi, will bring me my tea. I don't need anyone else to come into my room at all!' Finally Father Herbert came and spoke to me and, you know, priests have a way of telling you to do the right thing and so on and I decided: no, I wouldn't starve to death. I wasn't to do that. I started going to tennis again and that. I decided not to worry about your father's carrying on. I just left him and decided now I can do without his company anyway. He goes to work every day and he comes home to eat. I ate at the table with him and didn't speak much at all and then at five each day, I used to hear the bell for closing time ring and I used to get my tools out and go into the garden and talk to Our Blessed Lady. Then he promised he'd given up this entire woman thing and so on and he sort of became a bit friendlier. Then I suspected that he was carrying on with others who were working in the shop. I used to pray to Our Blessed Lady and ask her to send me flowers. I used to call her Our Lady of the Flowers. I used to ask her that if it was true that he was carrying on, she must send me flowers in some way, even if they were on a card, to show me a sign of the truth. Then I would know he was doing this again.

One time I said the flowers' prayer and really nobody at all had flowers, the gardens were so dry. Doris had scrap in her garden and there was no post or anything and my novena had ended. That morning here came a bunch of flowers with a note from Doris with a couple of little sunflowers and a couple of statice, a piece of this and that and a letter. 'Dear Dot, I've decided to send you flowers today but I am sorry they are so scrappy.' So when Daddy came home I said to him, 'I want to tell you something; you are carrying on with the woman in the shop.' I forget her name now, Bern. I said,

'You are carrying on, that's why you are going to the shop so early to be with her before opening time so you can fiddle around with her.' I said, 'I know that's what you are doing and do you want to know how I know? I know because I prayed to Our Blessed Lady to send me flowers to show me the truth about you carrying on with black women again. She sent me flowers this morning that were scraps from Doris's garden but they are still flowers.' He said, 'Oh well, you got your answer then, didn't you?'

So, Bern, I knew that it was true so I never slept with him because I couldn't, you know. All right I suppose he had to go somewhere and then there was the nursemaid who had worked for me when you kids were small and she came back and I made her the housemaid. You know, one day I was coming through the house and there's that passage from the dining room to the kitchen and she was coming up and I can't remember her name now, Bern, but she was coming up and Daddy was going out to work and as he passed her he took hold of her breast so I knew that that was another one he was having. He had all these women and you see I couldn't sleep with him because of that. But he expected me to be friendly and that in spite of it all so I just took to my garden when he came home. I went to my tennis and while I was there he used to have this thing in his room. He used to carry on with her. Then the Bishop spoke to me. He spoke to Daddy first and then to me. He said that we should start over again, start a new life and let Sally and Pat run the stores for us. We should go and live at the coast somewhere and it was all sort of arranged that we should do this and then Daddy died. Daddy died before we could go. He had prostate trouble and went to Jo'burg to have it seen to and never came back. Never mind all that, I would have forgiven him. So all right, I went out with Don. I did that to spite Daddy but I got very fond of Don in the end and I didn't think I was any great sinner for that. I was, of course, but in my mind I wasn't.

I couldn't get divorced. I would have but the school kids were home and Cathy was already about thirteen, you know. Whenever we went to bioscope, Daddy would never come. Why? That was because he used to have black women in the house. One time I came home early and I smelt her, the woman, and I accused him in front of the kids, you know, I was so wild! I said, 'And what's more, I am going to divorce you now, religion or no religion. I'm going to divorce you!' Cathy cried and cried and said, 'Mommy, I swear to you on the body of Jesus that Daddy will never do it again. Please don't divorce him. I swear on Jesus' body. I promise you he'll never do it again!' So, Bern, can you get divorced over a thing like that when you hear your child cry like that? So I had just to put up with it all, you see, and we were going to start a new life.

Daddy then got this prostate thing and went up to Jo'burg for an operation. He was getting over the operation and getting better. It was Ascension Day and Rex phoned me to say he is fine and I wasn't to come up because he is fine and would soon be discharged. All he was talking about was getting back home. So I decided I wouldn't go up then on Ascension Day but I would go up and fetch him when he was discharged. I would have to go up in the truck but it was a nice little truck, a Mazda.

Five o'clock that day I went to tennis. Sally was staying with me and Pat was in Jo'burg trying to find a job. Sally and Father Herbert came around with the children in the car and Charles said to me, 'Dot, the priest wants to talk to you.' So I got up to go and talk to him and he said, 'Dot, take your racquet with you.' I was busy getting up as the car was parked a bit away from the clubhouse and I came back and took my racquet, never thinking anything strange about being told to take the racquet with me. Then Herbert told me Daddy had passed away at three o'clock; he died the same time as Our Lord went up into heaven. Basically he was a good and religious man but he had his failings; everyone has their failings. I think Monica was with him when he died. He got a thrombosis. It was sudden. He died of a coronary thrombosis. Aunty Molly and them came to visit and she said, 'Good heavens, what have they done to you, my brother, what have they done?' Meantime they had done nothing but the doctors had all gone away for the public holiday and there was no doctor on duty for that weekend. Maybe if there had been, they could have saved him but he actually died from his feet up. He was ice cold right up to his hands and he just passed away. That was the end of an era for me, Bern.

So I'll just tell you now about the funeral. We decided to go up to Jo'burg. Sally took the bigger truck and I took the smaller Mazda. Pat stayed behind, as they had to take stock in the shop. We went up and I stayed with Uncle Willie. Faith and Bernard stayed with Aunty Helen on the farm. Did you come up with us, Bern? You were on the Mission in Rhodesia at the time. I remember getting the police to phone through because we do not have a phone in Palapye. I remember Trish was very pregnant with Kitch. In fact Kitch was born just after Daddy died. I am not sure how Cathy got to Jo'burg from boarding school. Anyway, we had the funeral and everything. You know that I cannot remember much about it now, Bern. I do not think I cried. I think I cried when I saw him in his coffin at the parlour. I don't remember the Mass or the church or the cemetery. These things are blocked out of my mind. Then there was the business of getting home again. I can't remember if we even had a tea after the funeral or if we just started for home straight from the burial. I do remember us trying to say the rosary before we left home for Jo'burg and we couldn't get anything out. We just began to laugh and laugh until we had to give up and ask God to pray for us instead.

You know, Bern, you have never told me how it was for you in the convent. You never tell me anything really. You seem just to listen but never to share your real life with anyone. You were always that way. Never saying much about you. All I remember is your phone call saying that you were not going to make your final vows and that you were coming home. I remember telling you that you were young enough to pick up the threads of life again and that there was nothing to be worried about. Remember, we went flat hunting and furniture hunting. The only lounge suite we could find at the price I could pay was bright red. I know how much you love red even to this day. You, poor little number five, had to put up with what you called the angry colour! The flat overlooked Joubert Park. 'King's Ransom' was the name of the block. I got a job at Greaterman's so that we could live together. I said you needed a mother for the first year out so that I could be sure you would settle down again. I used to come home each night from work and there you were in your habit. You just could not take it off and put on the mini skirt and blouse. I felt so sorry for you, Bern, and you were so silent about it all. Then one day I came home and you had changed and you looked lovely in your blue mini. You went to the General Hospital to visit Sister Wendy Beckett; you said she was ill. She was your superior when you left, wasn't she, Bern? You were very close to her, I remember. You are still close to her. I think she is your spiritual mother. Tell me about your time in the convent now, Bern."

It is strange this journey through the mists:
I see with faith-eyes,
Although I am blind.
My sight is the Other's light,
There can be nothing of my own
That radiates and makes a flame
So that another's eyes can see.

An empty reed accepts the Piper's breath
And is the ecstasy
Of being created music
With no notes of,
"I want, I need,
I must hear me."

The Piper's song, the love chorus,
Resounds and plays
In all life sequences
Of the Sacred's mind.
Whole One, Piper's breath,
Conceive your tune
In my self made mists,
In the poor, clogged reed
That is me...

I say, "Mama, my story is long; another book perhaps. Let's have some tea!" Dorry's feet do the tap-tap and her fingers fiddle but her clouding eyes do not spill their rain. "You're a funny one, Bern," she says.

♥

Do you remember his hat?
Oiled and greasy!
A dog named Ruddles
That sat at his lap?
The gun, the guinea fowl trap?
Tall and thin
With knees that knobbed
And eyes that said, don't sin.
The hunting belt, the slap
The hunting king,
Who cried when thirsty cattle died.
Do you remember him?

THE tin roof of the church is creaking in the heat. It sounds like small explosions. My father always told me that it was called expansion, and when the evening came and the sun went to sleep, the creaking was called contraction. He said metal does that. I did not understand expansion and contraction but I believed my father because Dorry said so, too. The priest is at the altar talking to us about the rising of the Holy Spirit in us. He says it is the rising of the mind, the heart and the soul. He says Jesus did that and then after his death and the appearances to his apostles, he left the earth and went up into heaven. His ascension was visible as though he wanted to show us the way of hope in life after death. He left a visible truth for us.

I have an invisible truth in my mind. The altar server is snuffing out the Easter candle and I know that my father's life has been snuffed out. I know that he is dead. It is a silent knowledge but as sure as the heat and the creaking roof. I am praying, "Eternal rest give unto him oh Lord." It is three o'clock and I think; this is the time of his death. It is Ascension Thursday, 4th May. My father has died at sixty-three years old. My being feels drained and I am finding it hard to focus on the Mass. The choir is singing 'Hail Redeemer King Divine'. I am thinking of my father in the water pan grass, aiming at the ducks and telling Mottle to stay. I am thinking of the stories and the cows coming home. I am remembering his knobbly knees and his hat and the smell of stale whiskey. I see the village station and the sea of people that came to greet me when I passed through on the train to this mission. The Radibatana was tall and proud to say to them that here is his daughter, that here is his nun. The woman came to shake my hand. She showed me the small boy and the girl child. She did not know of my witness, of my seeing her in the moonlight with him. I am thinking of my half brother and sister and of their mother's loss. I am praying for Dorry's new chasm and her knowledge of their history and of their father. I think of my moon journeys and of the reality that is now. The thoughts are long. The choir sings. I join the queue for communion. I remember the stoep Masses and my father's voice reciting the responses. We kneel again and place our small hands on his bed. He is hailing Mary and racing through the litany of Saints. He is scolding us for laughter but without real heart. He is under the lion rug crawling to catch us. He is under the withaak's shade with the leopard sniffing at his veldskoen. The priest is saying, "The body of Christ." I am thinking the body of Hugh, still and silent forever.

I fiddle with my rosary beads that dangle from the belt of my habit. My long robes swish against the long, dry grass and the black remains of thorn tree twigs crack beneath my shoes. My mind is blank and my thoughts are dry. I move along the scorched river bank and find a place to sit. The shade is thin and the heat remains heavy. There is nothing to tell of his death; nobody to share this truth. I keep it and fold it and linger by the sand-river until I hear the bell for evening prayer.

We sing. We listen to silence. We sing. We say Amen. We leave the chapel for the evening walk. The stars are out and I tell of their shining. I talk of the seven sisters that my father showed. I say, "See the seventh, so small and distant?"

They say my mood is strange. I say, "My father is dead." They say nothing. We arrive at the front door. The phone rings. I say, "Dorry will tell that my father is dead." They say I have an imagination and why is my mood so strange? I say nothing. I feel his soul around my head. It lingers like a goodbye. I think of the trains that took my sisters to boarding school. I feel the loneliness of parting. I watch the red lights on the back of the guard's coach fade into the distance. My father fades and I am left alone with knowledge that I do not want to keep.

Sister Mary follows me to my room. She says, "Here now, sit on the bed." She takes a chair and arranges it carefully. She sweeps up her habit and seats herself. Her hands play with beads. She looks long and I say, "My father is dead." The silence stretches into sorrow. Mary says, "The police have phoned with a message from your mother. Your father died today. He died at three o'clock. He was in hospital for a small operation and had a heart attack. He was doing well and going home on Sunday." She takes my hand. It lies limp. There are no tears; they rise like mist-clouds that wither like desert rain that never reaches the ground.

> *Sitting quietly in my room,*
> *I hear your love whispers*
> *In the ticking of the clock.*
> *You seem to say,*
> *"There is no wasted time in tears.*
> *Weep now for the healing of the years."*
>
> *I hear your love whispers*
> *In the ticking of the clock.*
> *But tears...*
> *I simply cannot weep*
> *For the healing of the years.*

The train is rocking along the line. I have its rhythm in my head and I doze and dream. My bones feel heavy and hollow. I am afraid of the arrival because I have to see Dorry weep for my father. I see her figure on the platform. The train grinds and stops. She sees me and her arms are stretched out. She enfolds me and I feel her shaking. Her tears do not reach the ground.

Dorry takes me home. We say nothing and her small truck bullets the sand. The dust rises and smothers thought. I enter my home. I enter my past and feel the memory of fleas rise and the sound of the kiewit's call. I feel the brown river's water wash over my feet. Dorry says, "Time for tea, Bern." She leads me to my bedroom and tells me to freshen up and rest. I greet Trish and Pete, her husband. Sally is in the store with Pat. They have come back from Kenya. My mind is hollow and out of tune flute music echoes through my head. I remember again the moon but my feet do not walk there. We sit on the stoep and watch the sun go down. In its sinking, I feel comforted. Dorry asks that we say the Rosary. We gather around her bed. She says, "You lead us, Bern, you're the nun now."

I say, "Name the father, the father's name is Hugh!" Dorry begins the winding wheeze and then the chortle. The 'Catherine wheel' whizzes its colours in my head. By the time she has reached crescendo we are all in our own bubbles and pops. Laughter rises beyond our Rosary intentions and beyond our prayer. Dorry says, "God forgive us man and God forgive our nun! I don't know what your father would say, Bern!"

I say, "Two Saint Litanies for tomorrow!" I hear the weaverbirds' fever in the trees. We sit on the floor and let the laughter until we are tired out of trying to speak-laugh. Supper sobers us and although the stew is good we sit in silence and let the mood hang its head around us. Dorry says, "More?"

Sally says, "Enough shit for today!" Pat's eyes grow big and blue. Dorry begins the whole weaver ritual again. Pat says, "There is not respect for nuns!"

I say, "Nuns have none, either!" Lemonade hisses, fizzes and pops.

Dorry says, "Well, I just don't know, man!"

The land is wet and watered. The tyre tracks are deep and the middle-mannetjie steep. The car wheels turn and churn and then sink. We get out and push. We get in wet and weary. We slip and slide from one side of the road to the other. After eleven hours we arrive in Jo'burg. We go to Dorry's friend Helen. I walk alone in her garden and gather geese. I sit in silence and watch them hiss and fuss. I think in blank echo that my father has died. My uncle drives Dorry's truck behind us. Sally drives her Bedford. Pat stays to look after the shop. The trucks behind us keep their distance in case of skids in the mud.

We sit in Wilmot's Funeral Parlour. We wait. They tell us to enter the chapel. We see my father in his coffin. Dorry cries a little. We stare. We kneel and leave.

We follow the coffin into the church. Incense smokes the air. We sing. My father's brothers and sisters and friends cry. The priest speaks of eternity and of welcoming into the new kingdom. I think of nothing but the desert rain that does not fall.

We are in the cemetery. We look into the hole and watch my father's journey end. Sally starts to whimper, heave and run. I follow her to a tree and she gets sick. We sit while she regains he strength. "Monica is a real little bitch!" she says. "Monica says before Daddy died he told her that Pat is no good and that he has no time for him!"

I say, "Monica is full of nonsense. Now is not the time for fighting. Find your peace and pray." Sally weeps. I sit in silence until the train of cars begins to move and Dorry calls to find us.

We are back on the road to home. I am driving Dorry's truck. She says I must be careful of the thick sand. The rains have gone. We sit in silence and listen to the hum of the engine and to the soil slap. My uncle is with Sally and my aunt May. May is coming to stay with Dorry for a while. She says Dorry needs company now. They keep a good distance because of the dust. My uncle smells of brandy and sweat. I am pleased to be with Dorry. My aunt is afraid of the sand roads and the sway of the truck. I think Sally must be having a hard journey.

I am telling Dorry about my work in the convent and about the Mission. The truck is going smoothly through the sand. The roads have been graded and the sand is not too deep. I go a little faster. Before Dorry can warn me I hit a deep, hollow sand patch. The truck swerves and I turn the wheel and it swerves to the other side of the road. I cannot control it and we slide and wobble. Dorry shouts that her door is jammed. The truck leaves the road and we rush through the bush. A mopani bush bashes the front of the truck and forces the fan back. The noise is nerve wracking and I am left with the thought of explosions and other death. I shout that Dorry should follow me and jump. I open the door and jump. I roll over the sand and land next to a deep hole.

I think Dorry is trapped. She leans and switches off the engine. She helps me up. We find the side of the road and sit in the sand to wait for Sally. The wind-up, the wheeze and the chortle start again. She says I am a sight for sore eyes. She says, "I wish your father could see us now; he would turn in his very fresh grave!" We watch a snake coil in a tree and we hear Sally's truck rattle nearer. We stand in the road and wave. We push Dorry's truck back into the road and my uncle ties up the towrope. Dorry goes to the truck and my uncle says I must travel with Sally. I say I will not get into her truck. I will stand on the running board because I am afraid of skidding again. My uncle says nuns do not behave badly and that I should show strength and courage and set a good example. I feel hot fire rising. I see him under the syringa tree molesting me. I flare and my language blooms into 'Bloody Bastard and Drunken Swine of hell'. I shout about bad brandy breath and sweltering armpit sweat. I say, "Shut your bloody mouth up!" He stands in shocked silence. He grapples with nun truth and fumbles for Dorry's truck door. Sally says, "That is a bit of a spit, Bern!" May says that we are all shook up and Elvis has nothing on us. I stand and hold onto the open window and the side mirror. Sally starts the truck and we move along slowly. The dust smothers and I cough. My eyes clam closed and my mouth dries in a crust. Sally says I am a sight to behold and my habit will never recover. She persuades me to get into her truck. May says she has to sit by the door in case she is sick. I am already sick but I sit in the middle. Dorry waves from her window and I see her shoulders shake. I do not hear the weaver's chortle.

Sally is putting her foot down harder and we are picking up speed. I am saying, "Slow down!" May is beginning to panic but it is too late. We skid from one side of the road to the other. Sally wrestles with the wheel. She says, "Shit!" The truck tilts onto two wheels. Sally wrestles with the wheel. We land back on four. May is hysterical. I am silent and sick and ready for other deaths. Sally lifts her foot and does not brake. The truck slows and settles and stops. Dorry jumps out of her truck. My uncle sits and stares. He is very pale. We get out of the truck and sit at the side of the road. Sally says 'Shit!" May weeps. Dorry says, "Ye gods, man!" I say nothing. My habit is as sandy as a desert.

Dorry says, "What a terrible day! Your father is getting his own back for us laughing so much at the rosary attempt!" We rest and gather our strength. Sally says we will travel slowly. I stand on the runner board. My uncle says nothing. We reach the narrow bridge near our village. I tell Sally to stop. She says just stay on the running board and do not panic. I tell her to stop. She sighs and stops and says she is going to report me to the priest in the village. I get off the running board and walk into the bush. The world swirls and I am sick. When I have buried my mess, I walk back to the bridge. Sally is waiting on the other side.

Dorry tells me to go and bath and rest. The village priest comes and Sally tells him all about our journey and my father's funeral. He looks at me and smiles. He says, "Give that woman there some brandy!" I think that this is the end of my father's death. I think that Dorry will be alone. I think that I will no longer have to be a nun and a saint.

♥

The Alps rise clear and ragged,
Pointed to the sky
As Jesus on the cross hanging out to dry
Like a scarecrow on the scene.

The white, veiled sleet
Fogs the world of vision,
Like Mary at God's feet
Trying to stay alive and sane.

And there the twisted, dark ravines
That savage at the fear
Like Judas freshly dead,
Hanging from his broken neck
That gives him nothing
For his doubt and pain
But gory images of hell.

And on the velvet peaks,
Untouched and so serene,
Here am I
Gliding along the convent corridors
Where silence prays to reign,
But for my rosary beads banging out beatitudes;
Like bullets shot and shattered in
My slow awakening brain.

The Bow End of Rain

Where the gullies meet the sky,
The sun shines soft on slants of hills;
To lend some comfort
To the open eye.
Dorry's knees are swollen;
She has arthritis in her hands and feet
But still,
She sits in quiet peace to praise the years
She's seen go by.

It's time for landing,
The world is flat and emptied
Of all that's lofty and ideal.
There's nothing more to mend the mind.

The doors have opened
And I am left to lug along
The baggage of my past
That has me trapped-
And will, until I grasp
With sure, stayed heart,
The fact that feet
Are meant to tread the ground
And walk the ragged hills
Unshod.

THESE many years have passed. My life in the convent lasted eight years. I have told Dorry that I cannot tell of it now. It will take another book. I do not know if I will ever write it. In spite of my fear of teaching, I became a teacher and later a school principal. I met and married Peter, my husband. Yet another book!

I think that my life has been a mountain and a marsh. Sometimes I have had to climb very high to see its implications and at others I have had to tread in the murk and mud of marshes, feeling my way to new horizons. My under water feet have trod carefully and in spite of that, have sunk to depths of uncertainty that I have never before experienced. I have not known how to survive. Somehow life has done that for me.

Dorry is old now and I sit with her here in my study. I watch her as her feet fold and her fingers tap-tap. I listen to her voice that is sometimes alive with anger and sometimes as soft as gentle rain. She weeps and she laughs. She tells me of all she has been and we travel along her history and mine, like two souls searching for life's truth and meaning. She says I must write this book. I have written it and she will never read it. Neither will Sally or Monica because they too have died. There is sadness in that because Dorry used to say that we can tell a tale or two because we have seen the rain and the bow end of it. I believe her.

♥

You were once my House
With look through windows
And a door of welcoming:
I could safely walk through
Fragile mysteries of my past.
I could frame and hang my history
On your Walls
For the eyes of Truth to see.
I could conjure new metaphors
For the Future.
I could feel free.

But now, I am my House;
Worn and weather-beaten,
Shelled by storms:
I could not fight the winds
And bring my being to Calm.
I am bereft.
I have only vagaries of Wholeness left.

THERE is soft light lending the bush a gentleness that wraps me up in velvet. The pink tinged grass glows; a vague mist among the thorn trees reminds me that life is mystery, seen and unseen. Joan, my friend who is travelling with me, voices the splendour and we say how even the tin shanties along the road look beautiful in the light. In the cold morning air the birds' chorus rises like unleashed and heady praise for the new day. It makes me want to stop the car and to sit a while just to be in silence, a part of it. I can't stop as we are heading

for home. Later I pull into the garage for petrol and my cell phone clicks off. I pay no attention to the power of being 'switched off'. A button pressed will bring back conversation and a line to the rest of the world. Some time along the way, when Joan is driving and I have had time to absorb a million different day flavours and I've watched the tractors harvest the dead heads of once flamed sunflowers, Joan says, "Punch in the phone code." I say the numbers in my head and press buttons that will take me into a new and foreign place - a journey that turns day into night and joy into a deep sense of fear and anxiety.

I listen to the message beeper and turn on the voice mail. I hear Sally's words quiver across the air like a spider's web entwining my mind in a spiral of panic. "Mommy's in the chair in a coma. I don't know what to do!" Already in the instant of her message my world changes colour. The light that was so soft is an inharmonious glare. The dead and seeding sunflowers are funeral sentries, broken and bent in pitiful lines of incomprehension. They stretch in never ending rows of withered life, life that has fled reality. Joan's sympathetic murmurs are helpless little sounds, lost in some distant part of my mind. I look out of the windows and am conscious of being encapsulated, trapped in a journey that cannot go any faster; stuck behind trucks that spew poison like the bad news that blocks any new thoughts. I am dialling and repeating the horror. I listen to Sally say it all again. Dorry is in hospital. A massive stroke, no hope of recovery. I try little comforts for her to cling to and then I am talking to my other sisters; giving them decapitated sunflowers and grinding their day's joy into a grief machine that seems to annihilate any sense of balance and normality. The car becomes my own tomb, a capsule in which to hold my pain and panic. The black road-strip undresses all my strength, all my layers of protective denial rub away in tyre friction and I am left burning in my recent memories of Dorry's voice.

I am here at Dorry's bedside. There is silence but for her quiet breathing. My bones are hollowed out like the passages of flutes. In the hollow is the echo of Dorry's life: the laughter, the sorrow and her music. Our journey has been long and intimate and it is hard to say that she will not speak to me again, not say 'Bye, bye, bye'; no hiss and wind up of her laughter for me. In the slow sorrow that creeps coldly and keeps silence in the well of my being, there is also peace and thanks for her coming and for her going. I tell her she can go back to God and that we will manage her death.

Dorry breathes her last. We stand around her and I hold her hand; Faith holds it with me. Our cousins pray. Our nieces, who are with us, weep and hold her other hand. We wait for the sound of her next breath. It does not come. The silence is like eternity that is not welcome. The nurse comes and takes the oxygen away. She says she is sorry that our mother has died. My lead feet move from the room where Dorry lies still. I phone my husband Pete and I ask him to give the news to Trisha and Sally and Monica. I look at Dorry's still body once more and I leave her and drive to Sally's house.

We take Dorry's photo with us up the aisle of the church. There are many people here with us. We walk up to the altar in line from Number One to Number Six. Kate, Number Seven, cannot be here with us but we carry her along anyway. We remember that she too is part of us and part of Dorry.

I am standing in the sanctuary in front of those who are at Dorry's Requiem Mass. In my mind is the image of a brown bread loaf - stodgy, steady and strengthening. I read our tribute. I hear my voice, sure and true. It tells of Dorry. It is our parting gift to her.

"Dorry is my mother. For fun, she calls me her precious 'Number Five'; there are seven of us sisters: Faith, Sally, Monica, Dorothy, Bernadette, Patricia and Catherine. There are nineteen grandchildren and fourteen great grandchildren. We are all hers, and all precious. We are woven together like an original tapestry; as individuals but at the same time we are integrated into her life's patterns. There seem to be no limits to Dorry's heart. It enfolds, protects, loves, laughs, grieves and fears for us all. She is like a flute reed that is hollowed out especially for our music. Our life's music, be it sad or glad, is also her music. She is a maestro in receiving and in giving song to the world. Her gentle yet rich and mellow voice has soothed us through the years.

I phone her two or three times a week. When she comes to answer the call she says, 'Is that you Bern? As soon as the phone rang, I said to Monica, that's Bern.' It doesn't matter what I talk to her about on the phone; when our conversation closes she always says, 'Bye, dear. God bless you, dear. I love you. Bye, bye, bye…' Then I hear the click and I also say, 'Bye, bye, bye, Mama.' Sometimes we go out for a meal and chat. We skinner about the whole of creation and I tell her that I mimic her on the phone and she says that I'm mad. Her sea-eyes laugh with her shaking body and she sort of heaves and hisses before the actual laugh sound breaks. Her laughter mops me up. If I had to describe it visually, I'd light a Catherine wheel and watch it twirl and hiss and spin me off into a brightly-lit world.

Dorry's tears are for herself and they are for us. They are for all that she cannot achieve, no matter how she tries. They are tears of faith and trust, never of despair. She knows the feel of human limitation. She says that she cries for the world inside, privately; but that she knows that God and our Blessed Lady are there too. She says that comforts her and gives her hope and courage.

Dorry is so huge in our lives, because she has lived with us in every detail of who we are and of where we have been. She is our tapestry too. Through her living strength and her weakness, her faith in us and in God, she has shown us a very deep and truthful way of being human, of how to live to our full potential in God.

We weep and we miss our beautiful mother. We know who she was to us and who she is for us. We know where she is now for us. We thank her for giving us life, for sharing it with us and for going before us, to show us, yet again, the way. Mama, we thank you for your life, for all you are to us and although we are sad - in faith, hope and love, we give you back to God."

♥

Far light beams.
It sheens through secret waves of mind.
Its fire, charges freedom's truth
And calms the churning waters.
They sleep.
The sailing boats, on the water's glass lie still.
This soft, lit day
A sacred peace will keep.

THERE are days of calm when the land looks velvet soft. My mind can travel easily along the shape of hills. My thoughts blend easily with the green grass blanket that weaves its way to where the blue hem of horizon greets it. I sit beside the river again under the morula tree's shade and watch the heat waves shimmer out images in the sun. Around me lie the little sand dunes that are moulded by the night winds. I lift the tops of them through my fingers and am strangely lulled by the feel of their flowing. Around my mouth lingers the salty taste of summer, and the sticky heat prickles through my clothes. It reminds me of the drought and the thirsty cattle and the herdsman with his whip. I hear again the lowing of the ox caught in the mud. I rub my back feverishly along the morula's bark and return to my world of half dreams and half reality.

I think of moon meanders that were so treasured on the journey I have come. I can no longer catch their silver, misted webs of past peace places. The moon remains a mystery silently contained.

Long before I hear its sound, I watch the dark dust cloud creep across the plain, whose journey ends at the river's bank. I stare above it at the drifting white halo of tickbirds. Were it not for the rhythmic sweep of wings, I would think them merely painted on a sky-blue page. Presently the cloud billows nearer until my tranquil world is blurred by swirling soil. Sharp explosions of rushing hooves blot out the softer thoughts and the softer sounds. I sneeze and blink away the tears of mud long after the cattle have reached the river's edge. The herdsman sits and sings beneath a thorn tree. There is no sign of sorrow in his voice. The river's life is deep and strong. The cattle are fat.

In my soul, there lingers, with the smell of dry earth, the memory of Dorry's going. It no longer hurts me as a child who has lost her mother, nor like a mother who has lost her child. It flows quietly and gently along the river with my thoughts that are one with the land and one with the sun. I travel back along the ways I walked with her, down the laughter times and the harsh sorrow roads. My memories settle like joy on the water, like reflections of sun promises, like the bow end of rain.

There is no more to be said. I move silently along the river's path, grateful for the journey that was Dorry's and that is still mine. I look to the future with love that is as giving as God and as careful as the rain.

THE END

GLOSSARY

ZULU:

umfaan: a young Zulu man

SETWANA:

morena: sir (also used when addressing God in prayer)

AFRIKAANS:

al: all

bliksem se donder se hell: infernal scoundrel of hell!

daarom: because

dan: then

derhalwe: so, therefore

dis: that is

doppie: tot (a measure of alcohol)

ek gaan met jou trou: I am going to marry you

en: and

jissie, man dis nou vrot1: Gee man, that is bad!

Jou donderskind: you darned fool!

impala: a large African antelope

kiewit: crowned plover: a bird common to southern Africa that warns game of intruders

klap: slap

koeksusters: Afrikaans cake that is plated and dipped into cold syrup immediately after cooking

kudu: an African antelope with long spiral horns

moenie huil nie: don't cry

nog: more

rys vleis en aartapplels: rice, meat and potatoes

sowel as: as well as

stoep: verandah; porch

stompie: cigarette end or cigarette butt

takkies: tennis shoes (canvas shoes)

toe: and then

tog: nevertheless

veldskoene: soft leather shoes that cover the ankles; used for walking in the bush

voetsek: be off!

wag 'n bietjie: wait a bit: refers to the small, hook shaped thorns of an acacia tree

wat: that

wildebeeste: wild cattle

withaak: umbrella-thorn tree (acacia tortilis)

OTHER:

Mopani: an indigenous tree that is common to northern Botswana. A worm (mopani worm) feeds off it during spring and this worm is considered a delicacy. It is usually cooked over coals in an open fire. It is generally eaten with maize (mealie) meal porridge.

morula: an indigenous tree common to Botswana. It bears a plum shaped yellow fruit used for brewing beer

syringa: tree bearing sweet smelling lilac blooms and that fruits small brown berries

MELROSE BOOKS

If you enjoyed this book you may also like:

The Freedom of Choice
Saradha Narayanan

"A fantastically emotional tale of interwoven troubled lives that addresses the social issues of adoption and organ transplant."

On a wet, gloomy Monday morning in March 2004, Rachel Thomas receives a letter from a private investigator that throws her comfortable, middle-class lifestyle into chaos. She is confronted with a deeply guarded secret from her past. Traumatic events that she has kept buried for fourteen years come back to haunt her and she must now find the courage to make a choice that may disrupt and destroy her marriage. Will she make the right choice?

Size: 234 mm x 156 mm	Pages: 272	
Binding: Royal Octavo Hardback	ISBN: 978-1-906050-52-8	£13.99

Passport To Paradise
Fr. Gabriel Finnegan

Written in a relaxed, conversational style this is a book by a 68 year-old retired Irish priest, Father Finnegan, who has had a long, varied and often exceptionally difficult life. Although he writes as a Roman Catholic, the book has an almost non-denominational quality.

Writing with enthusiasm and an unfailing cheerfulness, Father Finnegan is fluent and friendly and his words pour out easily. His narrative is enlivened by anecdotes of events in his life and by a constant stream of apt quotations. Dealing with some of the greatest questions of theology and ethics with a bubbling certainty (only one or two pockets of doubt) in which he hardly seems to be aware that there are other sides to the issues he raises. Faith, personal commitment to God, prayer and confession are simply taken as the norm for every human being and he gives a great deal of advice on how to deal with the things that get in the way of that, including lack of belief in hell and punishment, television and the internet.

Size: 198 mm x 129 mm	Pages: 96	
Binding: B Paperback	ISBN: 978-1 906050-24-5	£8.99

The Nazareth Route
Cecil Hargreaves

The Nazareth Route by Cecil Hargreaves focuses on the themes of "challenge" and the "form of vulnerability which consists in a willingness to get hurt and wounded." It is also about human dilemma.

The author outlines as many as thirty people across the world who have been seen to be among Jesus' modern Nazareth 'route-makers' and 'route-finders'.

Size: 234 mm x 156 mm	Pages: 320	
Binding: Royal Octavo Hardback	ISBN: 978-1-906050-44-3	£13.99

St Thomas' Place, Ely, Cambridgeshire CB7 4GG, UK

www.melrosebooks.com   sales@melrosebooks.com